ROGUE RIVER
Rendezvous

a gathering of Southern Oregon's finest recipes

The Junior Service League of Jackson County
Medford, Oregon

For additional copies of
Rogue River Rendezvous please write:

Rogue River Rendezvous
The Junior Service League
of Jackson County
526 East Main Street
Medford, Oregon 97504

Include your return address with your
check payable to **Rogue River Rendezvous** in the amount of $19.95 per volume
plus $3.00 postage and handling.

First Edition   October, 1992
Second Printing   July, 1993

Printed in the USA by

WIMMER
The Wimmer Companies, Inc.
Memphis • Dallas

The objectives of The Junior Service
League of Jackson County are to foster within its membership interest in
social, economic, cultural, civic,
educational and charitable aspects
of the community and to promote
voluntarism, to develop the potential
of its members for voluntary partici-
pation in community affairs and to
demonstrate the effectiveness of
trained volunteers.

The proceeds realized from the sale
of this book will be returned to Southern Oregon through community
projects benefiting children, troubled
families, at-risk teens, drug educa-
tion and cultural events.

Table of Contents

Menus	19
Appetizers	25
Soups	45
Salads	65
Breads	83
Oregon Catch & Seafood	107
Meats	127
Poultry	147
Vegetables, Rice & Brunch	165
Desserts	187
Contributors	214
Index	217

The pear symbol located in comment column denotes a cooking tip.

From its mile-high source on the slopes of the Cascades near Crater Lake to its union with the sea at Gold Beach, the legendary Rogue River shapes and defines a region that holds the very essence that is Southern Oregon.

The first explorers to enter the Rogue River Valley discovered a picturesque land of breathtaking native abundance — forests and meadows teeming with bear, deer, elk, quail and grouse; the river and its tributaries thick with salmon, steelhead and cutthroat trout, their berrylined banks crowded with fruit.

It was a natural place for a rendezvous. A classic tradition of the Old West, the rendezvous was an annual event that brought together trappers and traders, Indians and merchants to exchange goods and engage in fun and feasting on a variety of fresh foods readily available from nature.

Word of the utopia soon spread, attracting settlers who added to the valley's bounty by cultivating pears, peaches and apples that flourished in the fertile soils and raising cattle and sheep in the rich pasturelands. Later, newcomers introduced more exotic fare — wine grapes from Europe, tayberries from Scotland, ringnecked pheasants from China and wild turkeys from the southern United States.

A paradise for cooks as well as outdoors enthusiasts, the Rogue River Valley still attracts people from all over the world. And the tradition of the rendezvous continues in countless variations. Whether it's a streamside picnic, a fresh salmon barbecue or an elegant dinner following an evening at the theatre, a rendezvous along the Rogue is an opportunity to celebrate life and friendship by sharing fine food in splendid surroundings.

The best way to experience the Rogue and its wildlife is by boat, ideally a "Rogue River Special" drift boat during one of the legendary runs of salmon or steelhead. These boats are handled with the bow pointed downstream. The guide sits behind the anglers and rows against the current enough to allow lures or baits to drift ahead of the boat into prime fish holding areas. At the hands of a skilled oarsman, these seaworthy craft can turn quickly to avoid rocks and logs, or negotiate a whitewater chute and then pull off sharply into a back eddy to sweep a lure through every nook of a promising hole.

Fishing has a rich tradition here. Over the years, the Rogue has been the preferred destination of anglers including Zane Grey, Herbert Hoover, Clark Gable and George Bush. Each spring the Chinook salmon arrive by the tens of thousands in sizes typically ranging to 30 pounds or larger.

A successful salmon trip brings a royal reward. Fresh steaks or fillets grilled to perfection over a bed of glowing alder coals — a meal that embraces the essence of the region.

A river is water in its loveliest form; rivers have life and sound and movement and infinity of variation, rivers are veins of the earth through which the life blood returns to the heart.

— Roderick Haig-Brown
A River Never Sleeps

Along its 215 mile journey to the Pacific, the Rogue displays a kaleidoscope of moods, offering something to please any lover of rivers.

Near its headwaters, the river rages down a narrow gorge carved through volcanic rock, a vigorous mountain stream shaded by stands of fragrant firs and incense cedars. Here, a secluded picnic offers hikers an opportunity to dine to the music of a wild river in a setting as pristine as it was when members of the Takelma tribe were the only human inhabitants.

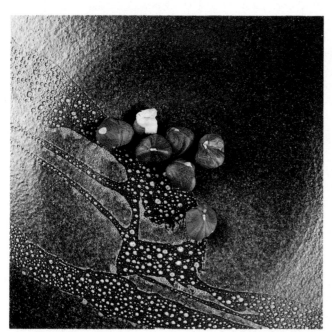

Strengthened by tributaries, the Rogue enters the upper valley below Lost Creek Lake as a broad, powerful river, its glassy stretches punctuated by riffles as it flows past homes perched along its banks.

In the broad reaches of the valley near Medford, the Rogue flows serenely past verdant pasturelands and the region's famed fruit orchards. Early settlers were quick to discover that the black loam soil produced fruit that was fabulously large, juicy and sweet. Orchards have flourished here since the mid 1880's and exports of Bartlett, Comice, Bosc and Anjou pears have given millions of people around the world their first taste of the Rogue River Valley.

Rogue River Rendezvous captures the spirit and flavors of the region in imaginative recipes featuring fresh ingredients from its forests, waters and fields. In the tradition of the rendezvous, this collection presents a unique blend of Pacific Northwest cuisine, offering novel interpretations of classic Oregon dishes with a contemporary flair. *Rogue River Rendezvous* is more than a cookbook, it's a journey down a fabled waterway, a sprinkling of local history and folklore and a taste of what one visitor described as "life as it should be."

A river in the backyard
helps elevate a casual outdoor
picnic into a special occasion,
especially when the menu
features Perfect Salmon Steaks,
Chilled Potato Cilantro Soup,
Oregon Chardonnay, Sesame
Asparagus, and Chocolate
Raspberry Tart.

A common sight along the river's wilder stretches is the high-rise nest of the osprey or fish hawk. The osprey enjoys a home with a view, building its nest out of sticks, bones and driftwood in the top of a prominent snag along the shore.

In the winter, ospreys are thought to migrate as far as South America, returning to the Rogue each spring as surely as the salmon. When it comes to fish-catching style, this bird has no equal. Boaters may be treated to the sight of an osprey patrolling the river, then suddenly plummeting a hundred feet, striking the water with talons extended, emerging wet and flapping with a luckless fish writhing in its grasp.

Below Grants Pass, the Rogue leaves civilization behind. For some 84 miles, the river cascades through an isolated wilderness accessible only by boat, plane or hiking trail. This section is so spectacular that Congress granted it Wild and Scenic status to protect it from any development.

This particular stretch of the Rogue has earned a well-deserved reputation as a classic river run, drawing whitewater enthusiasts from all over the world to challenge the Class III-V rapids. In less than 20 miles, you plunge into more than 40 named rapids which vary in difficulty according to the volume of water.

At Foster Bar, the Wild Section ends as do the journeys of many rafts and boats. Here stories are swapped of shooting Blossom Bar, Wildcat, Devil's Stairs and the infamous Coffee Pot of Mule Creek Canyon.

Just below Agness, the Illinois River joins the Rogue. Broad beaches favored by knowledgeable campers line the shores of this seven mile stretch called Copper Canyon.

Below Lobster Creek, the widening river gradually descends into a broad river delta, before emptying into the Pacific at Gold Beach. It was here that mail boats were first launched around the turn of the century, carrying supplies to the inaccessible stretches upriver. Today, jet boat companies carry visitors along the same route for a glance into the historic past of the famed river.

Join us now for a culinary journey along the Rogue and enjoy your own personal Rogue River Rendezvous!

Martin Vandiver, Photographer

Martin Vandiver has been a commercial photographer for an extended range of clients since 1972. His work has been used for market collateral, advertising, promotions and annual reports as well as covers and editorials for top magazines. His client list includes prestigious names such as CocaCola, Mobil Oil, Neiman Marcus and ITT. His work has been featured in publications such as *Architectural Digest* and *National Geographic.*

Martin came to the Rogue Valley from Dallas, Texas to become acquainted with the Rogue River through the lens of his camera. His personal Rogue River rendezvous is featured as a photographic journey through the pages of this book.

Dave Boutacoff, Narrative

David Boutacoff is a fly fisherman, wild game cook and writer living in Sonoma County, California. He has been fishing the Rogue and enjoying the traditions of the Rendezvous for 30 years.

Linda Boutacoff, Artwork

Linda Boutacoff's artwork reflects her love of nature and the Northwest, as well as her background in graphic design. Her award winning work is displayed in shows, exhibits and private collections throughout the United States. Linda is a member of the Arts Council of Southern Oregon, Rogue Valley Art Association, Upper Rogue Artists and the Watercolor Society of Oregon.

Linda resides on the upper Rogue River near Eagle Point, Oregon. Her proximity to the river and close association with those that spend time on the river, gave her the inspiration for the flies featured on the divider pages.

ROGUE RIVER RENDEZVOUS COMMITTEE

Co-Chairmen	**Michelle Hefley**
	Carole Schuler
Recipe Co-Chairmen	**Karen Meyerding**
	Leslie Meyerding
Marketing Chairmen	**Bonnie Hall**
	Kathryn Mahar
Editorial Coordinator	**Mignon Skinner**
	Cindy Prewitt
	Sharman Busch
	Mary Stebbins
	Michele Jones
	Cyd Bagley

TESTING CHAIRMEN

Appetizers	**Debbie Dixon**
	Janet Jamieson
Soups	**Michelle Hefley**
	Mary Stebbins
Salads	**Lynne Hunter**
	Joan Smith
Breads	**Carole Schuler**
	Catherine Barr
Oregon Catch & Seafood	**Leslie Meyerding**
	Dee Marchi
Meats	**Michelle Hefley**
	Maggie Silverman
Poultry	**Leslie Meyerding**
	Sue Naumes
Vegetables, Rice & Brunch	**Lynne Hunter**
	Bonnie Hall
Desserts	**Karen Meyerding**
	Debbie Dixon

DESIGN AND FORMAT

Linda Boutacoff
Jean Bolton Boyer

MARKETING COMMITTEE

Diane Somers
Claudia Lawton
Debbie Dixon
Sharon Withers
Susan Rachor
Debra McFadden
Dawn Heysell
Donna Dixon
Jan Carey
Connie Burns
Cheryl O'Reilly
Jan Mahon
Ellen Miller
Alma O'Connor
Dorathy Anderson-Thickett

LEAGUE PRESIDENTS

Connie Burns
Ellen Miller
Peggy Tomlins

COOKBOOK TREASURERS

Barbara Pinkham
Reni Ferguson

PHOTOGRAPHY	**MARTIN VANDIVER**
NARRATIVE	**DAVID BOUTACOFF**
ARTWORK	**LINDA BOUTACOFF**

ROGUE RIVER RENDEZVOUS MENUS

SUNDAY BRUNCH BUFFET

Rogues' Fizz

Melon Puree

Overnight Yeast Waffles
with Hazelnut Honey Butter

Red Potato and Clam Frittata

(Link Sausage)

Chocolate Almond Brioche

WHITEWATER PICNIC

Chilled Potato-Cilantro Soup

China Bar Chicken

Red Potato Salad with Sun-Dried Tomatoes

Basil Batter Rolls

Grand Marnier Brownies

COCKTAILS AT FIVE O'CLOCK

(Cocktails)

Ashland Artichoke Triangles

Aegean Eggplant Shell

Spinach Torte

Newport Shrimp

Chinook Salmon in Phyllo

HEARTHSIDE SUPPER

Stilton Cheese and Onion Soup

Rogue Caesar Salad

Brown Bag Sirloin Steaks

Rogue Polenta

Oregon Hazelnut Pears

HIKING THE ROGUE RIVER TRAIL

Chilled Cucumber Soup

Union Creek Chicken Salad
(in Pita Bread)

Chocolate Walnut Euphoria Cookies

CINCO DE MAYO

(Margaritas)

Posole

Salsa Sorbet

Chicken San Carlos

(Refried Beans)

Burnt Cream

MOTHER'S DAY TEA

Cheese Filled Pastry Puffs

Pear Tea Cake

Hazelnut Scone Hearts

Fresh Fruit Tray with Orange Cream Dressing

Chocolate Covered Shortbread
(Garnished with Candied Violets)

Tea

COZY AUTUMN EVENING

Winter Vegetable Salad

Braised Pork Tenderloin

Pear Puree

Baked Apples and New Potatoes

Gold Nugget Bread

Frozen Pumpkin Dessert

SYMPHONY UNDER THE STARS

Tarragon Chicken Pâté

Chilled Watermelon Strawberry Soup

Oregon Berry Salad

Gin Lin Char Shu Pork

White Chocolate Macadamia Cheesecake

RAFTERS BARBECUE

Spicy Cool Watermelon Salad

Tipsy Tenderloins

River Trail Vegetables

Pineapple Buttermilk Bread

Pecan Turtle Bars

CHRISTMAS EVE AT HOME

Brie Soup

Pacific Flyway Christmas Mallard

Wild Rice with Hazelnuts

Peas with Triple Sec

Overnight Light Rolls

Christmas Date Cake

ENGAGEMENT BRUNCH

(Champagne with Framboise)

Savory Tomato and Asparagus Pie

Chanticleer Parsnip Apple Pancakes
with Smoked Salmon and Sherried Crème Fraîche

Cream Cheese Braid

(Fresh Fruit in Icers)

Lemon Tea Cookies

EASTER DINNER
Asparagus Soup
Leg of Lamb in Wine Sauce
Red Potatoes in Lemon Butter
Garlic Spinach
Heavenly Yeast Biscuits
Kiwi Pavlova

FOOTBALL TAILGATE PICNIC
Tomatoes and Cheeses on Phyllo
Curry Oven-Fried Chicken
Couscous Salad
Blue Ribbon Apple Pie

LADIES GOLF LUNCHEON
(Daiquiris)
Pears, Parmesan, and Pepper
Cilantro and Black Bean Chicken Salad
Peasant Black Bread
Strawberries in Lemon Mousse

ELEGANT EVENING AT BLACK BAR
Baked Stuffed Shrimp
Herbed Walnut Salad
Raspberry Pork Tenderloin
Orzo with Myzithra and Basil
Sesame Asparagus
Chocolate Espresso Cheesecake

SUMMER CELEBRATION
Fresh Tomato-Dill Soup

Chilled Summer Corn Salad

Spinach Stuffed Artichoke Rounds

Perfect Salmon Steaks

Sourdough French Bread

Blackberry Peach Cobbler with
Grand Marnier Cream

SPORTSMEN'S FALL BOUNTY
Smoked Salmon Salad

Venison Pot Roast with Juniper Berries
and Huckleberry Relish

Wild Rice Roxy Ann

Sautéed String Beans

Apple Cake with Rum Sauce

AL FRESCO SUPPER
Hearty Minestrone Soup

Roasted Pepper Trio

Garlic Roma Tomatoes and Croutons

Veal Piccata

Pesto and Sun-Dried Tomato Twist

Poached Amaretto Pears

(Espresso)

FISHERMEN'S FEAST
Garlic Brie

Steelhead with Black Walnuts

Tomatoes Stuffed with Green Beans

Saffron Raisin Rice

Blueberry Peach Glacé Tart

APPETIZERS

ROGUE RIVER CHEIGNEY SPECIAL

This fly was developed by Joseph Cheigney, chauffeur for Mrs. Nion Tucker for 40 years. The unique mix of red and white bucktail produces a stunning rose hue resembling the spawned eggs upon which steelhead feed. Mrs. Tucker, the former Phyllis DeYoung of the DeYoung Museum in San Francisco, was bitterly opposed to the building of a dam. She was the proprietor of "Rogue's Roost" in the Laurelhurst area, which is now flooded by the Lost Creek Dam.

SMOKED SALMON CHEESECAKE

Smoked salmon is also known as "nova" and is used to refer to any smoked salmon regardless of its source. Quality is determined by the salmon and the smoking process used.

1½ tablespoons butter, at room temperature
⅓ cup plain, dry bread crumbs
3½ (8-ounce) packages cream cheese, at room temperature
4 large eggs
¾ cup (3-ounces) Gruyère cheese, shredded

⅓ cup half-and-half
3 tablespoons lemon juice
2 tablespoons fresh dill or 1 teaspoon dill weed
¼ teaspoon salt
½ cup thinly sliced green onions
1½ cups smoked salmon, chopped
fresh dill or parsley for garnish

- Preheat oven to 325 degrees.

- Line baking sheet with foil. Use butter to grease bottom and sides of 8 or 9-inch springform pan. Add bread crumbs; tilt and rotate pan to cover bottom and sides. Refrigerate pan while preparing filling.

- To prepare the filling: Using a food processor or electric mixer, beat cream cheese until smooth. Add eggs, Gruyère cheese, half-and-half, lemon juice, dill and salt. Mix just until smooth.

- Stir in onions and salmon until blended.

- Pour into springform pan and place on baking sheet. Bake for one hour and 15 minutes or until a toothpick comes out clean from center. Cool on wire rack for 30 minutes.

- Remove pan sides; cool completely. Cut into 12 wedges, or serve whole with a serving knife for individual servings. Serve on water crackers.

- Yield: 10-12 servings

CHINOOK SALMON IN PHYLLO

1 package phyllo dough, frozen
⅔ cup mayonnaise
2 tablespoons sour cream
1 teaspoon lemon juice

1 tablespoon dill
melted butter
½ medium size salmon fillet,
   cooked

- Thaw phyllo dough overnight according to package directions.

- Preheat oven to 375 degrees.

- Mix together mayonnaise, sour cream, lemon juice and dill.

- Using a pastry brush, brush one sheet of phyllo with butter. Place another sheet on top and brush with butter. Then add one more sheet and brush with butter. Cut the phyllo horizontally into 6 strips approximately 3-inches wide.

- Place a dab of the mayonnaise mixture in one corner of each strip. Add a piece of salmon and roll up like a flag to form a triangular shape. (Fold repeatedly on the diagonal.) Repeat process to make 24 triangles.

- Place on cookie sheet and bake until nicely browned, approximately 20 minutes.

- Yield: 24

These pastry triangles are baked in the oven and the layers of phyllo puff up making a delicate, crunchy appetizer for your next get together.

The Chinook salmon is one of the largest fish in the Rogue River. Chinook can be identified by black spotting on the dorsal fins and on both lobes of the caudal (tail) fin.

SALMON BAGUETTE

8 ounces cream cheese, room
   temperature
4 ounces (or more) smoked salmon
1 tablespoon grated onion

Tabasco sauce (optional)
fresh baguette, sliced into ½-inch
   thick rounds

- Beat cream cheese in mixer until smooth.

- Break up salmon in small bowl with a fork and mix into cream cheese. Season with grated onion, add Tabasco sauce if desired.

- Spread on toasted or room temperature baguette rounds and serve. The mixture may be refrigerated overnight and then brought back to room temperature when ready to assemble appetizers.

- Yield: 8-10 servings

Smoked salmon is available, often vacuum packed, in many grocery stores.

NEWPORT SHRIMP

Worcestershire sauce gets its distinctive flavor from various exotic ingredients such as: anchovies, tamarinds, shallots, molasses, soy and peppercorns. It is placed in vats and allowed to age for a minimum of two years before being bottled.

5 pounds shrimp, medium size in shell
1 cup salt to penetrate shrimp
8 sliced onions
2 cups vegetable oil

1½ tablespoons Worcestershire sauce
8-10 drops Tabasco sauce
1 (3-ounce) jar capers
juice of 1 lemon

- This recipe needs to marinate for at least 24 hours.

- Cook shrimp for 5 minutes in simmering salted water. Drain, peel and remove vein.

- To make marinade, mix onions, oil, Worcestershire sauce, Tabasco sauce, capers, and lemon juice, and place in baking dish or good quality sealable bag with shrimp. Marinate for at least 24 hours before serving.

- Yield: 5-6 dozen

OREGON SHRIMP PÂTÈ

There are many sizes of shrimp and, depending on variety, many different colors. Shells may be light gray, brownish-pink or red. When cooked, the shell will become reddish and meat will turn pink. Shrimp are available all year round, either fresh or frozen, in shell, or shelled and deveined. Canned shrimp are cooked and shelled.

Dijon mustard comes from the ancient Province of Burgundy, France.

1 pound cream cheese
3 tablespoons fresh lemon juice
1 teaspoon sugar
1 pound Oregon shrimp meat, well-drained
1 tablespoon fresh parsley, chopped

1 dash white vermouth
3 medium green onion tops, chopped
1 teaspoon Dijon mustard
salt and pepper to taste

- Whip cream cheese, lemon juice and sugar in food processor or electric mixer. Add half of the shrimp. Whip until shrimp is broken into pieces. Add parsley, vermouth, onions, mustard, salt and pepper; whip. By hand, fold in remaining shrimp. Spoon into bowl and chill.

- Serve with crackers, bread rounds or raw vegetables.

- Yield: 4-6 servings

BAKED STUFFED SHRIMP

2 pounds large fresh shrimp
5 tablespoons butter, divided
2 tablespoons shallots, minced
¼ cup onion, chopped
1 green pepper, seeded and
   chopped

1 cup bread crumbs
1 teaspoon salt
⅛ teaspoon pepper
1 egg, beaten
parsley for garnish

- Preheat oven to 400 degrees.

- Shell and devein 6 shrimp. Cook shrimp in 3 tablespoons butter until pink. Remove and chop. Add shallots, onion, and green pepper to skillet. Cook 3-4 minutes, stirring often. Remove from heat. Stir in bread crumbs, cooked shrimp, salt, pepper and egg.

- Shell reserved shrimp, leaving tails on. Place shrimp, back down on a board. Make slit along underside of each shrimp. Do not cut through; remove vein.

- Mound stuffing mix in hollow of each shrimp. Bring tail over stuffing. Put shrimp, tails up, on greased shallow baking dish. At this point dish may be covered and refrigerated.

- Drizzle shrimp with 2 tablespoons butter. Bake 10-12 minutes. Transfer to warm plate and garnish with parsley.

- Yield: approximately 40 stuffed shrimp

Unbaked stuffed shrimp can be made ahead and frozen. For each serving, allow ½ pound uncooked shrimp in the shell or ⅓ pound if shelled. If cooked and shelled, allow ¼ pound per person.

The finished result is a picture in itself.

SHRIMP-DILL PUFFS

1 pound cooked small shrimp
1 cup fresh Parmesan cheese,
   grated
1 egg, beaten
¼ teaspoon cayenne pepper

¼ teaspoon dill
¼ teaspoon coarse ground pepper
¼ teaspoon lemon juice
fresh dill for garnish

- Preheat oven to 400 degrees.

- Mince shrimp; mix with Parmesan cheese, egg, cayenne, dill, pepper and lemon juice.

- Drop by teaspoonfuls onto baking sheet. Bake 15 minutes.

- Serve on fish platter, garnish with fresh dill.

- Yield: 40 puffs

Dill can be fresh or dried. It has a distinctive yet mild caraway-like flavor.

PECAN-CRAB BALL

Crabs are available live, cooked in the shell, cooked and frozen in the shell, or as fresh cooked, frozen or canned crabmeat.

8 ounces cream cheese, softened
2 tablespoons chives
¼ teaspoon garlic powder

¼ teaspoon salt
6 ounces crab meat, fresh or canned
¼ cup chopped pecans

- Blend cream cheese, chives, garlic powder and salt. Fold in crab meat. Shape into ball or log. Roll in pecans. Cover with plastic wrap and chill until ready to use.

- Serve with assorted crackers.

- Yield: 8-10 servings

GIN LIN CHAR SHU PORK

When pork tenderloins are fully cooked, they may be stored in the refrigerator or put in the freezer. So handy to have on hand for an impromptu gathering.

3 pounds pork tenderloin
1 cup water
6 tablespoons sugar
½ tablespoon salt
½ cup soy sauce
¼ cup sherry

1 clove garlic, peeled, crushed and minced
3 slices fresh ginger root, peeled and minced (may use candied ginger, chopped fine)

- This recipe is best marinated for 48 hours, never less than 6.

- Place pork in baking dish or good quality sealable bag.

- In small saucepan, heat water, sugar and salt until dissolved. Add soy sauce, sherry, garlic and ginger root. Cool to room temperature. Pour over pork and marinate in refrigerator.

- Preheat oven to 450 degrees.

- Remove pork from marinade and place in baking pan. Bake meat for 15 minutes.

- Reduce heat to 250 degrees and bake for another 40 minutes.

- Turn meat over and bake an additional 40 minutes.

- Remove from oven and cool. Slice into ½-inch slices and serve with hot mustard and sesame seeds.

- Yield: 10-12 servings

ROGUES' FIZZ

1 (6-ounce) can pink lemonade
6 ounces vodka
1 (6-ounce) can evaporated milk
1 raw egg
1 pint vanilla ice cream

3-4 ice cubes
fresh strawberries, sprigs of fresh
  mint, or slices of lemon for
  garnish

- Place all ingredients except garnish in a blender and puree. To make it less sweet just add more ice cubes. Garnish and serve immediately.

- Yield: 4 (1-cup) servings

To save time, freeze glasses ahead of time and stack them in the freezer; remove just before using.

A festive holiday drink to serve at Thanksgiving and Christmas.

CHINA BAR CHICKEN

2 whole chicken breasts, skinned
  and boned
1 bunch green onions, optional
½ cup sherry
3 tablespoons soy sauce

½ teaspoon Chinese five-spice
  powder
½ teaspoon fresh ginger, minced
2 cloves garlic, crushed

- Cut chicken into 1-inch cubes. Put chicken on skewers. Finish skewer by weaving a 1-inch long piece of green onion on the end if desired.

- Mix sherry, soy sauce, Chinese five-spice powder, ginger and garlic.

- Broil chicken for 8-10 minutes basting often with sauce.

- Yield: 15 skewers.

Five-spice powder is a blend of powdered star anise, cinnamon, peppercorns, fennel and cloves.

In the 1860 s, hundreds of Chinese miners lived and worked along the Rogue River. After the passage of the Chinese Exclusion Act in 1882, almost all of the Chinese miners disappeared from the valley. China Bar was named for Chow Long, one of the few Chinese left mining the Rogue by 1894.

TARRAGON CHICKEN PÂTÉ

In the Rogue Valley, these have been served on bread cut with a pear-shaped cookie cutter, with zest of an orange for the stem of the pear. Placed on a bed of herbs fresh from the garden or a bed of tender butter lettuce, this makes for a beautiful dish, lovely for a summer tea!

2 whole chicken breasts, skinned and boned
3 tablespoons sour cream
3 tablespoons mayonnaise
1 tablespoon fresh tarragon or ½ teaspoon dried
½ cup celery, chopped
¼ cup pecans, chopped
salt and fresh ground pepper to taste
juice of ½ orange
wheat bread, thinly sliced

- Preheat oven to 350 degrees.

- Bake chicken breasts about 25-30 minutes. Do not overcook.

- Cool and cut chicken meat into small pieces. Place in small bowl and add sour cream and mayonnaise. Gently stir in tarragon, celery, pecans and seasonings. Squeeze in juice of ½ orange.

- To serve, spread on thinly sliced wheat bread.

- Yield: 40 small sandwiches

SPINACH TORTE

In the past, basil was used only by royalty. Today basil is commonly used with garlic for flavoring in many recipes.

CREAM CHEESE FILLING:

1 (8-ounce) package cream cheese, softened
¼ cup butter, softened
1 tablespoon milk

SPINACH-CHEESE FILLING:

1 cup fresh spinach leaves
1 cup fresh parsley, stems removed
¼ cup pine nuts
¼ cup olive oil
1 clove garlic
1 teaspoon dried basil, crushed
1 cup Parmesan cheese, grated
parsley for garnish
French bread, thinly sliced or crackers

- To prepare the cream cheese filling: Combine cream cheese and butter in mixing bowl or food processor and beat until fluffy. Add milk. Set aside.

- To prepare the spinach-cheese filling: Using a blender or food processor, combine spinach, parsley, pine nuts, olive oil, garlic, and basil. Blend well, frequently scraping sides of container. Add Parmesan cheese and blend until smooth.

- Line a 7-½x3-½x2-inch loaf pan with plastic wrap. Spread ⅓ of cream cheese filling in bottom of loaf pan. Next spread ½ of spinach-cheese filling. Repeat layers ending with cream cheese layer on top. Cover and chill several hours before serving.

- Unmold by pulling plastic wrap. Serve on plate garnished with parsley. Serve with French bread and/or crackers.

- Variations: Add pimiento at last minute for red color. Swirl parsley and pine nuts or basil on top.

- Yield: 25-30 servings

CHINA RIFFLE MUSHROOMS

36 fresh mushrooms
fresh lemon juice
½ pound cooked ground pork, lean
¼ cup water chestnuts, minced
¼ cup green onions, minced

1 egg, slightly beaten
1 teaspoon soy sauce
1 clove garlic, pressed
¼ cup sesame seeds

A very attractive appetizer that tastes marvelous and can be made ahead and baked just before serving.

- Preheat oven to 350 degrees.

- Wash mushrooms; remove and reserve stems. If prepared in advance, rub caps with lemon juice to keep them white.

- Chop mushroom stems finely and combine with cooked pork, chestnuts, onions, egg, soy sauce and garlic. Stuff mushroom caps. Coat just bottoms with butter. Top with sesame seeds. Place in ovenproof dish and bake for 10 minutes. Serve immediately.

- Yield: 36

CURRIED CASHEW PÂTÈ

4 tablespoons butter
1 pound fresh mushrooms, chopped
½ cup onions, minced
2 cloves garlic, minced
1½ teaspoons curry powder
½-1 teaspoon salt

¼ teaspoon ground coriander
¼ teaspoon ground cumin
1 cup unsalted cashews, roasted
2 tablespoons oil
parsley sprigs for garnish
wheat crackers

This recipe freezes well and may be halved or doubled.

Serve with dry champagne, caviar and roast tenderloin for a fancy dinner, or take it on a picnic with wine and French bread.

- Melt butter. Add chopped mushrooms, onions, garlic, curry powder, salt, coriander and cumin. Cook until most of the liquid is cooked down.

- Finely chop the cashews in a food processor. Slowly add oil to make a cashew paste. Add mushroom mixture and mix until smooth.

- Put into a serving bowl and sprinkle with parsley. Serve at room temperature with wheat crackers.

- Yield: 6-8 servings

AEGEAN EGGPLANT SHELL

When shopping for eggplant, look for a vegetable that is firm, free from blemishes with a uniformly dark, rich purple color and a bright green cap. Avoid wrinkled or soft eggplant as they are usually bitter tasting.

The purple eggplant shell creates a showpiece appetizer.

1 package pita bread
1 large eggplant
1 tablespoon lemon juice
¼ cup olive oil
1 green pepper, seeded and diced
3 celery stalks, diced
2 green onions, diced
2 garlic cloves, finely minced
1 (2¼-ounce) can ripe olives, sliced
1 tablespoon red wine vinegar

2 tomatoes, peeled, seeded and chopped
3 tablespoons chopped cilantro leaves
3 teaspoons fresh basil leaves
1 teaspoon salt
⅛ teaspoon cayenne pepper
fresh basil or cilantro leaves for garnish

- Cut pita bread into quarters, wrap in plastic wrap, and set aside.

- Cut eggplant in half lengthwise. Use spoon to scoop out pulp, leaving a ½-inch shell. Reserve pulp. Brush inside of eggplant shells with lemon juice to prevent browning; set aside.

- In a medium saucepan, steam or cook reserved pulp in boiling water until tender, about 8 minutes; set aside.

- In a large skillet, heat oil. Add green pepper, celery, and onion. Sauté until tender, 3-4 minutes. Stir in garlic, olives, vinegar, tomatoes, cilantro, basil, salt, cayenne pepper and cooked eggplant pulp. Stirring occasionally, cook over medium heat 10-15 minutes or until vegetables are very tender.

- Spoon cooked vegetable mixture into eggplant shells. Serve warm or refrigerate 1 hour. Serve as a dip with pita bread triangles.

- Garnish with fresh basil or cilantro leaves.

- Yield: 3½ cups serving 8-10

GOUGÈRE (FRENCH PASTRY PUFF)

Gruyère cheese is from the Burgundy region of France and is best served with dry white wine or Beaujolais.

Delicious as an appetizer or on a luncheon menu served with spinach salad.

¾ cup milk
⅓ cup unsalted butter
½ teaspoon salt
1 cup all-purpose flour

4 large eggs
1 cup Gruyère cheese, finely diced
6 tablespoons Gruyère cheese, shredded

- Preheat oven to 375 degrees.

- Generously butter 10-inch tart pan with removable bottom.

- Bring milk, butter and salt to boil in a heavy saucepan; stirring until butter melts. Remove from heat. Add flour all at once and beat vigorously with spoon until mixture pulls away from sides. Set over low heat and stir 1 minute. Cool slightly.

- Add eggs, one at a time, beating well after each addition. Mix in half of diced Gruyère cheese. Spread batter in pan. Sprinkle with remaining diced and shredded cheese. Bake until pastry puffs (about 35 minutes). Cut into wedges with pastry or pizza wheel. (May be reheated at 350 degrees for 5 minutes).

- Yield: 6-8 servings

CHEESY ARTICHOKE ROUNDS

¾ cup mozzarella cheese, shredded
¾ cup Parmesan cheese, grated
½ cup mayonnaise
1 (14-ounce) can water packed artichoke hearts, drained and finely chopped

1 (4-ounce) can chopped green chilies, drained
French bread baguette, thinly sliced

Add shrimp or crab to create a spread for open face sandwiches. Serve with soup or salad.

- Preheat broiler.

- Combine all ingredients and mix well. Spread mixture on French bread slices. Place slices on ungreased cookie sheet and broil until cheeses are melted and mixture is heated through. Serve hot.

- Yield: 3 dozen

ASHLAND ARTICHOKE TRIANGLES

3 (6-ounce) jars marinated artichoke hearts, reserve oil from one jar
2 tablespoons sun-dried tomatoes, in oil, reserve oil
2 tablespoons oil reserved from sun-dried tomatoes
1-10 cloves garlic, to taste
½ cup onion, chopped
4 eggs
¼ cup seasoned bread crumbs
½ pound sharp Cheddar cheese, shredded

¼ cup Parmesan cheese, freshly grated
2 tablespoons fresh parsley, minced
¼ teaspoon salt
½ teaspoon pepper
⅛ teaspoon Tabasco sauce
½ teaspoon dried oregano
parsley or watercress sprigs for garnish

Artichokes, an edible thistle, are in season all year. The best supplies of artichokes are in March, April and May.

- Preheat oven to 325 degrees. Drain oil from 1 jar artichoke hearts into skillet. Add 2 tablespoons oil from sun-dried tomatoes. Sauté garlic and onions in oil for 5 minutes, then set aside.

- Drain and discard oil from remaining 2 jars artichoke hearts and chop all hearts finely. Set aside.

- Mince 2 tablespoons of sun-dried tomatoes and set aside.

- Beat eggs until foamy, blend in bread crumbs, cheeses, parsley, salt, pepper, Tabasco sauce and oregano. Add artichoke hearts and sun-dried tomatoes. Blend in onions and garlic; mix well.

- Pour mixture into 9-inch pie pan. Bake for 30 minutes. May be made ahead, then reheated at 325 degrees for 10-12 minutes. Cool to room temperature before cutting into 2-inch triangles. Garnish with parsley or watercress sprigs.

- Yield: 16 triangles

TOMATOES AND CHEESES ON PHYLLO

This light appetizer makes a great first course or is equally appropriate for a tailgate picnic.

7 (17x12-inch) sheets of phyllo dough, thawed according to package directions
8 tablespoons unsalted butter, melted
¾ cup Parmesan cheese, freshly grated
1½ cups (6 ounces) mozzarella cheese, coarsely shredded
1 cup onion, very thinly sliced

2 pounds Roma tomatoes, cut into ¼ inch slices
¾ teaspoon dried oregano, crumbled
1 teaspoon fresh thyme leaves, or ¼ teaspoon crumbled dried thyme
salt and pepper to taste
fresh thyme sprigs for garnish

- Preheat oven to 375 degrees. Stack each sheet phyllo dough between 2 sheets wax paper and cover with a dampened kitchen towel. Using pastry brush, brush baking sheet lightly with some of the butter. Place 1 sheet of phyllo on the buttered sheet and brush it lightly with more butter. Sprinkle the phyllo with 1½ tablespoons of the Parmesan, lay another sheet of the phyllo on top and press it firmly down so that it adheres to the bottom layer.

- Butter, sprinkle, and layer the remaining sheets of phyllo in the same manner, ending with a sheet of phyllo and reserving the remaining 1½ tablespoons Parmesan.

- Sprinkle the top sheet of phyllo with the mozzarella, scatter the onion evenly on top, and arrange the tomatoes in one layer over the onion. Sprinkle with the reserved 1½ tablespoons Parmesan, the oregano, thyme, salt and pepper.

- Bake on middle rack of 375 degree oven for 30-35 minutes or until the edges are golden.

- Arrange the thyme sprigs along the doughs' perimeter and with a pizza wheel or sharp knife cut the phyllo dough into squares.

- Yield: 2 dozen as appetizers or 8-10 servings as first course

The spectacular Rogue River Trail starts near Illahe and follows the river for 40 miles. While backpacking, continue your hike past Solitude Bar and on to Brushy Bar Creek, where you will find your ideal lunch spot under the evergreens.

PESTO AND CREAM CHEESE ON SUN-DRIED TOMATOES

Pesto may be purchased or homemade.

PESTO:

2 cups fresh basil leaves, lightly
   packed
4 cloves garlic, peeled
½ cup pine nuts

¾-1 cup olive oil
¾ cup fresh Parmesan cheese,
   grated
salt and pepper to taste

CHEESE FILLING:

1 cup sun-dried tomatoes in olive
   oil, drained, chopped medium
   in food processor or by hand
16 ounces Neufchâtel cheese (or
   cream cheese), softened and
   sliced

fresh basil, rosemary or pine nuts
   for garnish
crackers, deli bread slices or
   breadsticks

Pesto means pounded and is a thick sauce made of garlic, herbs, cheese, nuts and olive oil. Pesto can be stored in the freezer for up to a year.

- To prepare the pesto: Whirl basil and garlic in food processor or blender until coarsely chopped. Add pine nuts; process off and on for 15 seconds. With processor on, slowly add olive oil. Stir in cheese, salt and pepper. (Yields approximately 4 ounces. Excess pesto may be refrigerated or frozen.)

- Spread the tomatoes onto a rimmed serving platter, preferably one with a rimmed center and surrounding compartment for crackers. Cover carefully with cream cheese. (It is helpful to place slices of cheese side by side over tomatoes and then spread carefully with a knife.)

- Spread desired amount of pesto over cheese. The more pesto used, the more pungent the flavor. Refrigerate for at least one hour.

- Garnish with sprig of fresh basil or rosemary, scatter pine nuts on top.

- Serve with simple crackers (such as water crackers), deli bread or bread sticks.

- Yield: 8-10 servings

PESTO CHEESE TORTE

Olive oils are actually fruit juices and can differ depending on the areas where the olives have been grown. The olives also come in a wide range of colors, flavors and aromas.

After a long day on the river, pull this appetizer from the cooler and serve while camp is being set up.

PESTO LAYER:

2½ cups fresh basil leaves, lightly packed
1 cup Parmesan cheese, freshly grated
1 tablespoon olive oil

2 cloves garlic, minced
water, to create paste consistency
¼ cup pine nuts
salt to taste

CHEESE LAYER:

1 cup low fat ricotta cheese
4 ounces Neufchâtel (light cream cheese) or cream cheese
2 cloves garlic, minced
2 teaspoons lemon juice
¼ teaspoon cayenne pepper

fresh basil sprigs for garnish
French bread baguette, thinly sliced or
raw vegetables, sliced
cheesecloth

- To prepare pesto layer: In blender or food processor, blend basil, Parmesan cheese, olive oil, garlic, and enough water to make a smooth paste. Stir in pine nuts and season with salt to taste.

- To prepare cheese mixture: With an electric mixer, beat ricotta and Neufchâtel until well blended. Add garlic, lemon juice and cayenne pepper. Smoothly line 2-cup container with airtight lid with double cheesecloth, moistened and wrung dry.

- With a spoon or tiny spatula press ¼ of cheese mixture evenly into bottom of cheesecloth lined container. Press ⅓ of the pesto onto the cheese, repeat, finishing with last layer of cheese. Cover airtight and chill at least 2 hours or overnight.

- Remove lid, fold back cheesecloth and invert torte onto serving plate. Gently lift off cheesecloth. Garnish with basil sprig and serve with baguette or raw vegetables.

- Yield: 10-12 servings

CHEESE FILLED PASTRY PUFFS

CHILI CHEESE FILLING:

2 (3-ounce) packages cream cheese
1¾ cups sharp Cheddar cheese, shredded

⅓ cup drained diced green chilies
2 tablespoons sesame seeds

CARAWAY CHEESE FILLING:

2 (3-ounce) packages cream cheese
2 cups Jarlsberg cheese, shredded

2 tablespoons caraway seeds

PUFFS:

1 package (17¼-ounce) frozen puff pastry sheets, thawed

1 egg, beaten

Use your imagination to create any combination of herbs and cheeses for your own cheese fillings.

- To prepare fillings: Using preferred filling recipe, mix all of the filling ingredients together, except seeds. Save seeds to sprinkle on top of finished puffs.

- To prepare puffs: On a floured board, roll each pastry sheet into a 12x15-inch rectangle. On half of each sheet, drop rounded teaspoons of filling about ¾-inch apart to make 3 rows of 5 per row. Using pastry brush, brush egg on pastry between mounds and around pastry edge. Fold unfilled side of pastry over so edges meet. Prick each mound with fork and press firmly around each mound to seal well. Cut with a knife or ravioli cutter. Place on ungreased cookie sheet. Cover with plastic wrap and chill 30 minutes or overnight.

- Preheat oven to 400 degrees.

- Cut a ½-inch slit on top of each puff. Brush with remaining egg and sprinkle with seeds. Bake uncovered for 15-20 minutes. Serve hot or warm.

- Yield: 15 servings (30 puffs)

OREGON BLUE CHEESE BUTTER

4 ounces Oregon Blue cheese
4 ounces unsalted butter, softened
2 cloves garlic, peeled and pressed

¼ teaspoon coarsely ground black pepper

- Blend all ingredients to make smooth paste. Serve with sliced baguettes or freshly baked bread.

- Yield: 1 cup

OREGON BLUE CHEESE PROSCIUTTO TARTS

Make the shells and fillings for these tarts ahead of time. Assemble right before serving to preserve a nice flaky crust.

1 cup all-purpose flour
pinch of salt
2 tablespoons grated Oregon blue
   cheese
¼ cup firm butter
1 egg, beaten
1 (14-ounce) can artichoke hearts,
   drained

¼ cup thinly sliced prosciutto
2 tablespoons dairy sour cream
2 teaspoons fresh dill, chopped
1 red pepper, cored, seeded and cut
   into thin strips

- In a bowl, stir together flour, salt and cheese. Using pastry blender, cut in butter to coarse crumb consistency; add egg and mix to form dough. Roll into ball, wrap in plastic and chill for about 30 minutes.

- Lightly grease small tart pans. Preheat oven to 400 degrees.

- Between two pieces of floured plastic wrap, roll out dough until thin. Cut pastry into rounds and fit into tart pans. Chill 15-20 minutes.

- Prick shells and bake for 15-20 minutes. Cool and remove shells from pans.

- Drain artichokes and rinse well. Dry on paper towels. Cut into quarters. Cut prosciutto in strips and roll into cylinders.

- Mix sour cream and dill together.

- To assemble, spoon a small amount of sour cream mixture into each shell and top with artichoke quarter and prosciutto. Garnish with strip of red pepper and sprig of fresh dill if desired.

- Yield: 15 tarts

CHUTNEY CHEESE BALL

11 ounces cream cheese
¼ cup sour cream
3 tablespoons raisins
¾ cup cocktail peanuts
½ pound bacon, cooked crisp and
   crumbled

1 cup pear chutney (following
   recipe) or a purchased variety,
   divided
1½ teaspoons curry powder
crackers

- Mix cream cheese, sour cream, raisins, cocktail peanuts, bacon and ½ cup chutney and curry powder together; form into a ball and chill.

- Before serving, spoon remaining ½ cup chutney over the top and let drizzle down the sides.

- Serve with crackers.

- Yield: 12-15 servings

PEAR CHUTNEY

7 cups peeled pears, diced
1 pound brown sugar, firmly
    packed
2 cups white vinegar
1 medium onion, chopped
1 cup raisins

½ cup preserved ginger, diced
½ teaspoon ground cloves
½ teaspoon cinnamon
2 teaspoons mustard seed
1 clove garlic, minced
2 teaspoons salt

Chutneys are actually relishes that come in hundreds of flavors and varieties. They can also be made from an extensive list of ingredients which include mangos, bananas, onions, garlic, ginger and coconut.

- Combine pears, sugar and vinegar in large, heavy pan. Boil for 10-20 minutes.

- Add onion, raisins, ginger, cloves, cinnamon, mustard seed, garlic and salt. Reduce heat to slowly simmer chutney, stirring occasionally. Cook mixture 1-2 hours, to reduce liquid.

- Pour into sterile jars, seal with lids and refrigerate.

- Yield: 6 (8-ounce) jars

PEARS, PARMESAN, AND PEPPER

3 large ripe Bosc, Anjou or Comice
    pears
¼ cup lemon juice
1 small red onion, thinly sliced

1 French baguette
parsley spread (recipe below)
1 cup Parmesan cheese, grated
1 teaspoon coarse ground pepper

PARSLEY SPREAD:

1½ cups fresh parsley, firmly
    packed
1 cup Parmesan cheese, grated

½ cup olive oil
3 tablespoons lemon juice
salt to taste

Pears with cheese are always in harmony, but pepper and fresh parsley bring an element of surprise to this first course.

Pear trees not only produce delicious fruit, but their springtime blossoms make a white bouquet out of each tree.

- To prepare parsley spread: In a blender or food processor, combine parsley, cheese, olive oil, lemon juice and salt. Use immediately or cover and chill overnight. (Makes 1½ cups).

- To prepare pears: Peel, core, and cut each pear into 12 to 16 slices and place in a bowl with lemon juice. Set aside.

- Cut baguette in half lengthwise and place cut sides down on baking sheet and broil 6 inches from heat until golden brown, about 3 minutes. Remove from oven. Separate sliced onion into rings. Spread baguette halves with parsley mixture, top with onion rings. Drain pears and arrange diagonally across bread. Sprinkle with 1 cup grated Parmesan cheese, then pepper. Preheat broiler and broil until cheese begins to melt, about 4 minutes.

- Cut each loaf into individual pieces and serve on individual plates for a first course or arrange on a platter as hors d'oeuvres.

- Yield: 15-20 appetizers or 10 servings as first course

GARLIC BRIE

Brie is a soft, ripened French cheese, mild to pungent in flavor. Look for wedges with a creamy interior and chalky (edible) crust.

1 loaf French bread, cut in half lengthwise
¼ pound butter, softened

2-3 cloves garlic, finely minced
12 ounces Brie cheese
parsley for garnish

- Preheat broiler. Hollow out French bread. Mix butter and garlic together; spread on bread. Cover with thin slices of Brie; use generously. Place under broiler for 2 minutes, until the cheese is hot and bubbly. Garnish with parsley; slice and serve immediately.

- Yield: 8-10 servings

MOLDED TRIPLE LAYER HORS D'OEUVRES

Simple to prepare, this colorful, layered hors d'oeuvres may be assembled in advance. A good choice when you want elegant results and time is limited.

3 (8-ounce) packages cream cheese, softened
¼ cup butter
4-6 ounces ham, finely chopped
1 tablespoon white onion, finely chopped
dash of Tabasco sauce

¼ pound Cheddar cheese, grated
2 tablespoons milk
4-5 green onions, sliced, green tops only
crackers
sprigs of parsley for garnish

- In the bowl of a food processor or in a small mixer bowl combine cream cheese and butter. Beat or process until smooth. Divide into 3 equal parts.

- Layer One: Mix ⅓ cream cheese mixture with ham, white onions, and Tabasco sauce. Spread in bottom of 7-inch springform pan. Smooth and chill well.

- Layer Two: Process until smooth, ⅓ cream cheese mixture, Cheddar cheese, and milk. Spread over 1st layer and chill well.

- Layer Three: With processor turned on, drop handfuls of green onion tops onto spinning blade. Puree as much as possible. Drop the remaining ⅓ of cream cheese mixture by spoonfuls into the bowl. Spread over 2nd layer and chill overnight.

- Remove sides of springform pan, garnish with parsley and serve with a variety of crackers.

- Yield: 8-12 servings

MEDITERRANEAN NOT TO WORRY

3 pita bread rounds
6 ounces feta cheese, softened
2 tablespoons mayonnaise
24 slices hard salami

4 medium sized red tomatoes,
  sliced
small sprigs fresh basil for garnish

- Preheat oven to 300 degrees.

- Slice pita bread pocket into quarters and open up forming 8 single layer pieces of each. Place 24 pieces of pita bread on cookie sheet and bake until light brown.

- In a food processor or mixer, mix feta and mayonnaise until smooth. Spread on the pita bread. Then top with a slice of salami and a tomato slice, garnishing with a sprig of basil.

- Yield: 24

There are various strengths of feta cheese available: mild, medium and sharp. Depending on the flavor, feta is made from sheep or goat's milk and is usually sold in a brine solution made with milk or water and salt.

FOCACCIA ROMA

2 cloves garlic, minced
2 tablespoons olive oil
1 Roma tomato, sliced paper thin
1 loaf focaccia (Italian flatbread)

½ cup Parmesan cheese, grated
2 slices red onion, paper thin
½ teaspoon Italian seasoning
fresh ground pepper

- Add garlic to oil and set aside for 15-20 minutes for oil to take on flavor of garlic. Place tomato slices on paper towel to absorb excess moisture.

- Preheat oven to 400 degrees.

- Brush bread with garlic oil mixture and sprinkle with Parmesan cheese. Top with tomatoes and onion slices and sprinkle with Italian seasoning and fresh ground pepper to taste. Bake 10-15 minutes, or until top is bubbly and golden brown. Tomatoes should be fairly dry. Slice into small wedges and serve.

- Yield: 10-12 servings

When selecting tomatoes, look for firm, unblemished tomatoes with good red color. If tomatoes are not fully ripe, leave them stem end up, at room temperature out of sunlight until they turn red. Then refrigerate and use within two days.

Focaccia is Italian for flatbread, similar in texture to a thick pizza crust.

SOUPS

GOLDEN DEMON

A favorite of Zane Grey, the Golden Demon glows in the water on semi-lit days. Grey enjoyed such success with the Demon in New Zealand in the 1930's that he imported this bright dress fly to the Rogue. Millions of readers were introduced to Grey's battles with the Rogue's steelhead in his angling tales. Winkle Bar, the site of his seasonal cabin, is one of the most popular fishing riffles on the Rogue.

ASPARAGUS SOUP

When shopping for asparagus, look for straight spears with tips tightly closed. Refrigerate with a paper towel around the ends, and put in a sealed plastic bag. Asparagus will keep about one week.

2 pounds asparagus, cut into 1-inch
    lengths
4 tablespoons butter

4 tablespoons all-purpose flour
2 cups chicken broth
1 cup whipping cream

- Cook asparagus in ¾ cup boiling water until very tender. Reserve tips for garnish; press remaining asparagus through food mill. Add water to cooking liquid to make 2 cups.

- Melt butter. Stir in flour and cook until bubbly. Gradually add chicken broth. Stir in 1 cup cream and milled asparagus. Serve hot or cold. Garnish with spear tips.

- Yield: 4-6 servings

ILLAHE ARTICHOKE SOUP

A Rogue Valley favorite!

1 (14-ounce) can artichoke hearts or
    bottoms
3 cups chicken broth
3 tablespoons heavy cream

2 teaspoons lemon juice
salt and pepper to taste
freshly chopped chives for garnish

- Drain artichokes and place in blender with chicken broth. Puree until smooth.

- Add cream and lemon juice; mix well. Pour into bowl. Add salt and pepper. Cover and chill well.

- To serve, pour into bowls and garnish with chopped chives.

- Yield: 3-4 servings

CHILLED POTATO-CILANTRO SOUP

4 cups chicken broth
1 pound thin-skinned potatoes,
  peeled and chopped
¼ teaspoon white pepper
½ teaspoon ground cumin
1 (4-ounce) can diced green chilies

1 cup fresh cilantro, lightly packed
3 green onions, thinly sliced
1 cup sour cream
salt to taste
cilantro sprigs for garnish
sour cream for garnish

- In a large saucepan, combine broth, potatoes, pepper and cumin. Bring to a boil; reduce heat to a simmer and cover. Simmer for 15-20 minutes or just until tender.

- Combine half the potato mixture with chilies, cilantro and green onions in a food processor or blender; blend until smooth. Transfer to a large bowl.

- Blend remaining potato mixture with sour cream until smooth. Add to other mixture in large bowl. Season with salt to taste. Cover and refrigerate until completely chilled or up to one day.

- Serve in tureen or individual soup bowls with a cilantro sprig garnish placed in center of a small dollop of sour cream.

- Yield: 6-8 servings

Fresh cilantro, coriander, Indian or Chinese parsley are all names for one of the oldest and most popular herbs around. Cilantro is easy to keep on hand in your refrigerator. Place the bunch in a jar filled with enough water to cover the stems at least halfway and cover the leaves with clear plastic wrap.

OUR FAVORITE GAZPACHO

3 cups tomato juice, divided
2 tablespoons olive oil
3 tablespoons red wine vinegar
1 clove garlic
2 medium tomatoes, peeled and
  quartered
1 small cucumber, cut into pieces
½ medium green pepper, chopped

3 medium stalks celery, sliced
¼ medium onion, cut into pieces
4 sprigs parsley
1 ripe avocado
1 teaspoon salt
¼ teaspoon freshly ground pepper
1 cup croutons for garnish
cucumber slices for garnish

- Place 1 cup tomato juice, olive oil, vinegar and garlic into blender. Blend until garlic is finely chopped.

- Add half each of tomato, cucumber, green pepper, celery, onion, parsley, avocado, salt and pepper. Blend until vegetables are pureed. Transfer to a 2-quart container. Repeat with remaining tomato juice, vegetables and seasonings.

- Serve in chilled mugs or bowls topped with croutons and garnish with cucumber slices.

- Yield: 6 servings

*This recipe is from our last Junior Service League cookbook, **Our Favorites**. It is so delicious that we decided to include it again for you to enjoy.*

FRESH TOMATO-DILL SOUP

A cool, fresh addition to a summertime luncheon. Dill is relatively easy to grow and looks lovely in the garden.

2 medium onions, chopped
1 clove garlic, minced
2 tablespoons butter or margarine
4 large tomatoes (2 pounds), peeled and cubed
½ cup water
1 chicken bouillon cube
2½ teaspoons fresh or ¾ teaspoon dried dill weed

¼ teaspoon salt
⅛ teaspoon pepper
½ cup mayonnaise
fresh cilantro or parsley sprigs for garnish
mayonnaise for garnish

- In a 2-quart saucepan, cook onions and garlic in butter or margarine for 3 minutes.

- Add all remaining ingredients except the mayonnaise; cover and simmer 10 minutes. Remove from heat and cool.

- Place half of tomato mixture at a time in a blender; cover and blend until smooth.

- Pour into a large bowl and stir in the mayonnaise. Chill overnight.

- Garnish bowls of soup with a dollop of mayonnaise and a sprig of parsley or cilantro. May be served hot or cold. If soup needs to be thinned, use tomato juice to achieve desired consistency.

- Yield: 4-6 servings

CHILLED CUCUMBER SOUP

Be sure to include one of these chilled soups on your next picnic or backpacking trip by pouring into a chilled thermos.

2 cups cucumbers, peeled and coarsely chopped
1 cup chicken broth
¼ cup celery leaves, chopped
¼ cup chives, chopped
3 sprigs fresh parsley
1 tablespoon fresh basil or ½ teaspoon dried

3 tablespoons soft butter
¾ cup sour cream
salt to taste
pinch white pepper
⅔ cup cucumber, finely chopped for garnish
grated lemon rind for garnish

- Combine all ingredients in a blender and blend until smooth. Taste and adjust seasonings if desired.

- Serve chilled and garnish with finely chopped cucumber and a bit of grated lemon rind.

- Yield: 4-6 servings

CHILLED CANTALOUPE SOUP
THE WINCHESTER COUNTRY INN

4 cantaloupes, peeled, seeded and
    cut into 1-inch chunks
2 lemons, juiced
⅔ to ¾ pint sour cream or
    buttermilk

½ pint heavy cream (optional)
salt to taste

- Puree cantaloupe, lemon juice and sour cream in food processor or blender. Cream may be added and pureed until smooth if extra creamy texture is desired. Salt to taste. Chill for at least 2 hours.

- Yield: 8-10 servings

The Winchester Country Inn provides an atmosphere of sophisticated country living, but is located "in the heart" of the City of Ashland. The Inn was originally constructed in 1886 and the Victorian charm has been preserved with the use of handsome period pieces.

CHILLED WATERMELON STRAWBERRY SOUP
THE WINCHESTER COUNTRY INN

½ watermelon
2 pints strawberries, washed,
    stemmed and halved
2 lemons, juiced

1 tablespoon fresh cilantro
1 pint sparkling cider or
    champagne (dry or brut)
½ pint heavy cream

- Cut one end off watermelon and stand upright on flat surface formed by cutting. Trim the green peel off and cut into thin wedges. Knock the seeds out by running spoon or finger down the sides; place in food processor. Add strawberries, lemon juice, cilantro and sparkling cider. Process, slowly adding cream to achieve a very smooth texture.

- Chill at least 2 hours before serving.

- Yield: 10-12 servings

When measuring ingredients by pint, remember that one pint equals two cups.

FRESH RASPBERRY SOUP

1 pint fresh raspberries
1 cup white wine
4 tablespoons honey
1 cup fresh orange juice

1 tablespoon fresh lime juice
½ cup heavy cream
fresh raspberries and mint for
    garnish

- Place raspberries, white wine, honey, orange juice and lime juice in a blender and puree for 1 minute. Add cream and continue to puree until well blended. Strain into bowl and chill.

- To serve, ladle into bowls and garnish with fresh raspberries and mint leaves.

- Yield: 4-6 servings

A beautiful soup, creamy and rich with the wonderful flavor of raspberries.

CHILLED BLUEBERRY AND STRAWBERRY SOUP

A delicious blend of two berries grown in Oregon. For variety, try substituting freshly picked huckleberries in place of the blueberries. Delicious and colorful!

1½ cups fresh strawberries, hulled
1½ cups fresh blueberries
1 pint buttermilk

8 ounces plain yogurt
fresh strawberries for garnish

- Place all ingredients into a blender and puree until well blended. Strain into a bowl and chill for 1 hour.

- To serve, ladle soup into individual bowls and garnish each with a fresh strawberry.

- Yield: 4-6 servings

CHILLED MELON SOUP

3 cups cantaloupe, cubed
3 cups honeydew melon, cubed
2 cups orange juice

⅓ cup lime juice
2 cups sugar-free lemon-lime soda

- Combine 1½ cups of cantaloupe and 1½ cups honeydew in a blender. Add 1 cup of orange juice and half the lime juice. Blend until smooth. Transfer to a large bowl. Repeat the process with remaining melons and juices. Add to bowl.

- Stir in sugar-free soda; cover and refrigerate.

- Yield: 8 servings

CARROT-APPLE POTAGE

Don't forget to use the carrot curl and chopped green chives as an imaginative garnish for this delightful soup.

4 large green cooking apples,
    peeled and diced
2 large carrots, peeled and chopped
6 cups water
2 (14-ounce) cans peeled tomatoes
2 teaspoons basil

¼ teaspoon marjoram
salt and pepper to taste
2 teaspoons sugar
2 sprigs parsley
chopped chives and carrot curls for
    garnish

- In a large Dutch oven, combine apples, carrots and water. Bring to a boil; then simmer, covered, until carrots are tender (about 15 minutes).

- Add tomatoes with liquid, basil, marjoram, salt, pepper, sugar and parsley; simmer 5 minutes.

- Puree mixture in blender until smooth; return to clean pan and heat to a simmer.

- Serve in soup bowls garnished with chopped chives and one carrot curl.

- Yield: 8 servings

CARROT-DILL SOUP

2 tablespoons butter
1 medium yellow onion, diced
3 cups carrots, thinly sliced
2½ cups potatoes, peeled and sliced
4 cups chicken broth
1 cup water
½ teaspoon salt

¼ teaspoon ground black pepper
½ teaspoon dried dill weed
¼ cup sour cream for garnish
¼ cup sliced green onions for
    garnish or
dill weed for garnish

At the vegetable stand, look for firm, bright orange carrots with crisp green tops.

An excellent choice for a busy summer schedule.

- In a Dutch oven, heat butter and sauté onion about 5 minutes or until tender, stirring frequently.

- Add carrots, potatoes, chicken broth, water, salt, pepper and dill weed; bring to a boil. Cover; reduce heat and simmer 20 minutes or until vegetables are tender. Set aside.

- Blend half of the mixture in food processor or blender at a time. Serve immediately or place in airtight container and refrigerate up to 2 days or freeze up to 1 week.

- To serve, place thawed carrot puree in a saucepan and cook over medium heat until thoroughly heated, stirring occasionally. Ladle soup into bowls; top with sour cream and green onions or dill weed.

- Yield: 8 servings

ARTICHOKE AND HAZELNUT SOUP

1½ pounds Jerusalem artichokes
¼ cup butter
1 medium onion, chopped
⅓ cup hazelnuts, ground
½ teaspoon salt or to taste
2 cups chicken stock, warmed
2 cups milk, heated to scalding
    point

2 tablespoons all-purpose flour
¼ cup cold milk
2 egg yolks
⅓ cup cream
finely chopped parsley for garnish
coarsely chopped hazelnuts for
    garnish

A soup that is perfectly designed for the first course of a dinner with a Pacific Northwest theme.

- Wash, dry, peel and slice artichokes; set aside.

- Melt butter in heavy pan (3-quart or larger); sauté onion about 3 minutes. Add artichokes; cover and cook over low heat for 10 minutes, stirring occasionally. Add hazelnuts and salt; stir in chicken stock.

- Puree in blender. Stir in scalded milk.

- Make a thick paste of the flour and cold milk. Beat into soup with a wire whisk; simmer 3-4 minutes. Remove from heat.

- Beat egg yolks in bowl; add cream and beat until smooth. Pour in a thin stream into soup, beating constantly. Return to low heat. Warm to serving temperature, but do not boil.

- Serve in soup bowls garnished with finely chopped parsley and coarsely chopped hazelnuts. (May thicken or thin soup with milk as desired).

- Yield: 4-6 servings

MUSHROOM SOUP WITH CASHEWS

Cashews add an exciting flavor to this rich, creamy soup.

2 tablespoons butter
2 tablespoons all-purpose flour
2 cups chicken broth
1 cup heavy cream
2 cups fresh mushrooms, sliced

1¼ cups cashews, chopped
salt and pepper to taste
sliced mushrooms for garnish
chopped cashews for garnish

- Melt butter in medium saucepan; add flour and stir until blended. Stir in chicken broth and cream. Cook over medium heat until thickened and well blended.

- Stir in mushrooms and half of the chopped cashews; cook for approximately 2 more minutes.

- In a blender or food processor, blend only half the mixture until smooth and return all to the pan. Heat through; add remaining nuts and salt and pepper to taste. Soup may be garnished with sliced mushrooms and cashews.

- Yield: 6 servings

PARSNIP AND CURRIED CARROT SOUP

The spice blend called curry powder contains a blend of turmeric, cayenne, cumin, fenugreek and sometimes ground curry leaves.

With a perfect combination of curry powder and other flavors, this is a colorful soup with a creamy texture.

¼ cup salted butter
1½ cups leeks (white part only), chopped
1 pound carrots, peeled and chopped
¾ pound parsnips, peeled and chopped
8 cups chicken broth

¾ teaspoon curry powder, or to taste
½ cup whipping cream
salt to taste
fresh ground pepper to taste
2 tablespoons fresh parsley, chopped for garnish

- Melt butter in large, heavy pot over medium heat. Add leeks and sauté until soft, about 4 minutes.

- Add carrots and parsnips and sauté 3 minutes.

- Add stock and curry; bring to a boil. Reduce heat and simmer until vegetables are tender, about 30 minutes.

- Cool slightly. Puree soup in blender in batches. Cover and refrigerate at this point if made ahead of time.

- Return to pot when ready to serve. Add whipping cream and bring to a simmer. Season with salt and pepper. Be careful not to boil. Ladle into bowls and sprinkle with chopped parsley to serve.

- Yield: 8 servings

PUMPKIN SOUP

6 tablespoons butter
½ cup all-purpose flour
1 medium onion, grated
6 cups chicken broth
1 (16-ounce) can pumpkin
1 tablespoon salt

2 teaspoons lemon juice
¼ teaspoon pepper
⅛ teaspoon ground nutmeg
2 cups half-and-half
2 cups milk

For a special fall meal, serve this unique soup in individual, hollowed out pumpkins.

- In large Dutch oven, melt butter over low heat. Add flour; stir constantly until light brown. Add onion; sauté lightly.

- Add chicken broth, pumpkin, salt, lemon juice, pepper and nutmeg. Heat mixture to boiling point. Reduce heat and simmer covered for about 15 minutes, stirring occasionally.

- Add half-and-half and milk; heat until warmed. Do not boil soup. Ladle into bowls and serve at once.

- Yield: 8 servings

TAKELMA TACO SOUP

1 pound Italian sausage
1 pound lean ground beef
1 large onion, chopped
2 (16-ounce) cans stewed tomatoes
2 (16-ounce) cans black beans, drained
2 cups chicken broth
1 (16-ounce) can tomato sauce

1 (4-ounce) can tomato paste
1 (8-ounce) can diced green chilies, drained
1 package taco seasoning mix
cheese bread or tortilla chips
sour cream for garnish
chopped chives for garnish

A hearty soup that is an excellent main course. Serve in bowls with cheese bread or tortilla chips. Garnish with sour cream and chives.

- Brown sausage and ground beef in large Dutch oven. Add onions and cook until tender. Add tomatoes, black beans, chicken broth, tomato sauce and paste, green chilies and taco seasoning.

- Cook 4-8 hours on low or put in a crock pot on low all day.

- Ladle soup into bowls; garnish with sour cream and chives, and serve with cheese bread or tortilla chips.

- Yield: 6-8 servings

POSOLE

A wonderful south-western dish that will add fun to your next dinner party. Serve it in a terra cotta tureen surrounded by bowls containing an assortment of condiments.

2 (49½-ounce) cans chicken broth
2 pounds ham hocks, cut into 1-inch slices
1 pound chicken breasts
1 pound chicken thighs
1 teaspoon dried oregano

½ teaspoon cumin
2 large onions, cut into chunks
1 (29-ounce) can yellow hominy, drained
1 (29-ounce) can white hominy, drained

- Day before serving: In a 6-8 quart saucepan, combine broth, ham, chicken, oregano, cumin and onions. Bring to a boil; reduce heat, cover and simmer about two hours.

- Remove meat and set aside to cool. Strain broth through colander and return to pan.

- When cool enough to handle, remove meat and discard bones. Cut meat into chunks and return to broth. Refrigerate overnight.

- Serving day: Skim and discard fat; bring broth to simmer and add hominy. Cook on low for 30 minutes.

- Serve with condiment bowls of: tortilla chips, salsa, sliced green onions, thin slices of red pepper and thinly sliced iceberg lettuce.

- Yield: 8-10 servings

ZUCCHINI SOUP

An excellent way to use an overabundance of zucchini from your vegetable garden.

2 tablespoons butter
1 onion, chopped
2 tablespoons all-purpose flour
2 bay leaves
¼ teaspoon dried thyme
¼ cup fresh parsley, chopped
salt and pepper to taste

5 cups chicken broth
1 large zucchini, shredded
1 large carrot, shredded
1-2 cups milk
1 medium potato, shredded (optional)

- In large saucepan, sauté onion in butter. Add flour and spices. Add chicken broth and bring to a boil.

- Add zucchini and carrot; simmer until carrot is tender. (May freeze at this point, removing bay leaves before freezing.)

- Reduce heat and add milk; heat through but do not boil.

- If you desire a thicker soup, add the grated potato and heat through.

- Yield: 6 servings

EGGPLANT AND SWEET RED PEPPER SOUP

3 large Japanese eggplants or 2
    small regular eggplants
salt and pepper to taste
extra virgin olive oil or spray olive
    oil
2 sweet red peppers

1 tablespoon olive oil
1 large onion, sliced
5 cloves garlic, crushed
1 quart chicken stock
1 bunch fresh basil for garnish

Be sure to look for firm, glossy eggplants with smooth, taut skin and a green cap. Large eggplants, or ones with brown patches, have a tendency to be bitter tasting.

An elegant first course soup for a special dinner party. It takes some time to prepare, but is well worth the effort.

- Wash eggplants and cut lengthwise into spears (6-8 per eggplant). Lightly season with salt and pepper and drizzle with olive oil. Roast eggplants at 400 degrees for 45 minutes or until tender and golden brown.

- Puree in blender until all the black specks from the skins disappear. May use some of the chicken stock to make pureeing easier. Transfer to a large soup pot and set aside.

- Cut peppers in half and place face down on greased cookie sheet. Place under broiler until skins are scorched on all sides. Watch them so they don't burn. Remove from oven and seal in a plastic bag to soften skins. Peel off skins and remove seeds; discard. Puree peppers in a clean blender until smooth. Set aside.

- Heat 1 tablespoon olive oil in skillet. Sauté onion and garlic until tender. Cover and simmer over very low heat for 5 minutes. Add to roasted eggplant puree; add chicken stock, stirring to combine mixture. Do not add the red pepper puree.

- Cook over low heat for 15 minutes until flavors blend and mixture is heated through. Puree in blender until smooth. Return to soup pot to reheat and serve. (May need to add more chicken stock when pureeing.)

- Meanwhile, cut basil into tiny squares like confetti.

- To serve: place soup in individual bowls and spoon red pepper puree in center and swirl with tip of knife or chop stick, etc. Garnish with basil sprinkled in an attractive design.

- Yield: 6 servings

During the summer months, streams of cold mountain water come into the warmer waters of the Rogue River forming large pools that attract schools of salmon.

HEARTY LENTIL SAUSAGE SOUP

Fresh oregano is wonderful but, if it is not available, it's good to know that it is one of the few herbs whose flavor actually improves when it is dried.

2 cups dried lentils, washed and picked over
8 cups water
1 envelope dry onion soup
2 cloves garlic, minced
1 cup celery, chopped
2 cups carrots, sliced

1 bay leaf
2 teaspoons salt
½ teaspoon pepper
½ teaspoon crushed oregano
1 pound smoked sausage or polska kielbasa, sliced

- In a large soup pot or 6-quart Dutch oven, place lentils and cover with water; bring to a boil.

- Add onion soup mix, garlic, celery, carrots, bay leaf, salt, pepper and oregano. Bring to a boil; then reduce to simmer and cover. Cook for 45 minutes or until lentils are tender.

- Add sausage and cook for 20-30 minutes more. If soup is too thick, more water may need to be added at this time.

- Yield: 10-12 servings

POTAGE ESAU

Lentil soup has been made and enjoyed for generations!

"then Jacob gave Esau bread and potage of lentils; and he did eat and drink and rose up, and went his way . . ." Genesis 15:34

2 cups lentils, rinsed
¼ teaspoon pepper
1 tablespoon fresh mint leaves
¼ teaspoon ground cinnamon
½ teaspoon basil
1 bay leaf

¼ teaspoon leaf oregano
⅛ teaspoon ground cloves
2 tablespoons olive oil
2 tablespoons lemon juice
6 cups water

- In large Dutch oven, cover the above ingredients with water and bring to a boil. Simmer, covered, 1 hour until most of the water is absorbed.

Add:

2 carrots, peeled and chopped
3 celery stalks, sliced
½ green pepper, chopped

1 broccoli stalk, sliced
1 medium onion, peeled and chopped

- Simmer on medium heat for 30 minutes, stirring often.

Add:

1 (14-ounce) can peeled, whole tomatoes in juice
3 tablespoons tomato paste
1 tablespoon honey

1 tablespoon red wine vinegar
1 tablespoon red wine
2 tablespoons chicken or beef bouillon granules

- Bring soup to a boil; simmer for 1 more hour. Serve hot.

- Yield: 10-12 servings

BROCCOLI AND CHEDDAR SOUP

2 cups water
1 cup celery, chopped
1 cup carrots, chopped
1 small onion, chopped
1 pound broccoli, chopped
½ cup butter or margarine
½ cup all-purpose flour

salt to taste
¼ teaspoon white pepper
4 cups milk
Tabasco sauce, if desired
4 cups Cheddar cheese, shredded
1 cup ham, cubed
sprigs of fresh parsley for garnish

An excellent selection to serve friends after a football game on a fall afternoon.

- In a large saucepan, combine water, celery, carrots and onion; bring to a boil. Reduce heat and simmer until vegetables are tender, but crisp. Add broccoli and cook until tender. Do not drain vegetables.

- To make sauce while vegetables are cooking, melt butter or margarine in separate saucepan; add flour, salt and pepper. Cook for 1 minute, stirring constantly. Slowly blend in milk and cook until sauce is thick. If desired, add several drops of Tabasco sauce. Add shredded Cheddar cheese and cook until melted.

- Combine cheese mixture with cooked vegetables. Add ham cubes and stir until well blended and ham cubes are warm.

- Garnish with parsley and serve hot.

- Yield: 12 servings

CHEDDAR CHOWDER

2 cups boiling water
2 cups potatoes, peeled and diced
½ cup carrots, sliced on diagonal
½ cup celery, sliced on diagonal
¼ cup onion, chopped
1½ teaspoons salt
¼ teaspoon pepper
¼ cup margarine

¼ cup all-purpose flour
2 cups milk
2 cups sharp Cheddar cheese, shredded
2 cups ham, cooked and cubed or 1 pound bacon, cooked, drained and crumbled

The good thing about choosing to make this soup is that the ingredients are usually on hand.

- In a large saucepan, bring water to a boil. Add potatoes, carrots, celery, onion, salt and pepper. Cover and simmer 10 minutes or until vegetables are just tender. Do not overcook.

- Meanwhile, melt margarine in a medium saucepan on medium heat. Add flour, then milk and stir well until smooth and thick. Do not boil. Add cheese to white sauce and stir until melted. Do not boil.

- Add ham or bacon to undrained vegetables. Add white sauce to vegetables.

- Heat through, being careful not to boil, and serve hot.

- Yield: 6-8 servings

STILTON CHEESE AND ONION SOUP

THE WINCHESTER COUNTRY INN

Be sure to follow cooling directions with leftover cheese soups. If a foam that looks like beer appears when reheating, discard remaining soup.

4 onions
1-1½ quarts homogenized whole or raw milk
white pepper and salt to taste
1 cup all-purpose flour

¾ pound butter, melted
2 pounds Stilton cheese, crumbled (blue cheese may be substituted)

- Peel onions and cut in half. With the flat side down, slice each half against grain to form long skinny strips. In Dutch oven sauté onions in butter. Add milk and bring to a simmer. Season with a small amount of white pepper and salt.

- Add flour and melted butter. Bring temperature back to simmer.

- Add crumbled cheese by sprinkling into soup. Simmer soup for 1 hour. Be sure not to boil. Adjust seasonings before serving.

- Cool slowly to 70 degrees, with lid off, before refrigerating.

- Yield: 12 servings

STEAK AND FRESH SPINACH SOUP

This is a quick, easy soup to prepare. It is sure to become a specialty at your house!

1 tablespoon cornstarch
2 tablespoons water plus 2 cups water
vegetable cooking spray or 1 tablespoon oil
½ pound lean, boneless sirloin steak, cut into 1x¼-inch strips
1 (14½-ounce) can whole tomatoes, undrained and chopped

2 cups fresh spinach, shredded
¾ cup zucchini, thinly sliced
2 tablespoons tomato paste
1 tablespoon sugar
½ teaspoon beef bouillon granules
¼ teaspoon onion powder
¼ teaspoon dried whole thyme

- Dissolve cornstarch in 2 tablespoons cold water and set aside.

- Coat a large saucepan or Dutch oven with cooking spray. Heat; then add steak strips and sauté 2 minutes.

- Add cornstarch mixture, 2 cups water, tomatoes, spinach, zucchini, tomato paste, sugar, bouillon, onion powder and thyme. Bring to a boil. Cover; reduce heat and simmer for 5 minutes. Serve immediately.

- Yield: 4 servings

BRIE SOUP

½ cup onion, chopped
½ cup celery, chopped
4 tablespoons butter
¼ cup flour
2 cups half-and-half
1 cup skim milk

2 cups chicken broth
¼ pound Brie, cut into cubes with rind
½ pound Monterey Jack cheese, shredded
sliced almonds for garnish

A recipe featured in the Medford Mail Tribune cookoff.

- In a medium saucepan, sauté onion and celery in butter. Remove from heat; add flour and blend with a whisk until smooth. Add the half-and-half, milk and chicken broth. Return to medium heat and heat until thick, stirring constantly. At this point soup may be refrigerated until just before serving.

- When ready to serve, reheat soup base; add Brie and Jack cheese. Stir until cheese is melted. Puree in blender, ⅓ at a time, until smooth. Return to saucepan and reheat before serving. Garnish with sliced almonds.

- Yield: 6-8 servings

ROGUE RIVER SALMON SOUP

FISH STOCK

3 cups clam juice
½ cup white wine
1 medium onion, chopped

1 bay leaf
2 sprigs parsley
4 peppercorns

SOUP

1 (14-ounce) can pink salmon or 1 pound fresh cooked salmon
3 tablespoons butter
1 medium onion, chopped
½ cup celery, finely chopped
3 cups fish stock
3 tablespoons all-purpose flour

1 cup whole milk
salt to taste
¼ teaspoon lemon pepper seasoning
3 tablespoons cream
chopped parsley for garnish

When freshly cooked salmon is not available, high-quality canned salmon may be substituted. If using canned salmon, be sure to drain it well and lightly rinse with cold water several times to wash away the oils used for the canning process.

A true reflection of the Rogue River. Serve this soup for an intimate gathering or a grand gala!

- To Make Stock: Place all stock ingredients in medium saucepan and mix well. Heat on medium for 5-10 minutes. Remove from stove and set aside.

- Soup: If using canned salmon, drain and mash in bowl. Mash fresh cooked salmon with fork.

- Melt butter in large, heavy saucepan. Add onion and celery; sauté until soft but not brown. Add fish stock, cover and simmer for 5 minutes.

- In a small jar with lid, shake flour and a little milk together to make a smooth paste. Add remaining milk and shake until smooth. Stir milk mixture into soup. Add salmon; season with salt and lemon pepper. Stir in cream; heat but do not boil. Serve in soup bowls garnished with chopped parsley.

- Yield: 8-10 servings

ITALIAN SAUSAGE AND BEAN SOUP

Treat your family to the heavenly aroma of this hearty soup on a cold, rainy day. Serve with a loaf of "Peasant Black Bread" for a meal to warm the heart.

1 pound navy or small white beans
1 pound mild Italian sausage
1 tablespoon vegetable oil
2 medium onions, chopped
2 cloves garlic, minced
4 stalks celery, sliced thin

2 carrots, sliced
1½ quarts beef broth
1 (15-ounce) can stewed tomatoes
1 teaspoon basil
1 teaspoon oregano
3-4 small zucchini, sliced (optional)

- In a Dutch oven, place beans in 5-6 cups cold water. Bring to a boil, reduce heat and simmer 1½-2 hours or until just tender.

- Slice sausage into ¼-inch thick slices. In a 10-inch skillet, brown sausage in oil. Remove from skillet; drain well.

- Add onions, garlic and celery to oil in skillet. Add more oil if necessary. Sauté until onions are transparent.

- In a very large kettle, combine sausage and sautéed vegetables, carrots and beans. Add beef broth and stewed tomatoes; stir in basil and oregano and simmer 30 minutes. Skim off any fat. If desired, add zucchini in the last ten minutes of cooking time. Serve hot.

- Yield: 10-12 servings

WILDCAT BLACK-EYED PEA SOUP

Rinse and sort through beans in a colander before cooking. A food processor makes this soup a snap to prepare.

1 pound dried black-eyed peas
1½ quarts water
2-2½ quarts chicken stock
½ cup dry sherry
1 small smoked ham hock
1 medium onion, finely diced
1 celery stalk, finely diced
1 small carrot, finely diced

1 bay leaf
1 garlic clove, minced
½ teaspoon dried marjoram
¼ teaspoon dried thyme
salt and freshly ground pepper to
    taste
sprigs of parsley for garnish

- Soak peas overnight in 1½ quarts water or to generously cover.

- In a large saucepan or Dutch oven, combine chicken stock, sherry and ham hock; bring to a boil. Add onion, celery, carrot, bay leaf, garlic, marjoram, thyme, salt and pepper; bring to a boil. Drain peas in a colander and check over. Add peas to soup and simmer until tender, about 1 hour, uncovered.

- Check seasonings; add salt and pepper if desired. Add more chicken stock for desired consistency.

- Serve immediately or refrigerate and reheat at meal time. Garnish each serving with parsley sprig.

- Yield: 8-10 servings

HEARTY MINESTRONE SOUP

1 cup dried kidney beans
2 cups water
6-7 cups beef broth
3 strips very lean bacon
2 medium red onions, chopped
2 cloves garlic, finely chopped and
  crushed with a little salt
⅓ cup olive oil
1 potato, peeled and chopped
2 medium carrots, chopped
½ cup fresh fava beans or sliced
  zucchini

¼ cup celery, coarsely chopped,
  including some of the leaves
1 tablespoon fresh basil, chopped,
  or 2 teaspoons dried basil
2 cups plum tomatoes, peeled,
  seeded and coarsely chopped
1 cup cabbage, shredded
½ cup dry red wine
1 cup cooked pasta, any tiny shape,
  cooked al dente
salt and pepper to taste
Parmesan cheese, grated
parsley and lemon rind for garnish

Canned red kidney beans can be substituted in this recipe if you haven't the time to soak dried beans.

- In a Dutch oven, soak kidney beans in the water overnight, or, bring the water to a boil; boil the beans for 5 minutes and let them stand in the water for 1 hour. Pour off the water. Add the beef stock and bring to a boil.

- Add the bacon, onions and garlic to the beans and simmer for 1 hour.

- In a heavy saucepan, heat the olive oil. Add potatoes, carrots, fava beans (or zucchini), celery and basil; cook for a few minutes; stir in tomatoes and cabbage, and mix well. Add to the beans and cook the mixture over medium heat for about 30 minutes. Stir in wine and cooked pasta. Season the soup with salt and pepper to taste.

- Serve with grated Parmesan cheese. Combine grated lemon rind and chopped fresh parsley to use for garnish.

- Yield: 10 servings

GOLD BEACH SHRIMP AND CORN CHOWDER

1 pound russet potatoes, peeled
  and chopped
1 large white onion, diced
1 large red bell pepper, seeded and
  chopped
4 cups water
1 (16-ounce) bag frozen cut corn

1 (17-ounce) can cream style corn
2 cups half-and-half
1 teaspoon salt
½ teaspoon pepper
½ pound uncooked medium
  shrimp, peeled and deveined
chives for garnish

"Chowder" is derived from the French word "chaud–ière," or cauldron.

- Place potatoes, onion and bell pepper in heavy, large Dutch oven. Pour water over and bring to a boil. Reduce heat and simmer until potatoes are tender, about 20 minutes. Stir in both kinds of corn and half-and-half. Season with salt and pepper. Simmer 20 minutes.

- Add shrimp and cook until opaque, about 8 minutes. Garnish with chives.

- Yield: 8-10 servings

ANAHEIM CHILE CHICKEN SOUP

Add some spice to your life and try this easy south-western chicken soup.

3-3½ pound broiler-fryer chicken, cut up
6 cups chicken broth
1 medium onion, chopped
1 (14½-ounce) can tomatoes
1 tablespoon fresh tarragon leaves or 1 teaspoon dry whole tarragon
1 teaspoon grated lemon peel
½ teaspoon pepper

1 pound potatoes, scrubbed and cut into ½-inch cubes
2 medium-size mild green Anaheim chilies, stemmed, seeded, and chopped
1 large firm, ripe avocado, peeled, pitted and diced for garnish
2 tablespoons lime juice for garnish

- Rinse chicken and pat dry. In a large saucepan, combine all chicken (except breasts) with broth, onion, tomatoes with liquid, tarragon, lemon peel and pepper. Bring to a boil over high heat; cover and simmer for 20 minutes. Add chicken breasts and simmer covered about 15-20 minutes more or until breast is no longer pink in center of thickest part (cut to test). Remove chicken and let stand until cool enough to touch.

- Add potatoes to broth; cover and simmer gently until potatoes are tender, 25-30 minutes.

- Skin and bone chicken; tear meat into bite-size pieces.

- When the potatoes are done, skim and discard the fat from the broth; add chicken and chilies. Heat soup just until ingredients are hot.

- Mix avocado with lime juice. Serve soup hot with garnish, if desired.

- Yield: 6-8 servings

SIGNATURE CLAM CHOWDER

A prize-winning recipe sure to earn you a blue ribbon on a chilly winter evening.

5 slices bacon, chopped
1 medium onion, chopped
4 large potatoes, peeled and cubed
salt and pepper

2 (6½-ounce) cans chopped clams, undrained
1 (12-ounce) can evaporated milk
parsley sprigs, paprika and butter for garnish (optional)

- In a Dutch oven, fry bacon until very crisp; drain but don't wipe out pan. Add onions, potatoes, salt and pepper. Drain juice from both cans of clams into Dutch oven and add enough water to barely cover mixture. Simmer until potatoes are soft but not mushy, about 1 hour.

- Add clams and mash in pan with potato masher. Add evaporated milk; heat until hot but not boiling. Serve garnished with parsley, paprika and a small dab of butter.

- Yield: 6-8 servings

BLACK BEAN AND JALAPEÑO SOUP
THE MCCULLY HOUSE INN

3 large yellow onions, chopped
6 cloves garlic, minced
1 large bunch cilantro, chopped
4 jalapeño peppers, chopped
2 quarts chicken stock

1 quart black turtle beans, soaked
    overnight in cold water to
    cover, drained
fresh salsa for garnish
sour cream for garnish

Look for other McCully House Inn recipes throughout this book.

- In large saucepan, sauté onion, garlic, cilantro, and peppers. Add the chicken stock and beans; bring to a simmer and cook until tender, about 1½ hours. Puree ¾ of the bean and broth mixture in a blender or food processor. Add puree to whole beans that are left. Simmer 5-10 minutes. Adjust seasoning and add more chicken stock if needed.

- Garnish with fresh salsa and sour cream.

- Yield: 6-8 servings

CHICKEN VEGETABLE SOUP THAI STYLE

2 tablespoons peanut oil
½ cup onion, chopped
1 large carrot, peeled and sliced
    diagonally
1 celery stalk, sliced diagonally
2 cloves garlic, minced
6 cups chicken broth

1 (16-ounce) can coconut milk
¾ cup chunky style peanut butter
1 medium potato, diced
2 cups cooked chicken, chopped
¼-½ teaspoon red pepper flakes,
    according to taste

Chicken soup with a twist. The spiciness of this soup may be varied by the amount of dried red pepper flakes used.

- Heat oil in large saucepan over medium heat; sauté onion, carrot, celery and garlic until soft, but not brown.

- Remove from heat and stir in broth, coconut milk and peanut butter. Add potatoes, chicken and red pepper flakes; bring to a boil. Reduce heat and simmer until potatoes are tender, 15-20 minutes.

- Yield: 8-10 servings

SALADS

GREEN BUTTED SKUNK

Topping any angler's list, the Skunk and the Green Butted Skunk stand together as the two most popular steelhead flies developed in the past twenty-five years.

RED, WHITE, AND BLUE FRUIT SALAD

The perfect salad for that patriotic Independence Day barbecue or picnic. Serve it to show your true colors!

2 cups seedless watermelon, cubed
2 cups honeydew melon, cubed
1 cup green seedless grapes
1 cup blueberries

1 cup fresh blackberries (optional)
2 tablespoons fresh mint, chopped
1 cup raspberries
2 kiwi fruit, sliced

- Combine melon, grapes, blueberries, and blackberries in a large decorative bowl. Toss with chopped mint. Sprinkle raspberries on top and arrange kiwi fruit around edge. Chill. Serve with Raspberry Poppy Seed Dressing.

RASPBERRY POPPY SEED DRESSING

1½ cups sugar
2 teaspoons dry mustard
2 teaspoons salt
⅔ cup raspberry wine vinegar

1 slice sweet red onion
2 tablespoons poppy seeds
2 cups salad oil

- Combine sugar, mustard, salt, vinegar, and onion in bowl of food processor fitted with knife blade. Process 5 seconds to blend. With processor running, pour oil slowly through food chute. Process 15-30 seconds or until mixture is thick and oil is fully incorporated. Stir in poppy seeds. Store in quart jar. Refrigerate unused portion.

- Yield: 8 servings

SPICY COOL WATERMELON SALAD

3 pounds or 1½ quarts watermelon,
    seedless is best, chilled
⅓ cup white or Walla Walla onion,
    thinly sliced rings, cut in half

¼ cup fresh mint leaves, minced
Spicy Dressing
salt to taste

A unique blend of spices makes this salad a perfect addition to a backyard summer barbecue. While poolside dining, serve this spicy cool salad as a sidedish.

- Cut watermelon into 1-inch cubes and remove seeds if necessary. Place watermelon in salad bowl. Toss with onion and mint. Lightly toss salad with dressing. Season with salt.

SPICY DRESSING

1½ tablespoons white wine vinegar
½ teaspoon chili powder

3 tablespoons vegetable oil

- Mix in glass measuring cup and pour over salad. May be prepared 3-4 hours ahead and chilled. Add dressing at serving time.

- Yield: 6 servings

OREGON BERRY SALAD

1 pineapple, peeled, cored and cut
    into ½-inch pieces
2 cups raspberries, rinsed

2 cups strawberries, washed,
    hulled and sliced
1 cup blueberries or blackberries,
    rinsed

The climate in Oregon provides the perfect balance to grow many varieties of mouth-watering berries. While strolling through the woods, imagine happening upon a fragrant blackberry patch and selecting your own fresh berries.

- Layer fruit in a serving bowl. Pour Strawberry Dressing over top. Chill. Do not mix fruit and dressing until ready to serve.

STRAWBERRY DRESSING

⅓ cup fresh lime juice (3-4 limes)
3 tablespoons sugar

4 strawberries, cleaned and hulled

- In a blender or food processor, puree lime juice, sugar, and strawberries. Strain mixture through a sieve.

- Yield: 8 servings

FRESH FRUIT TRAY WITH ORANGE CREAM DRESSING

The Orange Cream Dressing is a perfect complement to this fresh fruit tray. Use your decorating imagination to arrange the fruit, and this dish becomes the brightest beacon on any table!

1 fresh pineapple	red grape clusters
3 nectarines, peaches, or pears	pecans
2 oranges	Orange Cream Dressing
½ honeydew melon	

- Twist crown from pineapple. Cut pineapple in half lengthwise. Remove fruit from shells, core and cut into spears. Slice nectarines. Peel and slice oranges and melon.

- Arrange fruit on tray. Garnish with grapes and pecans. Serve dressing on the side.

ORANGE CREAM DRESSING

1 cup sour cream	1 tablespoon fresh orange juice
2 tablespoons honey	½ teaspoon orange peel, grated

- Combine dressing ingredients until smooth.

- Yield: 8 servings

MELON PUREE
HERSEY HOUSE

When melons are fully ripened, the blossom end should have a pronounced aroma and give slightly to gentle pressure. Most varieties are sold slightly underripe and need to stand at room temperature for a few days to fully develop their flavor.

1 cantaloupe or canary melon	fresh mint leaves to taste
1 honeydew melon	

- Seed and peel melons. In a blender, process each melon separately, a small amount at a time. Add mint leaves when blending honeydew. (Both purees should be very smooth after blending.)

- Pour into 2 equal size pitchers. Pour simultaneously into flat sauce bowl, one color on each side. Garnish with additional fresh mint leaves.

- Yield: 2 ounces of each melon will yield a small bowl of puree.

STRAWBERRY SPINACH SALAD

¾ cup almonds, slivered or sliced
1 tablespoon butter or margarine
1 pound spinach, torn into bite-size
   pieces

1 pint fresh strawberries, sliced
   (may substitute fresh
   blueberries or raspberries)

DRESSING:

2 tablespoons sesame seeds, lightly
   toasted
1 tablespoon poppy seeds
½ cup sugar
2 teaspoons onion, minced or
   grated

¼ teaspoon paprika
¼ cup cider vinegar
¼ cup white wine vinegar
½ cup vegetable oil

This light and tasty salad can truly be savored all summer long, beginning with the onset of the strawberry season and followed by delectable raspberries and blueberries.

- Melt butter in a small skillet and sauté almonds until lightly toasted. Remove and set aside to cool.

- Combine spinach, almonds, and strawberries in a salad bowl. Store in refrigerator if not serving immediately.

- For dressing, toast sesame seeds in a dry skillet by shaking over medium heat. Mix or shake sesame seeds, poppy seeds, sugar, onion, paprika, vinegars, and oil in a jar or plastic container with a tight fitting lid.

- Toss salad with dressing just before serving.

- Yield: 12 servings

WINTER VEGETABLE SALAD

1 head cauliflower
1 bunch broccoli
1 bunch green onions, sliced
½ cup sugar
⅓ cup cider vinegar

½ cup mayonnaise
6-8 slices bacon, cooked and
   crumbled
¼-½ cup sunflower seeds

Cauliflower originally came from Cyprus while broccoli originated in Italy and the root word broccolo means cabbage sprout. The combination of cauliflower and broccoli creates a colorful salad which may be prepared in advance.

- Cut cauliflower and broccoli into flowerets. In large bowl, combine cauliflower, broccoli and onion; set aside. Mix sugar, vinegar and mayonnaise well, and add to chopped vegetables. Refrigerate 8 hours or overnight. Stir occasionally. Before serving, add bacon and sunflower seeds. Additions: fresh mushrooms.

- Yield: 6 servings

FRESH BROCCOLI SALAD WITH CUSTARD DRESSING

An excellent salad to serve for dinner as an accompaniment to pork tenderloin; may be prepared in advance and combined just before serving.

4 cups fresh broccoli flowerets
½ cup golden raisins
5 slices bacon, cooked and crumbled
1½ cups fresh mushrooms, sliced

½ cup slivered almonds
1 (11-ounce) can mandarin oranges, drained
½ medium purple onion, sliced ⅛-inch thick

DRESSING:

1 egg and 1 egg yolk, beaten
½ cup sugar
1½ teaspoons cornstarch
1 teaspoon dry mustard

¼ cup white wine vinegar
¼ cup water
2 tablespoons butter or margarine
½ cup mayonnaise

- Combine broccoli, raisins, bacon, mushrooms, almonds, oranges, and onion in a large mixing bowl.

- Whisk egg, egg yolk, sugar, cornstarch and mustard in the top of a double boiler. Slowly add vinegar and water. Place over hot water and stir constantly until mixture thickens. Remove from heat; add butter and mayonnaise. Chill.

- Pour dressing over salad; toss well. Refrigerate up to 2 hours and serve chilled.

- Yield: 10 servings

HERBED WALNUT SALAD

The nutty flavor of Romaine and walnuts creates a perfect balance when teamed with this tangy dressing.

½ cup walnuts, coarsely chopped
¼ teaspoon salt
3 tablespoons Romano cheese, grated
¼ teaspoon basil
½ cup salad oil
2 tablespoons ketchup

¼ teaspoon herb seasoned pepper
1½ tablespoons lemon juice
1 teaspoon onion salt
1 teaspoon brown sugar
1½ quarts Romaine and butter lettuce, torn into bite-size pieces

- In a small, lightly oiled skillet heat walnuts on low 8-10 minutes, stirring until slightly browned. Remove from heat; sprinkle on salt, cheese, and basil. Set aside.

- Make dressing by combining all remaining ingredients except Romaine and lettuce. Toss greens with walnuts. Add dressing to taste.

- Yield: 4-6 servings

QUINOA SALAD

1 cup Quinoa
2 cups brown rice, cooked
1 cup tomato, chopped
⅓ cup pine nuts

¼ cup cilantro, chopped
½ cup celery, chopped
⅓ cup red onion, chopped

DRESSING:

1 cup sugar
¾ cup vinegar

2 teaspoons salt
2 tablespoons chili sauce (Thai or other)

- Rinse Quinoa. In large saucepan, bring 2 cups water to a boil. Add Quinoa. Reduce heat, cover, and simmer 20 minutes or until the water is absorbed and the germ of grain is visible. Cool. In a large bowl mix remaining salad ingredients and cooked Quinoa.

- Heat dressing ingredients over low heat to dissolve. Mix into salad to taste. Serve cold.

- Yield: 10 servings

Find Quinoa (pronounced keen-wa) in the health food section of your grocery store.

Whole grain Quinoa is an excellent source of high quality protein. Pack this for your picnic instead of pasta. Add your own fresh vegetables and you've created an original.

ROASTED HAZELNUT SALAD

1 head Romaine, torn into bite-size pieces
1 avocado, peeled and cubed
2 tomatoes, seeded and cubed

½ cup Oregon hazelnuts
½ cup alfalfa sprouts
⅓ cup green onions, sliced
½ cup mozzarella cheese, shredded

DRESSING:

2 tablespoons white wine vinegar
1-2 tablespoons Dijon mustard

⅓ cup olive oil
freshly ground pepper, to taste

- To roast hazelnuts, place on a cookie sheet in a 275 degree oven for 20 to 30 minutes, until skins crack. To remove skins, rub warm nuts between your hands or in a towel. (Or, microwave 3 to 4 minutes on full power.) Chop nuts saving a few whole nuts for garnish.

- In a large salad bowl toss Romaine, avocado, tomatoes, nuts, sprouts, onions, and cheese.

- In a small bowl, whisk together vinegar and mustard. Gradually drizzle in olive oil. Whisk; add pepper. Chill and pour over salad just before serving. Garnish with whole roasted hazelnuts.

- Yield: 10 servings

The warm smell of roasting hazelnuts will remind you of the cozy atmosphere in your grandmother's kitchen. Serve with salmon or steelhead.

COUSCOUS SALAD

Couscous is the Arabic word for semolina, which is the firm heart of durum wheat, and is either ground into flour or granules.

1 carrot, shredded
6 green onions, sliced
1 red pepper, chopped
1 green pepper, chopped

2 tomatoes, chopped
½ cup cilantro, chopped
5 cups cooked couscous (about 2 cups uncooked)

- Mix vegetables and couscous in a large bowl. Prepare dressing and mix.

DRESSING:

⅓ cup red wine vinegar
juice of one lemon plus 1 tablespoon lemon zest, minced
¼ teaspoon cinnamon
¼ teaspoon cloves

½ teaspoon turmeric
½ teaspoon ground ginger
2 cloves garlic, minced
⅔ cup olive oil

- Mix all ingredients, except olive oil, in blender or food processor. Slowly add olive oil until blended. Pour over salad and mix.

- Yield: 12 servings

CHILLED SUMMER CORN

This colorful salad resembles brightly colored confetti and would certainly create a festive atmosphere at any gathering. Serve with "Perfect Salmon Steaks".

6 ears corn
1 green pepper, seeded and sliced
1 red pepper, seeded and sliced
2 small yellow squash, sliced

2 small zucchini, sliced
½ cup green onion, chopped
½ cup cilantro, chopped

DRESSING:

3 tablespoons oil
¼ cup white wine vinegar
1½ teaspoons chili powder

2 cloves garlic, minced
1 teaspoon oregano
½ teaspoon cumin

- Boil corn 5 minutes. Remove from water. When cooled, cut corn off cob and place in a large salad bowl. Add remaining salad ingredients, mixing well.

- Combine dressing ingredients in jar with lid. Shake until well blended. Pour over salad. Chill. Serve salad cold.

- Yield: 8 servings

GARLIC ROMA TOMATOES AND CROUTONS

1½ pounds ripe plum (Roma) tomatoes, cut into large cubes
1 cup red onions, cut wafer thin
½ cup fresh basil leaves, chopped
2 tablespoons fresh chives, minced

⅓ cup extra virgin olive oil (use good quality)
1½ teaspoons red wine vinegar
salt and pepper to taste
1½ cups large garlic croutons

The homemade croutons are worth the extra effort as they really make this salad special. Parmesan cheese has a mildly piquant flavor and it's best to grate the cheese just before using it.

- In medium salad bowl combine tomatoes, onions, basil and chives. Mix olive oil, wine vinegar, salt and pepper. Pour over tomatoes. Just before serving, toss salad with croutons.

- Yield: 4 servings

CROUTONS

½ loaf slightly stale French bread
1½ tablespoons olive oil
1½ tablespoons butter
2 cloves garlic, minced

1 teaspoon fresh parsley, minced
3 tablespoons Parmesan cheese, freshly grated

- Cut French bread into large cubes. Leave uncovered. In a medium skillet, heat olive oil and butter. Add bread cubes. Using a wooden spoon, toss over medium heat 4 minutes. Add garlic and parsley. Continue tossing 10-15 minutes or until golden brown. Place croutons on tray or in bowl and toss with Parmesan cheese. Cool to room temperature.

- Yield: 3 cups

GARBANZO-FETA SALAD

A change from the ordinary with a Greek flair; delicious with "Savory Spring Leg of Lamb" and toasted, buttered pita bread quarters.

2 (20-ounce) cans garbanzo beans, drained
1 medium red onion, thinly sliced
8-10 lettuce leaves
½ cup fresh or frozen lemon juice
¼ teaspoon pepper

1¼ cups olive oil
1 - 1½ teaspoons salt
2 teaspoons Dijon mustard
¼ pound feta cheese, crumbled
2 tablespoons fresh parsley, chopped

- Combine beans and onion slices in a salad bowl.

- In a 1-quart jar with a lid, combine lemon juice, pepper, olive oil, salt, and mustard. Shake until smooth. Pour over beans and refrigerate at least two hours or up to 2 days.

- When ready to serve, add feta cheese and parsley; toss. Salad may be served on individual lettuce leaves or in lettuce-lined salad bowl.

- Yield: 8-10 servings

BLUE, SHRIMP, AND SPINACH

A good blue cheese is ivory colored, firm, springy and has evenly distributed blue-green veins. The distinctive flavor of blue cheese enlivens this main course salad.

½ pound mushrooms
Italian dressing, your favorite bottled or Homemade Italian Dressing
1 bunch spinach

1 (4-ounce) package crumbled Oregon blue cheese
½ pound cooked salad shrimp
5 ounces cashews
3-4 green onions, sliced

- Wash and slice mushrooms. Place in small bowl and cover with Italian dressing. Marinate overnight.

- Wash and dry spinach. Tear into pieces. Add blue cheese, shrimp, cashews, and green onions. Drain mushrooms, reserving dressing. Add mushrooms. Toss with reserved dressing, to taste.

- Yield: 6 servings

HOMEMADE ITALIAN DRESSING

½ cup white wine vinegar
1 clove garlic, halved
¾ cup vegetable oil (or ½ cup olive oil + ¼ cup vegetable oil)

1 teaspoon Italian herbs
½ teaspoon pepper

- Combine ingredients in jar with a screw top. Let stand overnight. Shake to mix before adding to salad.

- Yield: 1 cup

RAVIOLI SALAD

1 package (about 25) cheese ravioli, cooked, drained and chilled
¾-1 cup sliced mushrooms
½ cup black olive slices
1 cup zucchini strips
1 (6-ounce) jar marinated artichoke hearts

Homemade or purchased Italian dressing
¾ cup salami slices, cut into strips
¼ cup Parmesan cheese, grated
1-2 quarts salad greens
1 cup tomato wedges or cherry tomatoes, cut into halves for garnish

The combination of plump pasta pillows and zesty Italian dressing creates a memorable meal. Crusty French bread and red wine would be a good addition with "Rogue Pears" to complete the meal.

- Place ravioli, mushrooms, olives, zucchini and artichokes in a medium bowl. Pour dressing over ravioli mixture and refrigerate several hours or overnight.

- When ready to serve, combine ravioli mixture with salami and Parmesan cheese. Attractively arrange greens in a large salad bowl or on individual plates. Garnish with tomatoes.

- Yield: 4-6 servings

TOMATOES STUFFED WITH GREEN BEANS

6 medium-sized firm ripe tomatoes
9 ounces green beans, washed and snapped into ½-inch pieces
3 tablespoons oil (olive or salad)
1 tablespoon red wine vinegar
2 teaspoons lemon juice
¼ teaspoon salt
¼ teaspoon dry mustard

¼ teaspoon oregano leaves
⅛ teaspoon paprika
1 dash thyme
¼ pound very small mushrooms, thinly sliced
¼-⅓ cup green onions, thinly sliced
1 teaspoon parsley, minced

A perfect way to feature the red ripe tomatoes from your garden; this beautiful salad is as pleasing to the eye as it is to the palate and may be prepared in advance.

- Cut tops off the tomatoes, scoop out pulp and invert to drain. Cover and chill at least one hour.

- Cook and cool green beans. Refrigerate.

- Make dressing by combining oil, vinegar, lemon juice, salt, mustard, oregano, paprika and thyme. Set aside.

- In a large bowl combine mushrooms, green beans and green onions. Pour dressing over vegetables, stir lightly to mix, cover and refrigerate 1 hour, stirring once to mix flavors. Stuff tomatoes with bean mixture and sprinkle parsley on top. Refrigerate covered until ready to serve.

- Yield: 6 servings

SPINACH APPLE SALAD

Try making your own raspberry vinegar. See our "Fruit Vinegar" recipe on page 157.

4 cups packed spinach leaves, washed, torn into bite-size pieces
⅔ cup thinly sliced celery

¼ cup finely chopped green onion
1 Red Delicious apple, cored and cut into 1-inch chunks

SESAME DRESSING:

¼ cup raspberry vinegar
3 tablespoons sesame oil
¼ teaspooon salt

1 teaspoon sugar
1 tablespoon toasted sesame seeds

- Toss spinach, celery and green onion. To prepare dressing, combine vinegar, oil, sugar and salt. Mix well. Add sesame seeds.

- Just before serving, add apple to spinach. Pour dressing over salad; mix.

- Yield: 4 servings

ASPARAGUS MUSHROOM SALAD

Shiitake mushrooms, firm hearty mushrooms often used in Japanese cooking, are available dried or fresh and add a unique touch to this salad.

This recipe enables one to fully appreciate the delicate flavor of this late spring vegetable, a beautiful way to showcase Oregon's native asparagus.

3 pounds asparagus
⅓ cup corn oil
2 large shallots, minced
2 large garlic cloves, minced
1 pound mushrooms, quartered
½ pound shiitake mushrooms, fresh or dried

½ cup fresh orange juice
2 tablespoons fresh lemon juice
2 tablespoons soy sauce
1 tablespoon sesame oil
½ teaspoon coarsely ground pepper

- Steam asparagus for 3 minutes. Rinse under cold water. Cut the asparagus diagonally into 1-inch lengths.

- Sauté shallots, garlic and mushrooms in corn oil for 5 minutes. Add remaining ingredients and simmer 5 minutes.

- Add asparagus; toss to mix. Transfer to a serving dish and serve at room temperature.

- Yield: 8 servings

MANDARIN SALAD

1 pound salad greens (Romaine, Butter or Red Leaf) torn into bite-size pieces
1 (11-ounce) can mandarin oranges, drained

¼ pound bacon, cooked and crumbled
1 large avocado, sliced
¼ medium red onion, sliced into rings

- Combine salad greens, mandarin oranges, bacon, avocado and onion in a salad bowl. Pour Mandarin Dressing over all; toss. Serve immediately.

- Yield: 6 servings

Romaine has dark green leaves which are long and rather coarse. It has an appealing pungent flavor and is also known as cos lettuce. On the other hand, butter lettuce is very fragile and has a subtle, sweet taste. Red leaf, another branch of the lettuce family, has reddish-bronze leaves that provide a nice contrast when combined with other greens.

MANDARIN DRESSING

¼ cup white wine vinegar
4 teaspoons sugar
½ teaspoon dry mustard
½ teaspoon salt

2 teaspoons fresh lemon juice
⅔ cup vegetable oil
1 tablespoon poppy seeds

- Combine vinegar, sugar, mustard and salt in a blender. With the machine running, gradually add lemon juice and oil. Stir in poppy seeds.

- Yield: 1½ cups

UNION CREEK CHICKEN SALAD

6 cups cooked chicken, cubed
2 cups seedless grapes or fresh pineapple cubes
1 can sliced water chestnuts, drained
2 cups celery, chopped

1 cup cashews, dry roasted
1 cup mayonnaise
2 tablespoons soy sauce
2 tablespoons lemon juice
1 tablespoon curry powder

This makes a wonderful picnic or camping dish since it stores well on ice and may be served as a main dish or in pita bread as a sandwich.

- In a large bowl, combine chicken, grapes or pineapple, water chestnuts, celery and cashews. In small bowl, combine mayonnaise, soy sauce, lemon juice and curry powder. Mix well. Add to salad; toss gently.

- Salad may be made ahead. Add grapes, pineapple, cashews and dressing just before serving.

- Yield: 8 servings

RED POTATO SALAD WITH SUN-DRIED TOMATOES

This salad is a delightful change of pace from ordinary potato salad and would be a delicious addition to a picnic supper.

2 pounds small red potatoes, scrubbed
¼ cup dried tomatoes packed in oil, drained (reserve oil)
2 tablespoons from tomato oil
2 tablespoons vegetable oil (or oil from tomatoes)
5 tablespoons red wine vinegar

2 teaspoons Dijon mustard
2 small cloves garlic, minced
¼ cup fresh basil, chopped
½ cup celery, chopped
2 tablespoons fresh chives, minced or white onion, grated
salt and pepper to taste
parsley sprigs for garnish

- In a large, heavy saucepan, boil potatoes until just tender, about 25 minutes. Drain and cool. Measure 2 tablespoons oil from tomatoes and combine in small bowl with vegetable oil, vinegar, mustard, and garlic. Whisk thoroughly. Set aside.

- Cut cooled potatoes into ½-inch cubes. In a salad bowl, combine potatoes, tomatoes, basil, celery and chives. Toss lightly with dressing. Season with salt and pepper. Chill 1-2 hours.

- Yield: 6 servings

ALMOND SESAME SALAD

With these international ingredients, your palate will take a culinary "bon voyage". Serve with "Poached Whole Salmon with Sesame and Cilantro".

5 cups cabbage, chopped
½ cup green onions, chopped
1 (8-ounce) can water chestnuts, sliced and drained

½ cup slivered almonds, toasted
1½ tablespoons sesame seeds, toasted

- Toss all vegetables, almonds and sesame seeds in salad bowl.

DRESSING:

¼ cup salad oil
1 teaspoon sesame oil
2 tablespoons sugar
1 tablespoon fresh cilantro, chopped

½ teaspoon salt
¼ teaspoon black pepper
½ teaspoon ground ginger
2 tablespoons white wine vinegar
1 tablespoon soy sauce

- Combine dressing ingredients in small bowl and blend. Pour dressing over vegetables and toss. Cover and refrigerate 2-3 hours. Toss again before serving.

- Yield: 12 servings

SMOKED SALMON SALAD

2 heads butter lettuce
2 cups celery, thinly sliced
2½ Granny Smith apples, diced

½ cup walnut pieces
Tarragon Vinaigrette
¼ pound smoked salmon

- Arrange lettuce leaves on individual plates; top with celery, apples, and walnuts. Drizzle 1 tablespoon Tarragon Vinaigrette over each salad. Flake salmon into bite-sized pieces being careful to remove all bones. Divide among salads. Garnish with small clusters of grapes.

- Yield: 4 servings

Combine the flavors of the river and orchards to experience the best of the Northwest. Can anything compare to the taste of delectable morsels of smoked Rogue salmon?

TARRAGON VINAIGRETTE

¼ cup tarragon vinegar
¾ cup olive oil
¼ cup red wine
1 clove garlic, crushed

¼ teaspoon prepared mustard
¼ teaspoon pepper
½ teaspoon tarragon leaves, rubbed
  in palm

- Combine in jar. Shake well.

- Yield: 1¼ cups

SALSA SORBET

2 pounds tomatoes
1 jalapeño pepper
¼ cup cilantro, chopped

¼ teaspoon cumin
1 tablespoon Worcestershire
½ teaspoon Tabasco sauce

- Remove skin from tomatoes by blanching in boiling water for 20 seconds. Cut in half, gently squeeze out seeds and peel off skin. Place tomatoes in blender or food processor.

- Cut stem off jalapeño pepper, cut lengthwise, and remove seeds. Add jalapeño and remaining ingredients to blender; puree.

- Freeze overnight in a shallow airtight container. Set out at room temperature 15 minutes before serving, then whip with a blender or mixer.

- Serve in small bowls over avocado slices or red pepper rings.

- Yield: 2 cups, 4-6 servings

Jalapeño peppers belong to the Capsicum family. Capsaicin, which gives the pepper its heat, is found in greatest concentration in the membranes. It is a good idea to wear gloves when handling hot peppers as the oils may be very irritating to sensitive skin.

CUCUMBER DILL SORBET

Cucumbers, a member of the gourd family, originated in the foothills of the Himalayas and were first cultivated in India more than 3,000 years ago.

2 medium cucumbers, peeled and sliced
½ cup plain yogurt
1 rib celery, strings removed, sliced

2 tablespoons fresh lemon juice
½ teaspoon dried dill weed
2 tablespoons sugar

- Puree all ingredients in a blender or food processor. Freeze in a shallow airtight container. Set sorbet out at room temperature 15 minutes before serving. Whip with blender or mixer.

- Yield: 2 cups, 4-6 servings

CILANTRO BLACK BEAN CHICKEN

Fresh corn, usually at its peak from July to October, makes this salad exceptional. Backyard farmers like to gather corn as near mealtime as possible.

2 cups dried black beans, rinsed
4 (10-ounce) cans chicken broth, divided
1 cup red onion, chopped
¼ cup green onion, chopped
5 Roma tomatoes, chopped

1 red bell pepper, chopped
1 yellow bell pepper, chopped
3 cups chicken breast meat, cooked and cubed
2 cups fresh corn kernels, blanched two minutes (about 4 ears corn)

DRESSING:

½ cup Italian herb vinegar
¼ cup Dijon mustard
2 tablespoons honey
4 cloves garlic, minced
1 tablespoon fresh thyme, crumbled or 1 teaspoon dried thyme

¼ teaspoon cayenne pepper
1 tablespoon salt
black pepper to taste
1 cup olive oil
½ cup fresh cilantro, chopped
cilantro sprigs for garnish

- In a 3-quart saucepan, combine beans with 4 cups of broth. Bring to a boil and boil 2 minutes. Let beans set, covered, 1 hour. Add the remaining cup of broth and simmer approximately 1½ hours or until tender. Drain in colander; rinse with cold water.

- Blanch peppers in boiling water 1 minute. Drain.

- In a large bowl, combine red onion, green onion, tomatoes, bell peppers, chicken, corn and beans.

- In a blender, combine the vinegar, mustard, honey, garlic, thyme, cayenne, salt and pepper. With motor running, add the oil in a slow thin stream until dressing does not separate.

- Pour dressing over salad, add cilantro, toss and serve. More cilantro may be added to taste. May be served in a lettuce-lined bowl or on individual lettuce-lined plates; garnish with fresh cilantro sprigs.

- Yield: 12 servings

ROGUE CAESAR SALAD

1 clove garlic
2 heads Romaine lettuce, washed,
    drained, torn into pieces and
    chilled

anchovies (optional, to taste)
grated Parmesan cheese for garnish
croutons

If you love Caesar salad, you'll be pleased with this healthy, eggless version.

DRESSING:

3 cloves garlic, minced
½ teaspoon pepper
2 teaspoons Dijon mustard
½ cup olive oil

4 tablespoons fresh lemon juice
1 teaspoon lemon zest
⅓ cup fresh Parmesan cheese,
    grated

- Rub inside of a large salad bowl with 1 clove garlic. Place lettuce in bowl.

- In a separate bowl mix garlic, pepper, mustard, oil, lemon juice and lemon zest. Beat with a small whisk. Add cheese. (Anchovies may be mashed into dressing, or mixed into salad with croutons.)

- Drizzle dressing over lettuce and mix. Just before serving add croutons; mix. Garnish with freshly grated Parmesan cheese and a whole anchovy.

CROUTONS

5 (½-inch) slices of French bread
2 tablespoons butter

garlic powder or finely minced
    fresh garlic to taste

- Preheat oven to 350 degrees. Spread bread slices with butter. Sprinkle with garlic powder or fresh garlic. Cut bread into cubes, place on cookie sheet. Bake 15 minutes until crisp, turning once. Cool.

- Yield: 6 servings

Grave Creek marks the beginning of the Wild Section of the Rogue River. The whitewater that greets rafters below the put-in point is a warning of things to come.

BREADS

CUMMINGS

An Oregon steelhead favorite for more than thirty years, this low water fly is used throughout the fall run. The Cummings, it is told, was conceived late one night over a quart of scotch by two fly tying addicts.

SPICY PEAR MUFFINS

Perfectly mixed muffins have nicely rounded tops and a pebbly surface.

Pears lend a flavorful moistness to these muffins. Try drizzling tops with a cream cheese icing!

2 cups all-purpose flour	1 cup diced fresh pear
1 tablespoon baking powder	1 egg
½ teaspoon salt	1 cup milk
¼ cup sugar	3 tablespoons oil

TOPPING

½ cup brown sugar, firmly packed	½ teaspoon cinnamon
⅓ cup nuts, chopped	½ teaspoon ginger

- Preheat oven to 400 degrees.
- In a medium bowl, combine flour, baking powder, salt and sugar.
- Toss diced pears with mixture.
- Add egg, milk and oil; mix briefly.
- Spoon into 8-12 greased muffin cups, filling each cup ⅓ full.
- Combine topping ingredients; divide in half. Sprinkle half evenly over muffin batter in the cups.
- Cover topping with remaining batter until ⅔ full.
- Sprinkle tops of batter with remaining topping mixture.
- Bake 15-18 minutes or until set and golden.
- Yield: 8-12 muffins

ORANGE PECAN MUFFINS

1½ cups sugar, divided
½ cup fresh orange juice
½ cup butter, softened
¾ cup sour cream
2 cups all-purpose flour

1 teaspoon baking soda
1 teaspoon salt
1 teaspoon grated orange peel
½ cup golden raisins
½ cup pecans, chopped

- Preheat oven to 375 degrees.

- Combine ½ cup sugar and orange juice; set aside.

- Cream butter and remaining sugar; blend in sour cream.

- Combine remaining ingredients and add to creamed mixture. Stir briefly until batter is mixed but not smooth.

- Spoon batter into greased muffin tins, filling each cup ⅔ full.

- Bake at 375 degrees for 15 minutes.

- While still warm, dip each muffin in sugar and orange juice mixture. Place on racks to cool.

- Yield: 12-18 muffins

When muffins are overmixed, too much gluten develops, causing toughness and tunnels.

A sweet muffin ideal for brunch or breakfast.

OREGON RASPBERRY-HAZELNUT MUFFINS

½ cup butter or margarine, room
    temperature
½ cup granulated sugar
½ cup brown sugar, firmly packed
2 large eggs
1 teaspoon vanilla or hazelnut
    liqueur

2 teaspoons baking powder
¼ teaspoon salt
2 cups unbleached flour
½ cup milk
1½ cups fresh raspberries
½ cup chopped hazelnuts
¼ cup coarse raw sugar, optional

- Preheat oven to 375 degrees.

- In mixing bowl, cream together butter, granulated sugar and brown sugar. Beat in eggs, vanilla, baking powder and salt. Stir in half of flour, followed by half of milk. Add remaining flour and milk.

- Fold in raspberries and hazelnuts.

- Spoon into muffin tins lined with paper baking cups, filling about ¾ full. Sprinkle with raw sugar if desired.

- Bake for 25-30 minutes or until tops are golden and toothpick inserted into center comes out clean.

- Yield: 12 muffins

A delicious muffin combining two of the Northwest's favorites.

APPLE CINNAMON MUFFINS

Good choices for cooking apples might be Granny Smith, Pippin, Newtowns, Jonathans or McIntosh.

¾ cup sifted all-purpose flour
1½ teaspoons baking powder
½ teaspoon salt
½ teaspoon nutmeg
½ cup sugar

¾ cup wheat germ
⅓ cup shortening
1 egg, beaten
½ cup milk
½ cup grated raw cooking apple

TOPPING

⅓ cup sugar
2 tablespoons wheat germ

1-2 teaspoons cinnamon
½ cup butter, melted

- Preheat oven to 350 degrees.

- To prepare muffins: Sift together flour, baking powder, salt, nutmeg and sugar; stir in wheat germ. Cut in shortening until mixture is fine consistency.

- Mix together egg, milk and grated apple. Add egg mixture to dry mixture and stir briefly. Do not overmix.

- Fill greased muffin tins ⅔ full. Bake for 25-30 minutes or until lightly browned; cool.

- To prepare topping: In a small bowl, mix together sugar, wheat germ and cinnamon.

- Brush muffins with melted butter and roll tops in cinnamon mixture.

- Yield 8-12 muffins.

TINY VANILLA GEMS

Our favorites in the miniature size! Serve with fresh fruit or with coffee.

2 cups all-purpose flour
¾ cup sugar
2 teaspoons baking powder
¼ teaspoon salt
1 large egg

1 cup milk
⅓ cup butter, melted and cooled
4 teaspoons vanilla extract
powdered sugar

- Preheat oven to 400 degrees.

- Sift flour, sugar, baking powder and salt into a large bowl.

- In small bowl, beat egg, milk, melted butter and vanilla to blend well. Briefly stir milk mixture into flour mixture just until moistened. Spoon batter into thirty-six greased 1-inch muffin tin cups (or 12 full-sized 2-2½-inch muffin tin cups), filling ⅔ full. (¾ full for full-sized tins.)

- Bake for 15 minutes (18-20 minutes for full-sized tins). Remove from oven and dust with powdered sugar.

- Yield: 36 (1-inch) muffins, 12 (2-inch) muffins

RIVER LODGE REFRIGERATOR MUFFINS

6 eggs
2 cups oil
4 teaspoons vanilla
1 cup buttermilk
4½ cups all-purpose flour
2 cups sugar
4 teaspoons baking soda
4 teaspoons cinnamon

1 teaspoon salt
4 cups finely grated carrots (use smallest part of grater)
2 finely grated apples
1 cup raisins
1 cup chopped nuts (optional)
1 cup coconut

A refrigerator muffin that may be stored for a couple of weeks and baked as needed. The perfect way to have hot muffins for break-fast with very little effort.

- Using an electric mixer, cream eggs, oil, vanilla and buttermilk. Add flour, sugar, baking soda, cinnamon and salt; mix only until blended. Add carrots, apples, raisins, nuts and coconut. Stir only until mixed.

- Mixture can be refrigerated for up to two weeks and baked as needed.

- Preheat oven to 375 degrees. Bake in well greased muffin tins for 20-25 minutes or until the tops spring back when touched. Tops should be golden brown; do not allow to become dark. Let stand 10 minutes before serving.

- Yield: 35 to 40 muffins

CHOCOLATE CHIP PUMPKIN MUFFINS

2 cups all-purpose flour
2 teaspoons baking powder
1 teaspoon baking soda
1½ teaspoons cinnamon
½ teaspoon salt
½ teaspoon ground cloves
¼ teaspoon ginger
¼ teaspoon allspice

2 cups sugar
4 eggs
2 cups canned pumpkin
1 cup vegetable oil
1 cup bran cereal or 1½ cups bran flakes
6 ounces chocolate chips
1 cup chopped nuts (optional)

Make a child smile . . . pop this bread or a muffin into a lunchbox or have ready as an after-school snack.

- Preheat oven to 350 degrees.

- In medium mixing bowl, sift together flour, baking powder, baking soda, cinnamon, salt, ground cloves, ginger, allspice and sugar. Set aside.

- In large bowl of an electric mixer, beat eggs until foamy; add pumpkin, oil and cereal. Mix well. Add to sifted flour mixture, stirring only until combined. Stir in chocolate chips and nuts. Spoon evenly in greased muffin tins, 10x4-inch tube pan, or 8x5x3-inch loaf pan.

- Bake for 30-40 minutes in muffin tins; 70 minutes in tube pan or 60-70 minutes in loaf pan. Cool completely on a rack before removing from pan.

- Yield: 18 muffins, 1 cake or 1 loaf

NORTHWEST BLUEBERRY MUFFINS

There are many blueberry muffin recipes available to cooks. As you make your choice, remember these are moist, flavorful and may be eaten at room temperature. This makes them perfect for a raft or camping trip.

2 cups sifted all-purpose flour
1 tablespoon baking powder
½ cup sugar
½ teaspoon salt
¼-½ teaspoon cinnamon (optional)

1 cup milk
1 egg, well beaten
½ cup butter, melted
1 cup fresh or thawed frozen
  blueberries

- Preheat oven to 400 degrees. In a medium bowl, sift flour with baking powder, sugar, salt and cinnamon; set aside.

- In large bowl, beat together milk, egg and melted butter. Add flour mixture and gently mix until batter is moist. (There will be lumps which will bake out). Fold in blueberries.

- Fill greased muffin tins ⅔ full and bake for 25 minutes or until golden brown. Paper baking liners may be used if desired.

- Yield: 12-18 muffins

CHERRY NUT BREAD

A lovely pink-tinted bread, perfect for teas. Pretty as a little girl's birthday cupcakes shared with her class. There's no need for frosting. May be baked in regular or miniature muffin tins.

½ cup shortening or butter
1¼ cups sugar
3 eggs
1½ cups flour
2 teaspoons baking powder
½ teaspoon salt

1 teaspoon vanilla
½ cup maraschino cherry juice
½ cup milk
½ cup maraschino cherries,
  chopped
½ cup walnuts, chopped

- Preheat oven to 350 degrees for loaf or 375 degrees for muffins.

- In large mixing bowl, cream butter and sugar. Mix in eggs and beat until creamy.

- In medium bowl, mix flour, baking powder and salt; add to butter mixture. Add vanilla, cherry juice, milk and mix until well blended. Fold in cherries and nuts.

- Grease and flour one 9x3x2-inch loaf pan, muffin pan or miniature muffin pan. Paper liners may be used if desired. Bake loaf for 60 minutes; muffins for 25 minutes or miniature muffins for 15 minutes.

- Yield: 1 loaf, 12 muffins, or 48 miniature muffins

PEAR TEA CAKE

½ cup dried pears, chopped
½ cup dried apricots, chopped
½ cup golden raisins
2 tablespoons pear brandy or
    apricot brandy
¼ cup butter
1 cup sugar

2 eggs
2 cups all-purpose flour
2½ teaspoons baking powder
½ teaspoon salt
1 cup milk
¾ cup chopped hazelnuts

Full of fruit similar to a fruit bread and flavored with Oregon-made pear brandy. Beautiful bottles containing a whole pear are made by securing the bottle around tiny, growing pears.

- In a bowl, soak pears, apricots and raisins in brandy for at least 1 hour.

- Preheat oven to 350 degrees.

- In mixing bowl, cream butter and sugar together. Beat in eggs.

- In a separate bowl, combine flour, baking powder and salt. Add flour mixture to egg mixture, alternating with milk, mixing just until blended.

- Fold in fruit and nuts; pour into greased and floured 9x5x3-inch loaf pan.

- Bake 1 hour or until toothpick inserted in center comes out clean. Cool for 10 minutes in pan and turn out onto wire rack.

- Yield: 1 loaf

FRESH OREGON PEAR BREAD

3 eggs
1 cup oil
2¼ cups sugar
2 cups peeled, grated fresh pears
3 cups sifted all-purpose flour
1 teaspoon baking soda

1 teaspoon salt
3 teaspoons cinnamon
1 teaspoon ground cloves
1 package (8-ounces) chopped dates
1 cup chopped nuts

Quick breads are leavened by baking powder, air, steam or baking soda and an acid such as buttermilk.

- Preheat oven to 350 degrees.

- Beat eggs and add oil, sugar, pears, flour, baking soda, salt, cinnamon and cloves; stir briefly. Stir in dates and nuts; pour into two greased and floured 9x5x3-inch loaf pans.

- Bake for 1 hour or until a toothpick inserted in center comes out clean. Cool on racks.

- Yield: 2 loaves

An aroma that stirs memories of old-fashioned gingerbread. A moist, dark bread sure to please.

ORANGE SCONES WITH SUN-DRIED CHERRIES OR CRANBERRIES

You may dry your own fruit by blanching and drying according to dehydrator instructions.

Dried cherries and cranberries are available in specialty stores. They lend a unique flavor that is different than their fresh counterparts with less moisture.

3 cups all-purpose flour
¾ cup sugar
½ teaspoon baking powder
1 teaspoon baking soda
2 teaspoons grated orange peel

½ cup butter or margarine, cold
¾ cup sun-dried cherries or cranberries
¾ cup buttermilk
sugar for topping

- Preheat oven to 400 degrees.

- In large mixing bowl, stir together flour, sugar, baking powder, baking soda and orange peel. Cut in butter or margarine using pastry blender or fingers until butter is worked into flour to fine crumb consistency.

- Toss cherries or cranberries in flour mixture.

- Add buttermilk until mixture holds together and is evenly moist. Add more if necessary.

- Knead about 10 times on a lightly floured surface.

- On greased cookie sheet, pat dough into a 9-inch round, mounding slightly in center. Sprinkle with granulated sugar.

- Bake until evenly browned and toothpick comes out clean, about 40 minutes. Cover with foil during last part of baking to prevent overbrowning.

- Serve cut into wedges with butter, honey butter or orange butter.

- Yield: 1 (9-inch) round

RHUBARB-RASPBERRY CONSERVE

8 cups diced rhubarb
5 cups sugar, pre-measured
2 oranges

2 pints raspberries
¼ cup orange liqueur

- Place diced rhubarb in a large non-metal bowl; coat with sugar. Let stand overnight.

- Add the finely grated zest of the oranges. Remove remainder of peels and seeds from oranges; cut into thin slices. Combine rhubarb, oranges and raspberries. Bring to a boil, stirring constantly; boil until thickened. Remove a spoonful and place in a cool dish to judge thickness. Stir in liqueur and ladle into sterilized half-pint jars; seal.

- Yield: 7 (half-pint) jars

HAZELNUT SCONE HEARTS
OLD STAGE INN

2 cups all-purpose flour
¼ cup sugar (granulated or dark brown, firmly packed)
1 teaspoon baking powder
½ teaspoon baking soda
½ teaspoon salt
½ cup unsalted butter

1 cup hazelnuts, chopped
2 tablespoons grated orange peel
¾ cup buttermilk
1 tablespoon cream or half-and-half
¼ teaspoon ground cinnamon
2 tablespoons sugar

- Preheat oven to 400 degrees.

- In bowl of food processor, mix flour, sugar, baking powder, soda, salt, butter and hazelnuts. Pulse briefly until mixture resembles coarse crumbs. Transfer mixture to medium bowl and add orange peel and buttermilk; mix with fork until dough cleans sides of bowl. Gather dough into a ball; turn out onto a lightly floured board.

- Pat the dough into a ½-inch thick circle. Using a 2½-inch heart (or other shape) cutter, cut into individual scones. Place 1½-inches apart on lightly greased baking sheet. Brush tops of scones with cream. Mix cinnamon and sugar; sprinkle lightly on scones.

- Bake for 15-17 minutes or until tops are lightly browned. Serve warm.

- Yield: 12 scones

Try omitting the topping and cut a slit in each unbaked scone to fill with a teaspoon of raspberry jam.

Built in Jacksonville about 1857 by William Bybee, this elegantly restored inn stands grandly on 3½ acres, embraced by maple and locust trees. Old Stage Inn combines the charm of yesterday with the amenities of today.

OVERNIGHT YEAST WAFFLES

2 cups all-purpose flour
1 package active dry yeast
¼ teaspoon ground cardamom
2 cups milk
2 tablespoons butter or margarine

1 teaspoon sugar
1 teaspoon salt
2 egg yolks
2 egg whites, stiffly beaten

- In a large mixer bowl, mix flour, yeast and cardamom.

- In a saucepan, heat milk, butter, sugar and salt until just warm (105 degrees), stirring to melt butter. Add to flour mixture and beat at medium speed for 2 minutes, scraping sides of bowl. Cover bowl tightly and refrigerate overnight.

- While preheating waffle iron, beat egg yolks until thick and lemon colored, about 2 minutes. Remove batter from refrigerator and add yolks. Gently fold in beaten egg whites. Pour into waffle iron and bake until golden brown.

- Yield: 12 (4x4-inch) waffles

These may change your mind about making homemade waffles. Make the batter the night before and pour into your waffle iron when your family is ready for breakfast. Batter yields crispy, lightly-flavored waffles a second morning too!

WHOLE WHEAT HAZELNUT PANCAKES
ROMEO INN

Light and subtly flavored with Oregon hazelnuts, these pancakes are perfect for breakfast, brunch or a light supper.

2 eggs
¾ cup all-purpose flour
¾ cup whole wheat flour
1¼ cups buttermilk
3 tablespoons vegetable oil

2 tablespoons brown sugar, firmly packed
2 teaspoons baking powder
½ teaspoon baking soda
½ teaspoon salt
½ cup toasted hazelnuts, chopped

- Whisk together all ingredients, adding nuts last. Pour batter onto a lightly oiled 400 degree griddle. Turn when tops are full of bubbles. Cook until second side is nicely browned.

- Serve with Orange Honey Syrup.

- Yield: 6 servings

ORANGE HONEY SYRUP

1 cup honey
⅓ cup fresh squeezed orange juice

1 tablespoon butter
½ teaspoon fresh grated orange peel

- Combine all ingredients in a small saucepan. Heat, uncovered over medium heat, stirring frequently, until butter melts and syrup is smooth.

- Yield: approximately 1¼ cups

HAZELNUT HONEY BUTTER

¼ cup roasted hazelnuts
½ cup unsalted butter, softened

¼ cup honey
⅛ teaspoon cinnamon

- Place hazelnuts in food processor fitted with knife blade; process 5-10 seconds or until nuts are finely ground. Add butter, honey and cinnamon; process, stopping to scrape down sides, until butter forms a smooth well blended paste.

- Yield: 1 cup

GOLDEN PUMPKIN BISCUITS

2 cups all-purpose flour
⅓ cup nonfat dry milk
¼ cup sugar
4 teaspoons baking powder
¾ teaspoon pumpkin pie spice

¼ teaspoon salt
½ cup shortening
¾ cup canned pumpkin
1 tablespoon water

Especially good served as an accompaniment to a Thanksgiving feast. Try with turkey or pork at dinnertime; for breakfast; tucked in a lunchbox; or as an after-school snack. Great hot or at room temperature, perfect for a river rendezvous.

- In a medium bowl, mix together flour, nonfat dry milk, sugar, baking powder, pumpkin pie spice and salt.

- Cut in shortening, using a pastry blender or two table knives, until pieces are the size of small peas.

- Blend in pumpkin and water just until ingredients are moistened.

- On a lightly floured surface, knead dough 10-20 times. Dough should be smooth and not sticky.

- Preheat oven to 400 degrees.

- Roll out into a circle, ½-inch thick. Using a biscuit cutter, cut into 10-12 biscuits. Place 2 inches apart on an ungreased cookie sheet.

- Bake for 12-15 minutes or until golden brown.

- Yield: 10-12 biscuits

ALMOND PUFF PASTRY

1 cup butter, divided
2 cups sifted flour, divided
2 tablespoons plus 1 cup water

½ teaspoon almond extract
3 eggs

GLAZE

⅔ cup powdered sugar
2 tablespoons milk

sliced almonds for garnish

A must for a morning coffee, an early meeting or holiday breakfast. This almond flavored pastry melts in your mouth.

- Preheat oven to 350 degrees.

- With a pastry blender or 2 table knives, cut ½ cup butter into 1 cup flour. Add 2 tablespoons of water and mix well with a fork. With your hands, spread the soft mixture into 2 rectangles measuring 12x3-inches on an ungreased cookie sheet. Leave 2-3 inches between rectangles.

- In a saucepan, bring 1 cup water and ½ cup butter to a boil; add the almond extract. Remove from heat and beat in remaining 1 cup flour. Add the eggs, one at a time; beat well with a wooden spoon after each egg is added, until mixture looks smooth. Spread dough evenly over rectangles on cookie sheet. Bake until lightly browned and set, approximately 60 minutes.

- Top with a thin glaze of powdered sugar and milk, mixed and drizzled on with a spoon. Decorate with sliced almonds.

- Note: Do not underbake. Inside must be done or pastry will not retain its shape.

- Yield: 2 large pastries

OVERNIGHT LIGHT ROLLS

Oil, butter or shortening makes bread more tender, flavorful and gives a browner crust.

Too busy to add homemade rolls to a special dinner menu? Make this dough a day ahead and take from the refrigerator about two hours before serving for fresh baked rolls on the day you need them.

1 package active dry yeast
2 teaspoons sugar plus ½ cup sugar
½ cup warm water (105-110 degrees)
1½ cups warm milk

2 eggs, beaten
1½ teaspoons salt
7 cups all-purpose flour
½ cup vegetable oil
3 tablespoons butter, melted

- In a large mixing bowl, dissolve yeast and 2 teaspoons sugar in warm water until foamy (5-10 minutes). Add milk, eggs, ½ cup more sugar, salt, 1 cup flour and vegetable oil; mix well with mixer at low speed or with wooden spoon. Add remaining flour and mix with wooden spoon until stiff dough is formed. Cover and leave in refrigerator until morning.

- Remove from refrigerator and leave at room temperature for about 15-20 minutes. Pinch off dough into 24 equal parts. With fingers, take the top portion of dough and smooth it to the bottom and pinch seam together. Place rolls, pinched side down in greased muffin pans. Cover and allow to rise at least 1 hour. Rising time may be shortened by placing tins over pans of hot tap water and covering with a towel. Other roll shapes such as crescents may be used with larger amounts of dough.

- Preheat oven to 350 degrees. Bake for 12-15 minutes. Brush tops with melted butter and serve immediately.

- Yield: 24 rolls

BASIL BATTER ROLLS

The savory pesto garlic taste of these easily prepared rolls may be varied by increasing or decreasing the amount of garlic and pesto used.

Ingredients combine into a batter rather than a dough that is conveniently spooned into muffin cups. A perfect accompaniment with barbecued or roasted meats.

1½ cups warm water (105-110 degrees)
2 packages active dry yeast
4 cups unbleached flour
¼ cup sugar

1½ teaspoons salt
⅓ cup shortening
1 egg
1½-2 tablespoons pesto (or to taste)
2 cloves garlic, finely minced

- In a large mixing bowl, add water and yeast, stirring to dissolve; leave for about 10 minutes.

- Add 2 cups flour, sugar, salt, shortening and egg. Beat with mixer at medium speed for 1½-2 minutes. Add pesto and garlic. Add remaining 2 cups flour and stir in by hand until flour is absorbed. Cover and allow to rise until doubled (about 1-1½ hours).

- Stir down batter in 20-25 strokes. Spoon into 18 greased muffin tins filling each half full. Let rise until batter reaches top of tins (20-45 minutes).

- Preheat oven to 400 degrees. Bake for 12-15 minutes or until golden brown. Brush tops with butter after removing from oven, if desired.

- Yield: 18-24 rolls

HEAVENLY YEAST BISCUITS

2 tablespoons sugar, divided
¼ cup warm water (105-110 degrees)
1 package active dry yeast
2½ cups all-purpose flour

½ teaspoon baking soda
1 teaspoon baking powder
1 teaspoon salt
½ cup shortening
1 cup buttermilk

These yeast biscuits truly have celestial qualities. The lightness of yeast is combined with the ease of a quick bread for heavenly lightness.

- In a small bowl, dissolve yeast and 1 tablespoon sugar in warm water until foamy (5-10 minutes).

- Mix flour, baking soda, baking powder, salt and remaining 1 tablespoon of sugar in a medium bowl; cut in shortening. Warm the buttermilk to lukewarm (no hotter than 105 degrees). Stir the yeast mixture into buttermilk. Add yeast mixture to the dry ingredients and mix well.

- Turn dough out onto floured board and knead lightly 4 or 5 times. Roll out ¾-inch thick and cut with biscuit cutter. Place on a greased cookie sheet or in greased baking pans, leaving 1-2 inches between biscuits.

- Let dough rise slightly (20-30 minutes) before baking. Preheat oven to 400 degrees.

- Bake 12-15 minutes or until lightly browned. May also be used as dumplings.

- Yield: 12-18 biscuits

PINEAPPLE BUTTERMILK BREAD

1 (8¼-ounce) can crushed pineapple, undrained
3 tablespoons warm water (105-110 degrees)
2 envelopes active dry yeast
¾ cup buttermilk at room temperature

1 tablespoon sugar
4½ cups sifted all-purpose flour
¼ cup shortening
1½ teaspoons salt
½ teaspoon dill weed
vegetable oil

An unusual flavor combination that is not sweet. Try topping thick slices of "Pineapple Buttermilk Bread" with Havarti cheese. Pack bread, fresh fruit and your favorite bottle of wine in a picnic basket.

- Spoon 2 tablespoons syrup from pineapple into mixing bowl, add warm water and sprinkle with yeast; leave for 5 minutes to soften. Add buttermilk, sugar and 1½ cups flour; beat thoroughly (about 2 minutes at low speed using electric mixer or 200 strokes by hand). Beat in shortening. Stir in remaining undrained pineapple, salt and dill weed. Very gradually stir in remaining flour, mixing to a moderately stiff dough.

- Turn out onto floured board and knead about 5 minutes, until the dough is smooth and mounds up. Divide into 2 equal portions and shape each into a ball. Dough can be shaped into loaves and placed in greased 9x5x3-inch pans. Brush tops lightly with oil. Cover and allow to rise in warm place until doubled, (about 1-1½ hours).

- Preheat oven to 350 degrees. Bake on lowest rack of oven for 45-60 minutes. If top of loaves begin to brown deeply, place a small sheet of foil loosely over the top of loaf.

- Turn loaves out onto wire rack and once again brush tops lightly with oil; cool.

- Yield: 2 loaves

ORANGE SUNFLOWER BREAD

Try not to be discouraged by the number of ingredients! The results of your efforts will be a fragrant, orange-scented loaf of delicious bread. Serve with a meal or as sandwich bread.

2 packages active dry yeast
1½ cups warm water (105-110 degrees)
⅓ cup honey
⅓ cup margarine or butter, melted
1 cup nonfat dry milk
½ cup wheat germ
1 cup mixed-grain cereal (for hot cereal)
2 tablespoons orange peel
2 teaspoons salt
1 cup orange juice
2 cups whole wheat flour
3 cups all-purpose flour
1 cup unprocessed bran
½ cup sunflower seeds

- In the large bowl of an electric mixer, sprinkle yeast over the water; let stand 5 minutes. Stir in honey, butter, dry milk, wheat germ, cereal, orange peel, salt and orange juice. Mixing on low speed, gradually add the whole wheat flour and 1 cup all-purpose flour until well blended. Beat on medium speed for 5 minutes. Mix in bran and seeds. With a heavy-duty mixer or by hand, gradually mix in about 2 cups all-purpose flour.

- Knead 5-8 minutes with dough hook or on a well-floured board. Dough should be satiny and not dry. Add extra flour only to keep from sticking.

- Turn dough into a greased bowl, turn once to grease top. Cover and allow to rise in a warm place until doubled in size (about 1½ hours).

- Punch down dough and divide in half. Shape each half into a loaf and place in a well greased 5x9x3-inch loaf pan. Cover pans and let rise until doubled (50-60 minutes).

- Preheat oven to 375 degrees. Bake for 40-45 minutes until browned and hollow sounding when tapped. Cover with foil laid loosely over loaves during last part of baking to prevent overbrowning.

- Remove from pans and cool on a rack.

- Yield: 2 loaves

TAYBERRY JAM

3 quarts ripe tayberries, washed and sorted
¼ cup lemon juice
1 (1½-ounce) package powdered pectin
8 cups sugar, pre-measured

- In large bowl, crush berries thoroughly. Measure enough pulp to equal 5¾ cups and pour into 6-8 quart stock pot. Add lemon juice and pectin; stir well to dissolve. Place over medium-high heat, stirring constantly until mixture comes to a full rolling boil. Add sugar and increase heat to high, stirring constantly, to dissolve sugar. Return to full rolling boil and boil hard for 4 minutes. Continue to stir constantly to prevent scorching. Remove from heat and skim foam.

- Ladle jam into sterilized jars; filling to ¼-inch from the top of jars. Process in boiling water bath for 5 minutes to seal jars. Remove to counter and cool.

- Yield: 10-12 (half-pint) jars

CURRY BAGUETTES

1 package active dry yeast
1 tablespoon sugar
1 cup plus 2 tablespoons warm
    water (105 to 115 degrees)
cornmeal
3 tablespoons shallots, minced
2 tablespoons butter or margarine

2 cups bread flour
1 cup all-purpose flour
1 teaspoon salt
½ teaspoon curry powder
1 egg
½ teaspoon salt
¼ teaspoon paprika (optional)

- In a small bowl, dissolve yeast and sugar in warm water until foamy (about 5-10 minutes).

- Oil a large bowl and french bread or baguette pans or a cookie sheet. Sprinkle pans or cookie sheet with cornmeal.

- Cook shallots in butter or margarine until soft. Transfer to food processor fitted with steel knife; add flours, salt and curry powder. While machine is running, pour in yeast mixture and process until moist and smooth, about 15 seconds. If using an electric mixer, gradually mix in yeast and knead with dough hook for 10-12 minutes.

- Put dough in oiled bowl and turn so that dough is coated with oil. Cover bowl and place in warm area until doubled in size (approximately 1½ hours).

- Punch dough down and turn out onto a floured board. If necessary, work in enough flour so that dough is not sticky. Divide in half.

- Roll one half of the dough into a rectangle and roll up like a jelly roll, pinching ends and seams tightly. Place seam side down in bread pan or on a cookie sheet and repeat with the other half. Cover with a damp cloth and let rise again until doubled.

- Preheat oven to 425 degrees, placing rack in center position.

- Slash top of bread with sharp knife, diagonally, making ½-inch deep cuts approximately 4 inches apart. Beat egg, salt and paprika (optional) for wash and gently brush over loaves. (Do not drip wash into bread pan!)

- Bake about 25 to 30 minutes, or when loaves are golden and have a hollow sound when tapped on the underside. Cool on wire rack before serving.

- Yield: 2 baguettes

Bread flour is hard-wheat flour and contains a high percentage of gluten, which gives elasticity to yeast dough. It is readily available in grocery stores.

Reminiscent of the flavors of India, curry lends a subtly different taste and aroma.

PESTO AND SUN-DRIED TOMATO TWIST

Use purchased or homemade pesto, recipe on page 38. Pesto freezes beautifully for a year.

Call a few friends and have a dinner party to show off this impressive bread.

¼ cup plus 1 tablespoon butter
⅓ cup dry milk
2¼ teaspoons salt
¼ cup plus 2 tablespoons sugar
2 cups water, divided
⅓ cup dried onion flakes
3 packages active dry yeast
2 eggs, slightly beaten

7-8 cups all-purpose flour
1½ tablespoons pesto
2 tablespoons tomato sauce
½ teaspoon garlic, minced
¼ cup sun-dried tomatoes, chopped (may increase)
4 tablespoons fresh Parmesan cheese, grated

EGG WASH

1 egg mixed with 1 tablespoon water

- In a saucepan over medium heat, dissolve butter, dry milk, salt and sugar in 1½ cups warm water. Add dried onion. Cool to lukewarm.

- Dissolve yeast in remaining ½ cup warm water (110-115 degrees).

- Combine sugar mixture, eggs and yeast mixture. Add flour until a moderately stiff dough is formed. Divide dough in half. Add pesto to one half. Add more flour if needed to knead into a smooth ball (about 5 minutes). To the second half, add tomato sauce and minced garlic, kneading in more flour (knead about 5 minutes). Place each half in a separate greased bowl and turn to coat all sides. Cover each ball and let rise until doubled in size (about 45 minutes to 1 hour).

- Punch down each bowl of dough. Roll out the tomato dough into a 14x6-inch rectangle. Sprinkle with sun-dried tomatoes. Roll up into a long rope. Cut rope in half.

- Shape pesto dough into a second long rope about 2x14 inches; cut in half. Lay the ropes, side-by-side on a greased cookie sheet. Twist one pesto and one tomato rope together and seal both ends by pinching together. Repeat. Cover and let rise until doubled in size (about 45 minutes to 1 hour).

- Preheat oven to 375 degrees. Bake for 15 minutes. Remove from oven and brush with egg wash. Bake 15-20 minutes more or until golden brown and completely done. Sprinkle with grated Parmesan cheese. Cool on a rack.

- Yield: 2 loaves

PEASANT BLACK BREAD

½ cup warm water (105-110 degrees)
2 envelopes active dry yeast
2 teaspoons sugar
½ ounce unsweetened chocolate
1 tablespoon margarine
1 cup water
¼ cup dark molasses

2 tablespoons cider vinegar
1 tablespoon salt
½ cup 100% bran cereal
2-2¾ cups all-purpose flour
1½ cups rye flour
4 tablespoons crushed bran cereal for topping

- In a small bowl, dissolve yeast and sugar in warm water until foamy (5-10 minutes).

- Melt chocolate and margarine in a double boiler with 1 cup water or on reduced power in a microwave, stirring until smooth. Blend in molasses, vinegar and salt. Mix in cereal and allow to cool.

- Grease a large bowl. Mix yeast mixture into cereal mixture. Gradually stir in 2 cups all-purpose flour and all the rye flour.

- Turn dough onto lightly floured surface and knead 8-10 minutes or until dough is smooth and elastic. If necessary, knead in another ¾ cup flour to keep dough from sticking. Turn dough once in greased bowl to coat entire surface. Cover and allow to rise until doubled, about 1½ hours.

- Punch down dough and let rest 5 minutes. Grease two 9x5x3-inch loaf pans. Divide dough into 2 portions. Shape into loaves and place in loaf pans. Brush tops of dough with melted butter, sprinkle crushed bran cereal on tops of loaves. Let rise until doubled, 1½ hours.

- Preheat oven to 375 degrees. Bake about 45 minutes until loaves sound hollow when tapped. Cover loosely with foil during baking to prevent overbrowning. Remove from pans and cool completely on racks.

- Yield: 2 loaves

Yeast works best at room temperature (80-85 degrees). It is destroyed quickly at high temperatures but low temperatures slow yeast activity.

The finished loaf has a homey, old world appearance and the flavor is superb. Try with salads at a luncheon or with a meal, tucked under a woven napkin in a handcrafted bread basket.

APRICOT-ALMOND BUTTER

¼ cup sliced almonds
¼ cup chopped dried apricots

1 cup unsalted butter, softened
2 tablespoons amaretto

- Add almonds to food processor fitted with knife blade. Process 5-10 seconds or until finely ground. Add apricots and process until chopped. Add butter and amaretto, processing until smooth and well blended. Place in small bowl and refrigerate until ready to use.

- Yield: 1½ cups

SOURDOUGH FRENCH BREAD STARTER

For a more "sour" taste, allow the starter to sit out in a warm room for 2-3 days before using.

Ancient Egyptians baked yeast bread by keeping wild yeast alive in leftover dough . . . sour dough!

½ cup unbleached flour
½ cup self-rising flour
1 cup slightly warm water

½ cup unbleached flour
½ cup warm water

- Mix first three ingredients in a glass bowl, or a crock or jar (at least ½-gallon size with a loose fitting lid).

- Leave in a warm place for 24-30 hours. Mixture should start to show bubbles. When this happens, add ½ cup unbleached flour and ½ cup warm water (or enough to make a medium thin batter consistency). Be sure to use unbleached flour. Never use self-rising flour in starter again after the first step. Refrigerate starter in a glass jar with loose fitting lid when not in use.

- To use starter: Pour into mixing bowl and add equal amounts of unbleached flour and warm water, about 1½ cups each. Whisk well, cover, and allow to rise and bubble in a warm place before using (approximately 1½ hours). To hasten this process, put bowl of starter in a larger bowl of very warm water. Cover and use in 30-45 minutes.

- Return unused starter to jar and refrigerate.

SOURDOUGH FRENCH BREAD

Sourdough starter may be kept indefinitely in your refrigerator. If liquid turns dark, replace with an equal amount of fresh water.

Pictured on page 10. Light sourdough flavor is evident in this golden loaf.

1½ cups warm water (105-110 degrees)
1 tablespoon dry yeast
2 tablespoons sugar
1 tablespoon salt

2 cups sourdough starter
4 cups unbleached flour
1 egg white, beaten
poppy or sesame seeds or mixture of both

- In a large bowl, whisk together water, yeast, sugar and salt. Add sourdough starter and stir well. Gradually add flour until dough is workable to knead by hand.

- Knead on floured surface until dough is smooth and elastic. Cover and leave in a warm place to rise until doubled in size.

- Punch down dough and shape into 2 loaves. Place in greased bread pans and make a deep depression on top of loaves with fingers dipped in flour to prevent crust from bulging and separating on top. Press down until fingers touch bottom of pan. If French loaves are preferred, divide dough into 3 loaves and place on a greased cookie sheet. Slash diagonally across tops of loaves with a sharp knife.

- Preheat oven to 400 degrees.

- If seeded crust is desired, paint unbaked loaves with egg white and roll in seeds. Seeds may be sprinkled and pressed onto loaf.

- Bake for 30-40 minutes until crust is golden brown. Cool on rack.

- Yield: 2 regular loaves, 3 French loaves

GOLD NUGGET BREAD

2 cups water
½ cup cornmeal
2 teaspoons salt
½ cup molasses
2 tablespoons butter

5-6 cups all-purpose flour
1 package yeast
½ pound medium sharp Cheddar
cheese or Jarlsberg Swiss
cheese, cut into ½-inch cubes.

- In medium-sized saucepan, combine water, cornmeal and salt. Bring to boil over medium-high heat, stirring constantly. Cook until slightly thickened; remove from heat. Add molasses and butter; cool to lukewarm (105 degrees).

- In large mixing bowl, combine 2 cups flour and dry yeast. Add cornmeal mixture; blend well. Stir in remaining flour to form a stiff dough. Knead on well-floured surface until smooth and elastic (about 5 minutes). Dough will be somewhat sticky. Place in greased bowl, turning to grease top. Cover; allow to rise in warm place until light and doubled in size (about 1 hour).

- Punch down dough. Work cheese into dough a quarter at a time, until cubes are evenly distributed. Divide into two parts. Shape into two round loaves, covering cheese cubes. Place in two 8 or 9-inch cake pans, well-greased and sprinkled with cornmeal. Cover; allow to rise in warm place until light and doubled in size (about 1 hour). If desired, bake loaves in two 1½-quart casseroles, well-greased and sprinkled with cornmeal.

- Preheat oven to 350 degrees. Bake for 55-60 minutes until deep golden brown.

- Yield: 2 loaves

Salt improves the flavor of yeast bread and also helps to control yeast growth. The amount of salt in a recipe varies with the texture desired.

Moist and full of melting cheese, the aroma of this bread will have family or guests crowding into your kitchen.

STRAWBERRY-PEACH-KIWI FREEZER JAM

1 pint ripe strawberries
¾ pound ripe peaches (about 3
    medium)
3 medium kiwi fruit
¼ cup lemon juice

1 (2-ounce) package powdered
    pectin
1 cup light corn syrup
4½ cups sugar, pre-measured

- Wash and stem strawberries. Crush berries and measure 1 cup. Rinse, peel, pit and fully crush peaches. Measure 1 cup. Stem and peel kiwi; slice and crush. Measure 1½ cups.

- In a large bowl or saucepan, stir together fruit and lemon juice. Slowly sift in pectin, stirring occasionally. Add corn syrup, stirring well. Gradually stir in sugar. Heat to lukewarm to dissolve sugar.

- Ladle into sterilized half to one-pint freezer containers leaving ½-inch headspace. Cover at once with tight lids. Freeze and transfer to refrigerator as needed.

- Yield: 7 (half-pint) containers

BRANDIED FRUIT BRAID

The liquid in bread is usually milk or water. Breads made with milk have a higher nutrient value, taste richer and brown better.

A bountiful harvest of fruits perfectly spiced and enclosed in sweet yeast bread.

FRUIT FILLING

½ cup raisins, chopped
½ cup dried apricots, chopped
½ cup golden raisins, chopped
2 cups unpeeled apples, chopped
¼ cup pitted prunes, chopped
½ can (3-ounces) frozen apple juice concentrate, thawed
¼ cup plus 2 tablespoons water

2 tablespoons honey
¼ teaspoon ground allspice
¼ teaspoon ground cinnamon
¼ teaspoon salt
1½ tablespoons brandy, apricot brandy, or apple juice
¼ cup almonds, walnuts or pecans, chopped (optional)

- In a large, heavy saucepan combine all ingredients except brandy and nuts. Bring to a boil, cover and simmer 40-50 minutes, stirring occasionally. Uncover and simmer about 15 more minutes until liquid is almost evaporated, stirring often.

- Remove from heat and stir in brandy. Stir in chopped nuts if desired. Cover and cool.

BREAD

1 package active dry yeast
¼ cup warm water (105-110 degrees)
¼ cup sugar
4 tablespoons butter, divided

1½ teaspoons salt
¾ cup milk, scalded
1 egg
2½-3 cups all-purpose flour

- Combine yeast and water in a small bowl.

- In a large mixing bowl combine sugar, 3 tablespoons butter, salt and milk. Cool to lukewarm. Stir in egg and yeast. Gradually mix in flour to form a stiff dough. Add half the flour using an electric mixer then switch to a dough hook for remaining flour. Knead with dough hook or by hand for 5-8 minutes or until smooth and satiny. Place in a greased bowl, turning once to grease all sides. Cover and allow to rise in a warm place until doubled in size (about 1-1½ hours).

- Punch down dough and divide into thirds. Roll each out on a floured surface into a 12x6-inch rectangle. Spread each with ½ cup or more of the fruit filling. Starting with 12-inch side, roll jelly roll fashion; seal edges.

- Place all 3 rolls side by side on a greased cookie sheet; braid together. Brush with 1 tablespoon melted butter. Cover and allow to rise in warm place until doubled in size (about 45 minutes).

- Preheat oven to 375 degrees. Bake for 20-25 minutes until golden brown. Cool on rack.

- Drizzle with confectioners glaze if desired. (See page 104, substitute vanilla for almond flavoring and exclude almonds).

- Yield: 1 large braid

CREAM CHEESE BRAID

½ cup sugar
½ teaspoon salt
2 packages active dry yeast
3½ cups all-purpose flour
¼ cup plus 2 tablespoons butter or
    margarine
⅔ cup water
2 eggs (1 egg separated)
8 ounces creamed cottage cheese,
    pressed through a fine sieve

8 ounces cream cheese, at room
    temperature
½ cup powdered sugar
1 teaspoon grated lemon peel
½ cup raisins or dates or sun-dried
    cherries, chopped
½ cup walnuts or almonds,
    chopped, optional

Sweet doughs have a higher percentage of sugar and may contain butter, milk and egg for richness.

A favorite at brunches, coffees and holiday break-fasts. If you love cream cheese pastries, you will add this to your list of favorites.

- In a large mixer bowl, combine sugar, salt, yeast and 1 cup flour.

- Heat butter and water to 120-130 degrees in a saucepan or in the microwave.

- Using an electric mixer, beat water into dry ingredients for 2 minutes at medium speed. Beat in one egg and ¾ cup flour. Beat 2 minutes. Stir in 1¼ cups more flour.

- Knead dough on a floured surface, or use a dough hook, for 8 minutes. Add remaining ½ cup flour while kneading. Shape dough into a ball and place in a greased bowl, turning to grease top. Cover and allow to rise in a warm place until doubled in size, about 1 hour.

- Blend cottage cheese, cream cheese, powdered sugar and lemon peel. Separate remaining egg, saving the white, and adding egg yolk to cottage cheese mixture, blending until smooth. Stir in raisins and nuts; refrigerate.

- Punch down dough. Place dough on floured surface, cover and let rest 15 minutes.

- Grease large cookie sheet. Roll dough into 15x12-inch rectangle. Spread filling in 4-inch strip lengthwise down center. Cut dough on both sides of filling crosswise into 1-inch strips. Place strips at an angle across filling alternating sides for braided effect. Place braid on cookie sheet. Cover; let rise until doubled.

- Preheat oven to 350 degrees. Beat egg white slightly. With pastry brush, brush braid with egg white. Bake 20 minutes or until richly browned.

- Cool 15 minutes and serve.

- Yield: 1 braid

CHOCOLATE ALMOND BRIOCHE

If you are in the mood for a special creation to emerge from your kitchen, this is the recipe you have been looking for. More effort than many breads, but two glorious loaves will be your reward. Freeze one for another moment or give it as a remarkable gift.

One recipe Brioche Dough - recipe
   follows

FILLING

¾ pound almond paste
1 egg white
4 tablespoons unsalted butter,
   softened

¼ teaspoon salt
¼ teaspoon almond extract
4 ounces semi-sweet chocolate,
   melted

GLAZE

6 tablespoons unsalted butter
1½ cups powdered sugar
¼ cup hot milk

½ teaspoon almond extract
½ cup toasted, sliced almonds

ASSEMBLY

- Filling: In a food processor or by hand, combine the almond paste, egg white, butter, salt and almond extract. Stir in the melted chocolate.

- Divide the dough in half, roll each piece into a rectangle about 10x14-inches in size and spread all over with half the filling. For each coffeecake, mentally score the dough into thirds vertically. With a sharp knife, make diagonal cuts down the side thirds and alternately fold the side pieces over so that they overlap across the middle third to resemble a braid. Seal the ends by pinching together and tucking under. Set the coffeecakes on foil-lined and greased baking sheets and leave in a warm spot to double in size (about 1 hour).

- Preheat oven to 350 degrees. Bake for 25 minutes. Remove to cooling racks and allow to cool to room temperature.

- Glaze: Melt butter in small pan and cook until it turns a golden brown. Blend in the sugar, remove from the heat and add milk, 1 tablespoon at a time, until the mixture is of spreading consistency. Add the almond extract and drizzle glaze over the cooled coffeecake. Sprinkle with almonds and allow the glaze to set.

- Yield: 2 coffeecakes

BRIOCHE DOUGH

2 packages active dry yeast
¼ cup warm water (105-110 degrees)
½ cup sugar, divided
5 cups all-purpose flour

1½ cups butter
1½ teaspoons salt
6 eggs
¼ cup warm milk (105-110 degrees)

Dough that has risen long enough will have doubled in size and will make an impression when touched with your fingers.

- In a small bowl, combine yeast, water and 1 tablespoon sugar with 2 tablespoons flour. Let stand 20 minutes or until foamy.

- In a mixing bowl, cream butter.

- In a large bowl, combine remaining flour, sugar and salt; add eggs. Work into a paste with wooden spoon or fingers. When smooth, add yeast mixture and milk.

- With a heavy-duty mixer, beat in butter; continue beating 5-10 minutes. Cover and allow to rise in a warm place until doubled in size (2-3 hours).

- Punch dough down and lightly knead in the bowl for 1-2 minutes.

- Roll out as instructed in assembly directions.

CHAMPAGNE-MARIONBERRY JELLY

1 quart marionberries, washed
¼ cup water
2 cups champagne
2 tablespoons lemon juice

1 (1¾-ounce) package powdered pectin
4 cups sugar, pre-measured

- Wash and sterilize 5-6 half-pint jelly jars. Prepare lids according to manufacturer's directions. Hold jars and lids in scalding water until ready to use.

- Crush berries in medium saucepan and add water. Bring to boil over medium heat. Reduce heat and simmer about 5 minutes to extract juice. Strain to remove pulp and seeds. Add water, if necessary, to obtain 1 cup of berry juice.

- Combine berry juice, champagne, lemon juice, pectin, and sugar. Stir to dissolve pectin and place over medium-high heat, stirring constantly, until juice comes to a full boil. Continue stirring constantly. Boil hard for 2 minutes. Remove from heat and skim foam.

- Remove jars from hot water and fill with hot jelly, being careful not to drip on rim of jar. Fill to ¼-inch from top and wipe rims with clean, damp cloth. Place lids on jars and process in boiling water bath for 5 minutes to seal jars. Remove to counter and cool.

- Yield: 5-6 (half-pint) jars

OREGON CATCH & SEAFOOD

BUCKTAIL COACHMAN

When evening falls on the Rogue, the traditional Bucktail Coachman tops the water. With its origins in England, the coachman pattern has been utilized in more steelhead and trout flies than any other English or American design. The original coachman was Tom Bosworth, employed by the British royal family during most of the nineteenth century.

About Salmon:
The salmon is a pink fleshed fish that is spawned in the cold running rivers of the Pacific Northwest, such as our own Rogue River. They migrate downstream to the Pacific Ocean where they live and mature over several years, then return upstream to reproduce and die. The Rogue yields mostly Chinook and a few Silver (Coho) Salmon. The Chinook is prized for its flavor. The Jack Salmon is an immature salmon that returns to the river prematurely. They are usually male, smaller than 24 inches and are lower in fat. During the spring and fall runs Rogue River fishermen catch salmon from the river bank and from specially designed drift boats.

NORTHWEST DRIFTERS' SALMON

A wonderfully mild and slightly sweet flavor as prepared by one of the Rogue's finest river guides.

salmon fillet, 1 to 1½-inches thick
fresh lemon juice
salt and lemon pepper
brown sugar

white or Walla Walla sweet onion,
    thinly sliced
mayonnaise

- Preheat oven to 350 degrees.

- Place fillet skin-side-down in ovenproof pan that accommodates fish snugly. Pierce salmon with fork and sprinkle generously with fresh lemon juice. Sprinkle entire surface with salt and lemon pepper. Let stand for 15 minutes.

- Cover with ¼-inch layer of brown sugar. Top with layer of very thinly sliced onion. Cover with ⅛-¼ inch layer of mayonnaise.

- Bake uncovered on center rack of oven for 25-30 minutes. Salmon is done when meat loses transparency. Do not overcook. Top will be light golden in color.

- Yield: Average fillet serves 4-6

SALMON IN PARCHMENT WITH LIME-DILL BUTTER

¼ cup cold butter
2 cloves garlic, peeled and sliced
1 tablespoon minced fresh dill
1 tablespoon lime juice
1 pound salmon fillet, cut into 4
    equal portions

4 sprigs fresh dill
fresh whole chives
parchment paper
olive oil

- Preheat oven to 500 degrees. Blend ¼ cup butter with garlic, 1 tablespoon dill and 1 tablespoon lime juice. Set aside.

- Cut 4 pieces of parchment that are 6 inches longer and 4 times wider than fish pieces. Brush parchment with oil one inch from the edge of paper near center, covering area the same size as fish. Place fish portion over oiled area and top with 1 tablespoon of butter mixture. Arrange small sprig of dill and whole chives over butter. Fold parchment to enclose salmon, turning edges under. Place seam sides down on cookie sheet, brushing tops of paper packets with olive oil.

- Bake until fish is opaque, about 10 minutes. Watch carefully as oven temperature is very high. Transfer to dinner plates and serve, allowing guests to open packets at their places.

- Yield: 4 servings

Parchment paper may be purchased at specialty cook shops.

These are great fun to open at the table. The aroma is wonderful and the fish is moist and tender. The short baking time and ability to prepare the unbaked packets early in the day, make these a nice choice for dinner parties.

HALF MOON OVEN BARBECUED SALMON

3 tablespoons butter
1 large onion, thinly sliced
1 large salmon fillet, whole side if
    possible with skin on

mayonnaise to cover
garlic salt
4 teaspoons A.1.® Sauce

- Preheat oven to 375 degrees. Melt butter in skillet over medium heat. Add onions and cook until soft; set aside.

- Place salmon on aluminum foil and spread generously with mayonnaise. Sprinkle with garlic salt to taste and distribute A.1. Sauce evenly over entire surface.

- Cover with additional foil and bake 12-15 minutes or only until fish flakes. Uncover and top with sautéed onions. Return to oven for 5 minutes to heat through.

- Yield: 4-6 servings

The number of servings is dependent on the size of the fillet, but keep in mind that salmon is rich and servings need not be too large.

An outdoor covered grill also works well on those occasions when we want to escape the kitchen.

SALMON WITH SUN-DRIED TOMATO SALSA

For best results use those luscious red, ripe tomatoes from the summer garden. Everyone should have at least one plant in their backyard. Grow Roma or San Marzano varieties of Italian plum tomatoes for cooking and canning - they have lower water content.

½ cup white wine
3 tablespoons olive oil
½ teaspoon salt
½ teaspoon pepper
6 salmon steaks, 1-inch thick
4 small ripe tomatoes
¼ cup diced sun-dried tomatoes

3 shallots, diced
2 tablespoons chopped cilantro
2 tablespoons minced garlic
¼ cup diced green pepper
2 teaspoons lemon juice
salt and pepper to taste

- Whisk together wine, oil, salt and pepper in small bowl.

- Place salmon steaks in shallow glass pan and pour wine mixture over fish, turning to coat. Cover with plastic wrap and marinate one hour, turning once.

- To make salsa, drop ripe tomatoes into boiling water bath for 1 minute. Remove. Peel, core and cut into halves. Squeeze to remove seeds. Dice and place in large bowl. Add remaining ingredients and stir to mix. Cover and set aside.

- Preheat broiler or grill. Cook on grill or broil for 5-7 minutes on each side. Serve immediately, topped with salsa.

- Yield: 6 servings

POACHED WHOLE SALMON WITH SESAME AND CILANTRO

This is a spectacular, yet simple way to serve whole salmon. Pour oil over fish at tableside for a beautiful presentation and enjoy the delicate oriental style flavor.

1 whole salmon, any size; head and
   tail intact if desired
½ cup chopped cilantro
½ cup sliced green onion
1-2 tablespoons coarsely grated
   fresh ginger

¼ cup sesame oil
¼ cup canola oil
5-6 cloves garlic, peeled
soy sauce

- Poach salmon in 1 inch of simmering water in large covered pan. (Fish poaching pan works best.) Cook for 10 minutes for each inch thickness of fish. (About 40 minutes for a salmon 4 inches in diameter at thickest part.)

- Gently remove to heat proof serving platter. Discard poaching liquid or save to use as fish stock.

- Cover salmon with cilantro, green onion and ginger in that order.

- Heat oils and garlic in small saucepan or skillet over medium-high heat until garlic browns and oil is very hot. Carefully pour hot oil over salmon, wilting greens.

- Sprinkle with soy sauce to taste. Serve immediately.

- Yield: Approximately ½ pound per serving

SALMON IN WHITE WINE MARINADE

4-6 salmon steaks or 1 large fillet
¾ cup butter or margarine, melted
¼ cup dry white wine
⅓ cup lemon juice
2 teaspoons Tabasco sauce

3 tablespoons finely chopped green
   onion
1 teaspoon salt
¼ teaspoon marjoram
¼ teaspoon pepper
¼ teaspoon thyme

Light and flavorful way to prepare salmon in your oven for those indoor days.

- Place salmon in shallow glass baking dish. Combine remaining ingredients and pour over salmon. Refrigerate 1-2 hours, turning occasionally.

- Preheat oven to 350 degrees.

- Bake uncovered in preheated oven for 20-30 minutes or until fish just turns opaque.

- Yield: 4-6 servings

PERFECT SALMON STEAKS

fresh salmon steaks, ¾ to 1-inch
   thick
garlic powder
coarse ground black pepper

bottled liquid smoke flavoring
4 tablespoons margarine or butter,
   melted

A step by step guide to cooking flawless salmon steaks time and time again. This method has been used for 25 years by a local physician/fisherman without failure and is sure to work for you.

- Season steaks liberally with garlic powder, pepper and liquid smoke flavoring.

- Start charcoal in a barbecue grill large enough to accommodate the number of steaks used. When charcoal is burning well, spread it evenly under grill. Heat the grill, clean it with a wire brush and oil lightly.

- There are three small areas of grey meat on a salmon steak: one at the top and one on each lateral line. (See picture.) Place steaks on grill and check time. Bubbles of milky juice will appear in the grey areas when the steaks are half done.

- When each steak has 1 or 2 bubbles of "milk," check the elapsed time and carefully turn steaks.

- Baste with margarine and cook for same amount of time it took for bubbles to appear, usually 5-8 minutes per side.

- Yield: 1 steak per serving

"Perfect Salmon Steaks"

grey
areas

GRILLED LEMON SALMON

Salmon, pure and simple. A delicate treatment for a richly flavored fish.

4 salmon steaks, approximately
    1-inch thick
garlic powder
ground black pepper

1 medium white onion, sliced
1 lemon, sliced
2 tablespoons butter, melted
2 tablespoons dry white wine

- Preheat gas grill at medium setting, or use charcoal grill.

- Sprinkle both sides of salmon steaks with garlic powder and pepper. Place fish on large sheet of aluminum foil. Top each steak with a slice of onion and lemon; drizzle butter and wine over all. Seal foil, enclosing salmon. Poke holes in foil to allow smoky flavor to enter and steam to escape. Cook 20-25 minutes.

- Yield: 4 servings

BACON WRAPPED SALMON STEAKS

Put these on the grill some warm summer evening, add fresh fruit and red potato salad and sit back in a lounge chair for a wonderful al fresco supper.

6 salmon steaks, 1-inch thick
hickory smoke salt
black pepper, freshly ground

6 strips thinly sliced bacon
¼ cup unsalted butter, melted
6 lemon wedges

- Sprinkle salmon steaks with hickory smoke salt and ground pepper. Wrap slice of bacon around middle of steak like a belt, securing with toothpick and brush one side with melted butter.

- Place salmon on preheated grill buttered side down and cook 5 minutes. Brush remaining side with butter and turn gently. Continue grilling for 5 additional minutes or until fish is just opaque. Squeeze lemon wedge over steaks and serve immediately.

- Yield: 6 servings

GRILLED LIME-SESAME SALMON

May spray grill with non-stick coating before heating. Never spray aerosol onto lighted grill.

Simply marinate salmon steaks for great flavor with an oriental flair.

½ cup lime juice
½ cup corn oil
2 tablespoons soy sauce
2 tablespoons sesame oil

2 tablespoons honey
4 salmon steaks, 1-inch thick
thinly sliced lime for garnish

- Early in day, combine first 5 ingredients in nonmetal container large enough to hold salmon. Add salmon, turning to coat well. Marinate at least 6 hours.

- Grill over medium coals, 5-7 minutes per side, turning once carefully, until fish is opaque and flakes easily. Do not overcook.

- Serve topped with thinly sliced lime.

- Yield: 4 servings

SALMON AND HAZELNUTS IN PHYLLO

1 package frozen phyllo dough
2 salmon fillets
juice of ½ lemon
1 teaspoon dried dill
½ teaspoon garlic salt
2 tablespoons butter
½ pound mushrooms, sliced
1 (14-ounce) can of artichoke
   hearts, drained and coarsely
   chopped

6 green onions, chopped
1½ tablespoons capers
¼ cup white wine
salt and white pepper to taste
⅓ cup roasted hazelnuts, chopped
½ cup butter, melted
1 egg
1 teaspoon water

- Thaw phyllo dough according to package directions. (Overnight in refrigerator)

- Preheat oven to 325 degrees. Place salmon fillets in greased shallow baking pan. Sprinkle with lemon juice, dill and garlic salt. Bake 15-20 minutes or until fish just turns opaque. Remove from oven and set aside.

- Melt 2 tablespoons butter in 10 to 12-inch skillet. Sauté mushrooms until limp; add artichoke hearts, green onions, capers, wine, salt and pepper. Heat through and set aside.

- Increase oven temperature to 375 degrees.

- Open phyllo and unfold on work space. Remove one sheet, keeping remaining sheets covered with damp dish towel. Brush single sheet with melted butter and place another sheet on top of it. Brush it with butter and repeat process with third sheet.

- Divide each salmon fillet into 4 equal serving portions, making eight total.

- Place 1 salmon piece over bottom ⅓ of phyllo, leaving borders all around. Top with ⅛ of mushroom mixture and sprinkle with chopped hazelnuts. Turn up bottom edge of dough. Then fold in sides, partially enclosing the salmon. Roll up jelly roll fashion and carefully place seam side down on ungreased baking sheet. Repeat with 7 remaining pieces of salmon.

- Beat egg with water and glaze each bundle with egg mixture. Sprinkle with pinch of chopped nuts.

- Bake for 30 minutes or until heated through and pastry is crisp and golden brown. Serve warm.

- Yield: 8 servings

Toss any extras in the freezer. They keep beautifully, but must be reheated in the oven, not the microwave.

Working with phyllo may seem intimidating at first, but give it a try. It's fun and becomes much easier once it is demystified.

These delightful little bundles are impressive on a luncheon menu with a steamed vegetable and fresh fruit or as an elegant main course for a special dinner party.

SALMON STEAKS GENOESE

Fine cuisine can't get much easier than this. A little salmon, a little pesto and presto...dinner is served!

4 teaspoons prepared pesto
4 salmon steaks, 1-inch thick

freshly ground pepper

- Spread ½ teaspoon pesto on each side of salmon steaks. Allow to rest covered, for 30 minutes.

- Preheat broiler or grill. Cook 5-7 minutes per side, turning once. Season to taste with freshly ground pepper. Serve immediately.

- Yield: 4 servings

SHRIMP AND CRABMEAT PANCAKES GREENWOOD
UNDER THE GREENWOOD TREE

Under the Greenwood Tree, homesteaded in 1861 by the Walz family, provides a parklike ambiance which includes magnificient gardens, sweeping croquet lawns and 300 year old oak trees. This romantic Bed and Breakfast is located in Medford.

CREPES

1 cup white flour
½ teaspoon salt
2 eggs
1 cup milk

2 tablespoons salad oil
½ teaspoon dill
¼ cup butter, melted

- Blend all ingredients and chill for one hour. Cook in a little butter, using a 7-inch skillet.

FILLING

½ cup shallots (or green onions
    plus 1 clove garlic)
¼ pound mushrooms, sliced
1 cup butter, divided
5 tablespoons flour
2 teaspoons salt
¼ teaspoon white pepper

1½ cups light cream
½ cup white wine
2 egg yolks, beaten
½ pound crabmeat
½ pound cooked, shelled shrimp
3 tablespoons French cognac,
    warmed

- Sauté shallots and mushrooms in ½ cup butter for 5 minutes. Blend in flour, salt and pepper. Blend in cream and wine; bring to boil and cook 10 minutes. Add eggs and stir. Set aside.

- In separate pan, sauté crab and shrimp in remaining butter for 3 minutes. Add cognac and ignite. When flames die down, add half the cream sauce. Place 3 tablespoons of mixture on each crepe and roll up. Top with reserved sauce and serve.

- Yield: about 10 servings

CRAB AND ZUCCHINI SAUTÉ

¼ cup peanut oil
½ teaspoon chopped fresh ginger
½ small onion, chopped
½ pound Dungeness crab meat
2 tablespoons dry sherry
white pepper to taste
1 large zucchini, sliced
3 tablespoons peanut oil

1 clove garlic, crushed
½ teaspoon salt
½ teaspoon sugar
6 tablespoons chicken stock
1 tablespoon cornstarch
1½ tablespoons cold water
1½ teaspoons sesame oil

The Dungeness crab is the crab of the Pacific Coast. They are large, meaty and bright pink when cooked. Their season runs from September through April, so shop for crab only in months with an "r".

Wonderful as an entree served with rice or as the first course of a Chinese meal.

- In a 12 to 14-inch sauté pan, heat ¼ cup peanut oil over medium heat. Add ginger and chopped onion and begin to sauté. Add crab meat and cook about 2 minutes. Add sherry and white pepper. Continue cooking for 1 minute and remove from heat.

- In separate pan, sauté zucchini in 3 tablespoons peanut oil over medium heat. Add garlic, salt, sugar and 4 tablespoons chicken stock. Add crab mixture and 2 tablespoons chicken stock to zucchini.

- Mix cornstarch and water in small container and add to other ingredients stirring until sauce is clear and thickened. Season with sesame oil and additional white pepper if desired. Serve hot.

- Yield: 4-6 servings

CALAMARI MARINARA

1 tablespoon olive oil
4 cloves garlic, peeled and chopped
1 cup chopped onion
1 cup chopped mushrooms
2 pounds prepared squid
1 (28-ounce) can whole tomatoes,
    including liquid

1 teaspoon oregano
1 teaspoon dried basil
1 teaspoon sugar
½ teaspoon pepper
½ teaspoon salt
1 pound fresh fettucine or linguine,
    cooked and drained

Preparing squid may not be for the faint of heart, so you may want to ask the fish market to do it for you, but here goes! Pull heads off squid and pull out backbone. Rub off most of outside colored membrane and push out innards. Cut into ½-inch rings and rinse well in colander under cold water. Voila!

- Heat olive oil in 10-inch heavy skillet. Add garlic, onion and mushrooms. Stir and cook over medium heat until tender, about 5 minutes. Add squid, tomatoes and liquid, oregano, basil, sugar, pepper and salt. Simmer 30 minutes, or until liquid is reduced by ½ to ⅔. Serve over hot fettucine or linguine.

- Yield: 4 servings

Where there's smoke, there's......salmon!

Smoked salmon was a staple of the Pacific Northwest Indians. It could be considered one of the most significant foods of our regional cuisine. In the following recipes the fish is cured in a seasoned brine and cooked in a smoker, over low consistent heat in the midst of wood smoke for 8-16 hours. Smokers may also be used to "cold smoke" or "smoke flavor" meats. With this technique, meat is placed in a preheated smoker and exposed to wood smoke for shorter periods of time, usually 20-30 minutes. This is not a curing process therefore, the meat must be cooked after smoking.

RENDEZVOUS SMOKED SALMON I

Different wood shavings impart a different smoke flavor to the fish. Alder, cedar and pear woods are Rogue Valley favorites.

This recipe includes the "basics" for smoking salmon. The following recipes include variations in the brine and slight variations in method. They are all outstanding, but you may find a particular favorite.

1 (15-20 pound) salmon
1 pound brown sugar, divided

¾ cup tender-quick meat cure
2 quarts cool water

- Fillet salmon leaving skin on. Cut fillets crosswise into 2 to 3-inch strips. To make brine, stir ½ pound sugar, meat cure, and water together in a 3-gallon, nonmetal container. (A crock works well.) Add salmon and, using hands, gently mix salmon into brine. Add water if necessary, to cover fish. Turn top pieces skin side down and let stand overnight in cool place.

- Early next morning, rinse fish under cool tap water. Lay fish skin-side- down on a clean dish towel. Let dry, at room temperature, about 4 hours or until fish has a dull, tacky glaze.

- Place fish on smoker racks, positioning thick pieces at the bottom of the smoker. Fill hot plate one-third full of wood chips and start smoker, keeping smoker temperature just under 140 degrees.

- After smoking for three hours, sprinkle remaining brown sugar over fish, add more wood to hot plate and continue smoking process. Depending on thickness of fish and size of smoker, tail sections may be removed after 6-8 hours while thicker pieces may require 8-10 hours.

- The dryness of the finished fish is a matter of personal preference, although moist fish is usually most desirable. Remove from racks, cool and refrigerate. Smoked fish will keep in the refrigerator for about 1 month. Vacuum pack and freeze for several months.

RENDEZVOUS SMOKED SALMON II

1 (10-12 pound) salmon
½ cup non-iodized salt
¼ cup granulated sugar

1 teaspoon pepper
1 quart cool water
½ -1 pound brown sugar

Use this recipe to smoke trout. Soak 10-12 12-inch trout in brine for 6 hours followed by 2-4 hours in the smoker. The brine is also good for venison soaked 12-24 hours.

- Prepare salmon according to previous recipe. Combine salt, granulated sugar, pepper and water in a nonmetal container. Soak salmon for about 12 hours. Smoke according to preceding directions. In a small bowl, blend brown sugar with just enough water to make a thick paste adding carefully and slowly. Brush fish with brown sugar glaze 2-3 times during last half of smoking. Finish and store according to previous directions.

RENDEZVOUS SMOKED SALMON III

1 (10-15 pound) salmon
2 cups dark brown sugar, packed

2 cups rock salt

A unique taste of cedar smoke, this brine involves no additional water.

- Fillet salmon and cut crosswise into 2 to 3-inch wide strips. Mix brown sugar and rock salt thoroughly in large nonmetal container. Add salmon and toss gently to coat. Refrigerate for 12-24 hours. Salmon will cause sugar/salt mixture to reduce to thick syrupy liquid. Make sure fish is completely immersed while marinating.

- Smoke salmon over cedar chips for 12-16 hours as described in first recipe. Refrigerate for up to 1 month or seal and freeze to store for longer periods.

RENDEZVOUS SMOKED SALMON IV

1(10-12) pound salmon
½ cup non-iodized salt

1 cup dark brown sugar
1 teaspoon Tabasco sauce

Tabasco sauce adds a slightly spicy flavor to this curing brine.

- Fillet and cut salmon according to previous directions. Mix salt, brown sugar and Tabasco sauce with enough water to cover salmon. Soak overnight. Smoke according to the instructions included with your smoker.

STEELHEAD AND BLACK WALNUTS

Steelhead and walnuts; a perfect autumn combination. As you enjoy this delicious fish, think of the fisherman that probably braved the cold and rain to claim his prize from the icy river. Steelhead is a trout that spends part of its life cycle in the ocean, returning to the fresh water of the Pacific Northwest rivers to spawn.

½ **pound butter or margarine**
2 **tablespoons beef suet or water**
1½ **pounds steelhead fillets, cut in 2x3-inch pieces**
¼ **cup cracker crumbs**

¾ **cup flour**
2 **egg whites, stiffly beaten**
1 **cup black walnuts, coarsely ground**

- Melt butter in electric frying pan and add 2 tablespoons melted beef suet or water to keep butter from browning too much. Heat to 375 degrees.

- Place cracker crumbs and flour in paper bag. Add fish pieces and shake bag to coat.

- Dip each piece of steelhead in egg white, then gently roll in walnuts.

- Place in frying pan and cook 5-6 minutes on each side being careful not to overcook. Turn fish gently to prevent nuts from falling off. Drain on paper towels and serve immediately.

- Yield: 4 servings

STEELHEAD WITH CREAMY OLIVE SAUCE

Great sauce for a true Northwest delicacy. For a tangier sauce use ½ green olives with pimiento in place of ½ the black olives. The sauce keeps very well and is still good the next day.

1 **large steelhead, boned and butterflied**
¼ **cup butter**
salt and pepper
2 **tablespoons butter**
2 **tablespoons dry sherry**

¼ **cup green onions, sliced**
¼ **cup mushrooms, sliced**
1 **cup black olives, sliced**
1 **cup sour cream**
½ **teaspoon garlic powder**
½ **teaspoon Worcestershire sauce**

- Preheat broiler. Place fish skin-side-down on broiler pan. Dot with butter and season with salt and pepper to taste. Broil 5 minutes or until fish flakes easily. Remove from broiler and place on platter. Keep warm.

- In 2-quart saucepan, heat butter and sherry over medium heat until bubbly. Add onion and mushrooms; cook 1 minute. Stir in olives, sour cream and seasonings; cook, stirring 2-3 minutes until hot. Pour sauce over steelhead and serve.

- Yield: 4 servings

STEELHEAD WITH PINE NUTS

2-2½ pound steelhead fillet
salt and white pepper
flour
¼ cup vegetable oil
½ cup unsalted butter, melted
½ cup toasted pine nuts
2 tablespoons dry white wine

4 teaspoons minced fresh chives
¼ teaspoon minced fresh thyme (or
    pinch of dried)
1 tablespoon minced fresh parsley
3 teaspoons fresh lemon juice
salt to taste
fresh parsley sprigs for garnish

- Season steelhead fillet with salt and white pepper. Dredge in flour, shaking off excess.

- Heat oil in large skillet over medium-high heat. Sauté fillet, skin side up for 3 minutes. Turn and cook 3-4 more minutes or until fish flakes. Remove to warm platter.

- Add butter and pine nuts to pan. Cook over medium heat, shaking until butter begins to brown.

- Remove from heat. Stir in wine, chives, thyme, parsley, lemon juice and salt to taste.

- Spoon sauce over fish. Garnish with fresh parsley sprigs.

- Yield: 6-8 servings

Have all ingredients ready and waiting in small containers so that the sauce combines quickly to top warm fish.

The Italians refer to them as pignoli, American Indians and Mexicans call them stone nuts or piñions. We call them wonderful! Pine nuts lend a rich toasty flavor and the buttery sauce keeps steelhead moist and delicious.

PETRALE SOLE MACADAMIA

2 eggs
¾ cup grated fresh Parmesan
    cheese
2 tablespoons flour
4 Petrale sole fillets

3 tablespoons vegetable oil
3 tablespoons butter or margarine
½ cup salted, roasted Macadamia
    nuts, finely chopped
4 thin slices lemon

- Preheat oven to 425 degrees. Beat eggs in pie pan until blended.

- Mix cheese and flour on a double sheet of wax paper.

- Dip fillets in egg to coat, drain and dip in cheese mixture. Place oil and butter in a shallow baking dish and place in oven until butter melts. Remove pan from oven and swirl to coat bottom of pan with oil mixture. Place fillets in pan, turning once to coat with butter. Sprinkle fillets with chopped nuts. Bake uncovered until fish is barely opaque, about 8-10 minutes.

- Garnish with lemon twists and serve immediately.

- Yield: 4-6 servings

Fresh Parmesan cheese has no equal. Once you have tried it, you will never go back to the cheese in the can. Buy a chunk at the grocery or deli, grate it in the food processor and store it in a resealable freezer bag in the freezer. Take it out as needed.

BROOKINGS CLAM AND RED POTATO FRITTATA

Leeks grow in the ground buried up to their necks in soil, therefore they require thorough cleaning when they come from the market. To clean properly, cut off root end and ⅔ of green top, removing one layer of outer leaves. Rinse well under cool water and slice in half lengthwise. Rinse again, carefully cleaning the dirt from between the layers. Pat dry and slice to desired size.

Ideal as a brunch dish, this is a hearty Northwest version of the omelette.

6 tablespoons butter or margarine, divided
1 large red potato, diced
2 leeks, cleaned and sliced
1 (6.5-ounce) can chopped clams, drained

6 eggs
salt and pepper
½ cup shredded Swiss cheese
2 tablespoons chopped parsley

- Melt butter in 12 to 14-inch ovenproof skillet over medium-high heat.

- Add potatoes and cook, stirring often until potato is golden, about 20 minutes. Remove potatoes from pan and set aside.

- Reduce heat to medium and melt 1 tablespoon butter in pan. Add leeks and cook, stirring until leeks are limp.

- Stir in potatoes, clams and remaining butter; heat through.

- Beat eggs; add salt and pepper to taste.

- Pour over leek mixture and cook, using wide spatula to gently lift cooked portion allowing uncooked egg to flow underneath.

- Cook until softly set. Sprinkle with cheese and parsley. Broil 4 inches from heat until cheese melts and top is lightly browned. About 1 minute.

- Cut into pie shaped wedges and serve.

- Yield: 4-6 servings

RED SNAPPER ORIENTAL

Red snapper at its best. Serve with rice or on platter of cooked oriental noodles.

2 pounds red snapper
1 teaspoon salt
flour
½ cup butter
1 large onion, sliced
1 large green pepper, sliced
2 cloves garlic, pressed

1 tablespoon flour
1½ cups water
1 tablespoon rice or white wine vinegar
½ teaspoon powdered sugar
¼ teaspoon ground ginger
2 tablespoons soy sauce

- Sprinkle fish with 1 teaspoon salt, then flour lightly.

- Melt butter in large skillet over medium-high heat. Add fish and brown well on both sides turning carefully. Remove from pan and set aside. In same pan, add to drippings: onion, green pepper and garlic. Reduce heat and sauté until golden. Stir in 1 tablespoon flour, water, vinegar, sugar, ginger and soy sauce. Bring to boil and return fish to skillet. Cook covered, over low heat, 8-10 minutes or until fish flakes easily with fork, but is still moist.

- Yield: 6-8 servings

OREGON LING COD WITH PISTACHIO CRUST

½ cup shelled, salted pistachio
    nuts, finely chopped
⅓ cup fine dry bread crumbs
¼ cup minced fresh parsley
¼-½ teaspoon freshly ground
    pepper
¼ teaspoon salt

1 egg
4 (4-ounce) skinned and boned ling
    cod fillets
¼ cup butter or margarine, melted
2 green onions, sliced
1 tablespoon capers, drained
1 lime, cut in wedges

A wonderful way to prepare the ling cod caught off our Oregon Coast, of course other firm white fish may be used. This recipe is so good that the 4 ounce serving may not be enough. Make extra!

- Preheat broiler or covered grill. Mix pistachios, bread crumbs, parsley, pepper and salt on a rimmed plate.

- Beat egg in a 9-inch pie plate. Dip fish in egg to coat and place egg coated fillets on wax paper lined cookie sheet. Roll fillets in nut mixture.

- Melt butter in small frying pan over medium heat. Add onions and capers stirring just until the color of the onions brightens. Set aside.

- Place fish on broiler pan or foil covered grill. Pour butter over fish and cook approximately 5 minutes per side, turning once.

- Remove to platter and serve topped with onion and capers. Garnish with lime wedges.

- Yield: 4 servings

LEMON GRILLED ORANGE ROUGHY

½ teaspoon grated lemon rind
2 tablespoons lemon juice
1 tablespoon margarine, melted
½ teaspoon dried thyme
¼ teaspoon salt

¼ teaspoon paprika
⅛ teaspoon garlic powder
1¼ pounds orange roughy fillets
4 slices of lemon for garnish

It is best not to substitute any other white fish because orange roughy has a special flavor all its own.

- Combine lemon rind, lemon juice, margarine, thyme, salt, paprika and garlic powder in shallow dish. Place fish in dish and turn to coat. Preheat barbecue grill on high heat and place fish on grill. Cook about 5-7 minutes per side with grill cover on.

- Top fillets with lemon slice and serve.

- Yield: 3-4 servings

CAYENNE TROUT WITH BUTTERED ORZO

Orzo looks very much like rice, but it is not. It is actually a tiny rice shaped pasta! Cooked in boiling water, as with any other pasta, it is a fun and different accompaniment. Simply prepared and mildly spiced, this is a refreshing and elegant way to prepare rainbow trout.

¼ cup butter or margarine, softened
2 teaspoons minced garlic
¼ teaspoon rosemary, crushed
¼ teaspoon thyme, crushed
¼ teaspoon cayenne pepper

⅓ cup beer
⅓ cup chicken stock
2 teaspoons Worcestershire sauce
2 whole rainbow trout
¼ pound tiny shrimp

- Blend butter, garlic, rosemary, thyme and cayenne pepper in small bowl.

- Combine beer, chicken stock and Worcestershire sauce in 12 to 14-inch skillet and bring to boil over medium-high heat. Add butter mixture, stirring until blended. Add trout and cook over medium heat, turning once and basting often, until fish is white and flakes easily. Top with shrimp and heat through. Remove trout to plate and spoon shrimp sauce over buttered orzo.

- Yield: 2 servings

BUTTERED ORZO

½ cup dried orzo
2 quarts boiling water

2 tablespoons butter or margarine

- Add dried orzo to rapidly boiling water. Boil over medium-high heat, stirring often for 10-13 minutes. Drain and stir in butter until butter melts and pasta is well covered. Serve with Cayenne Trout.

- Yield: 2-3 servings

Gold was discovered in 1859 on the Rogue. Evidence of mining is still visible today. You can see stone tailings along streambeds, gouges from hydraulic mining, occasional shafts and abandoned equipment.

THREE PEPPER CAJUN SHRIMP

1 teaspoon butter
1½ pounds jumbo deveined
  shrimp
1 red onion, sliced in rings and
  halved
2 cloves garlic, minced
3 tomatoes, seeded and coarsely
  chopped
1 green bell pepper, seeded and
  chopped

1 yellow bell pepper, seeded and
  chopped
1 tablespoon cayenne pepper or to
  taste
1 (8-ounce) can mandarin oranges,
  drained
½ cup grated fresh Parmesan
  cheese, divided
juice of ½ fresh lemon

Three pepper Cajun spells HOT! Adjust the amount of cayenne pepper to suit your palate.

- Preheat oven to 350 degrees. Melt butter in large skillet over medium heat. Add shrimp, onion and garlic; sauté until shrimp just turns pink and opaque. Drain and add tomatoes, bell peppers, cayenne pepper and ¼ cup of Parmesan.

- Transfer to 9x13-inch baking dish and squeeze lemon over all. Bake 30 minutes. Sprinkle with mandarin oranges and remaining cheese. Return to oven for 10 minutes. Serve immediately over white or brown rice.

- Yield: 6 servings

CAJUN SHRIMP WITH PASTA

1 pound fresh angel hair pasta
½ cup butter
¾ cup chopped green onions
½ pound fresh mushrooms, sliced

1 pound fresh shrimp meat, shelled
  and deveined
1 tablespoon Cajun seasoning
1 pint half-and-half or heavy cream

Spice up your shrimp Cajun style. Vary the seasoning according to your passion for the hot stuff. This pasta dish is rich, creamy and beautiful.

- Cook pasta 1-1½ minutes. Drain and chill by running under cold water. Drain thoroughly.

- Melt butter in large saucepan and sauté onions and mushrooms over medium heat for 2-3 minutes. Add shrimp and Cajun spice; sauté 1 minute. Add cream and cook 5-10 minutes until sauce thickens. Add pasta to pan and toss well. Serve immediately.

- Yield: 4 servings

SHRIMP ROTINI

Scallops or crab also work beautifully in this dish, or use all three for triple seafood pleasure.

6 tablespoons butter or margarine, divided
1 cup chopped onion
1 cup dry white wine
2 tablespoons instant chicken bouillon granules
1 teaspoon dried basil
½ teaspoon salt
½ teaspoon pepper

12-16 ounces raw medium shrimp, shelled
10 ounces rotini pasta
2 medium tomatoes, peeled, seeded and chopped
½ cup grated fresh Parmesan cheese
½ cup fresh parsley, snipped

- Melt 2 tablespoons butter in large skillet over medium heat. Add onion and cook until tender, but not brown. Stir in wine, bouillon, basil, salt and pepper. Bring to boil and reduce heat. Simmer uncovered 12-15 minutes or until liquid is reduced by two-thirds.

- Meanwhile, cook pasta according to package directions. Drain and keep warm.

- Cut shrimp in half lengthwise and add to wine mixture. Cover and simmer 5 minutes or until shrimp are bright pink and tender. Stir in tomatoes and heat through.

- Melt remaining 4 tablespoons butter. Toss with hot pasta. Add shrimp mixture, cheese and parsley; toss until pasta is coated.

- Yield: 4 servings

CONFETTI SHRIMP

Five peppercorn blend is a mixture of black, white, green, pink and Szechuan whole peppercorns. They are perfect when spicy flavor is desired, but a peppermill is required.

Bright, beautiful colors and the delightful flavor combination of shrimp, sweet peppers and hazelnuts make this a splendid dish.

2 tablespoons olive oil
¾ cup diced red or white onion
4 cloves garlic, finely minced
1 each: green, red and yellow pepper, diced
1 pound medium shrimp, shelled
⅔ cup dry white wine

⅛ teaspoon freshly ground five peppercorn blend
1 teaspoon dried oregano
1 teaspoon paprika
½ cup roasted hazelnuts
1 tablespoon toasted sesame seeds
fresh fettucine or linguine, cooked and drained

- Heat oil in frying pan over medium heat. Add onion and sauté until soft; move to side of pan.

- Add peppers and cook until softened; move to edge of pan.

- Add shrimp to center of pan and stir, cooking until bright pink.

- Pour in wine and add seasonings, stirring until blended.

- Add hazelnuts and sesame seeds, tossing to blend.

- Serve immediately over hot fresh fettucine or linguine.

- Yield: 6-8 servings

PASTA WITH SALMON IN BASIL CREAM

2 tablespoons butter or margarine
2 tablespoons minced shallots or green onion
1 cup whipping cream
1 cup chicken stock
2 tablespoons dry white wine
¼ teaspoon garlic powder
¼ cup fresh basil leaves, lightly packed or ½ teaspoon dried basil

12 ounces fresh pasta
1 salmon fillet or steak, cooked, boned and in chunks
salt and pepper
sprigs of fresh basil or fresh parsley for garnish
fresh grated Parmesan cheese

Fabulous way to use left-over salmon. Rich and delectable. Don't forget the crusty French bread!

- Melt butter in 5 to 6-quart saucepan, over medium-high heat. Add shallots and stir until soft, about 2 minutes. If using dried basil, add at this time. Gradually stir in cream, stock and wine. Add garlic powder. Cook over high heat, stirring constantly until reduced to 1 cup, about 10 minutes. Reduce heat and add fresh basil. Keep warm over low heat.

- Bring 3-4 quarts water to a rolling boil. Add pasta and cook over medium-high heat for 3-5 minutes, until al dente. Drain.

- While pasta is cooking, add salmon to basil sauce. Season to taste with salt and pepper, and heat through. Place pasta on rimmed plates. Ladle sauce over pasta and garnish with fresh basil sprigs or fresh parsley. Serve. Pass fresh grated Parmesan separately.

- Yield: 4-6 servings

SCALLOP LINGUINE

1 tablespoon olive oil
2 shallots, minced
2 garlic cloves, crushed
2 tablespoons chopped Italian parsley
2 tablespoons minced fresh basil
¼ teaspoon red pepper flakes
1 teaspoon salt
1 (16-ounce) can tomatoes

½ cup dry white wine
2 tablespoons tomato paste
1 pound sea scallops
1 (9-ounce) package frozen artichoke hearts
12 ounces linguine, cooked and drained
2 tablespoons pine nuts
basil leaves for garnish

Single leaf "Italian" parsley is a flat leaf variety that is fuller in flavor than the curly type and is preferred for cooking. It is also quite high in vitamin C. If you are interested in growing parsley in your garden, consider buying plants. Seeds take a very long time to germinate.

- Heat oil in 3-quart saucepan; sauté shallots and garlic over medium heat. Add parsley, basil, pepper flakes, salt, tomatoes, wine and tomato paste. Cover and simmer about 20 minutes. Add scallops and artichokes; cook about 5 minutes longer.

- Place pasta on platter and pour scallop mixture over. Sprinkle with pine nuts and garnish with basil leaves. Serve immediately.

- Yield: 6 servings

The red pepper flakes are very flavorful, so measure carefully. A wonderfully savory dish that happens to be low in calories and high on health.

MEATS

CAREY SPECIAL

Renowned throughout the Pacific Northwest, the Carey Special was designed by a Canadian, Colonel Tom Carey. Growing in popularity each year, the darker colors of this fly are suggestive of the damsel, dobson and dragonfly larvae found in many lakes.

VENISON POT ROAST WITH JUNIPER BERRIES

The juniper berry imparts a slightly sweet, pine flavor. If juniper berries are unavailable, a dash of gin is a good substitute. Juniper berries can be purchased at the health food store.

4-5 pound elk roast or venison round or rump roast, fat trimmed
4 thick-sliced bacon slices, fried for 5 minutes and drained
1 cup dry red wine
¼ cup fresh lemon juice
1 onion, sliced
2 slices fresh ginger root

10 whole juniper berries
2 cloves garlic, minced
½ teaspoon salt
½ teaspoon pepper
⅓ cup salad oil
1 cup water
3 tablespoons cornstarch
½ cup water

- This recipe needs to be marinated for at least 8 hours.

- Place meat in a flat baking pan and pierce all over with fork.

- In a bowl, combine bacon, red wine, lemon juice, onion, ginger root, juniper berries, garlic, salt and pepper. Pour over roast and marinate in refrigerator for at least 8 hours.

- When ready to cook, transfer roast from marinade to a plate and wipe dry with paper towels. Reserve marinade.

- In a Dutch oven or heavy skillet with tight fitting lid, heat salad oil over moderate heat; add roast and brown on all sides. Add 1 cup water to marinade and pour over roast. Cover and simmer 2-2½ hours.

- Remove roast from pot and keep warm.

- Strain pan juices and return strained liquid to pan.

- Combine cornstarch and ½ cup water; blend into pan juices and stir over medium heat until slightly thickened. Return meat to pot and keep hot, without boiling, until serving time.

- Serve sliced with fresh fettucini noodles and sauce or with huckleberry relish.

- Yield: 6-8 servings

HUCKLEBERRY RELISH

1 quart huckleberries (or
blueberries)
½ cup semi-dry red wine
½ stick cinnamon

2 whole cloves
2 whole allspice
1 cup sugar

Huckleberries are a prized possession in the Northwest. Valued for making delicious pies, muffins, jellies and jams, huckleberry aficionados go to great lengths to keep their picking grounds top secret!

- Wash berries and place in large enamel or stainless steel kettle. Add remaining ingredients. Bring to a boil, skim off foam and reduce heat. Simmer 30 minutes. Strain berries through sieve, discarding cinnamon stick, cloves and allspice, reserving juice.

- Return juice to kettle and bring to a boil. Reduce heat and simmer juice until it thickens. Add berries and bring back to a boil.

- Use immediately, or pour into hot sterilized jars and process in hot water bath for 5 minutes. Recipe may be halved.

- Yield: 4 cups

VENISON MCINTOSH

5 elk or venison steaks, tenderized
if necessary
⅓ cup all-purpose flour
⅓ cup fresh Parmesan cheese,
freshly grated
oil for browning

⅔ cup red wine
⅔ cup water
2 or more cloves garlic, minced
¼ pound fresh mushrooms, sliced
salt and pepper to taste

If there isn't a hunter available to provide the venison, it's good to know that fresh game is becoming more readily available in specialty markets.

- Rinse steaks and shake off excess moisture. Mix flour and Parmesan cheese together. Dredge steaks in flour mixture and set flour mixture aside. Brown steaks in hot oil in 10-inch skillet. Turn once, carefully, with large spatula. When both sides are browned, add wine and water to completely cover steaks. Increase liquid if necessary. Add garlic, mushrooms, salt and pepper. Simmer, uncovered until tender, approximately 1 hour.

- Remove steaks from pan and adjust sauce just before serving by adding more liquid or sprinkling with reserved flour and Parmesan mixture to thicken.

- Spoon sauce over steaks and serve.

- Yield: 5 servings

LEG OF LAMB IN WINE SAUCE

This is a wonderful, traditional Easter meal.

Leg of lamb
4 or more cloves fresh garlic,
    slivered
2 tablespoons all-purpose flour

1 cup water
¼ cup white wine
½ lemon
salt and pepper to taste

- To prepare: Preheat oven to 325 degrees and plan ½ hour cooking time per pound of lamb. At the end of the cooking time turn the temperature up to 350 degrees and cook the entire leg of lamb for an additional 30 minutes. If using a meat thermometer, it should read about 155 to 160 degrees when it is time to take the meat out.

- Peel 4 or more cloves of garlic and cut into thin lengthwise pieces. Using the tip of a sharp knife make shallow incisions in the outside surface of the meat and insert garlic.

- To roast: Place lamb on a roasting rack in large roasting pan and cover loosely with a foil tent. Roast to desired doneness according to directions described above.

- To serve: Remove the meat from oven and pour off all but 2 tablespoons of the fat. To this add 2 cloves of minced garlic and heat briefly. Add 2 tablespoons flour and mix with a wire whisk. Pour in 1 cup of water and scrape crust from bottom of pan. Stir until smooth. Add ¼ cup of white wine and simmer. Add the juice of ½ of a lemon. Season to taste with salt and pepper. Adjust liquid to make a free-flowing sauce.

- Serve sauce in a gravy boat with the leg of lamb.

- Yield: 1 serving per pound of lamb

LAMB CHOPS WITH GARLIC AND ROSEMARY

Garlic and rosemary blend together for a perfect combination of flavors to enhance this lamb main dish.

4 cloves garlic, pressed or minced
2½ tablespoons plus 1½ teaspoons
    fresh rosemary, minced or 1
    tablespoon dry rosemary,
    crumbled
⅓ cup parsley, minced

2 tablespoons olive oil or water
4 lamb rib or loin chops, bone
    removed, cut ¾ to 1-inch thick
salt and pepper to taste
fresh rosemary sprigs for garnish

- Mix garlic, rosemary, parsley and oil.

- Slash fat around lamb chops at 1-inch intervals. Rub 1 tablespoon of garlic mix on each side of each chop.

- Place each chop between 2 sheets of plastic wrap. Pound meat with a flat-surfaced mallet. Pound meat evenly, until about ¼-inch thick. Cover and chill, if preparing ahead of time.

- Cook meat on a greased grill about 6 inches from heat, about 4-5 minutes per side for medium or until done to your liking.

- Season with salt and pepper and garnish with fresh rosemary sprigs.

- Yield: 4 servings

SAVORY SPRING LEG OF LAMB

½ cup soy sauce
1 tablespoon oregano
1 tablespoon thyme
1 tablespoon rosemary
½ teaspoon mace
1 teaspoon dry mustard

4 cloves garlic, peeled
2 bay leaves
½ cup extra virgin olive oil
1 (7-pound) leg of lamb
salt and pepper to taste

Oregon Pinot Noir is an excellent choice of wine to serve with this meal.

- This recipe needs to be marinated for at least 1 hour before roasting.

- To marinate: Combine soy sauce, oregano, thyme, rosemary, mace, dry mustard, garlic and bay leaves in a food processor fitted with a steel blade or a blender. Process, slowly adding olive oil to mixture until it forms a smooth paste. Cover the lamb entirely with mixture. Reserve some of the marinade to serve with the lamb as a sauce. Refrigerate for at least 1 hour.

- Preheat oven to 450 degrees.

- To roast: Place lamb on rack of large roasting pan and roast 15 minutes; reduce heat to 350 degrees and continue roasting for 12 to 15 minutes per pound or 140 degrees on a meat thermometer for medium rare.

- Allow lamb to rest for about 20 minutes before carving. Salt and pepper to taste.

- To serve: Slice, using the reserved marinade to spoon over lamb.

- Yield: 8-10 servings

HONEY APPLE PORK CHOPS

4 (¾-inch) pork chops
½ cup apple juice
¼ cup soy sauce
¼ cup honey

2 tablespoons lemon juice
½ teaspoon garlic powder
¼ teaspoon ground ginger
¼ teaspoon dry mustard

Pineapple juice may be substituted for apple juice in this recipe and is especially good with pork. A broiler chicken can also be used in place of pork chops.

- This recipe needs to be marinated 2-4 hours before grilling.

- To marinate: Place pork chops or chicken in a shallow glass baking dish or quality sealable plastic bag.

- Combine apple juice, soy sauce, honey, lemon juice, garlic powder, ginger and mustard in a glass jar with a lid. Shake to combine.

- Pour marinade over meat. Cover and refrigerate 2 to 4 hours, turning the meat several times.

- Barbecue or broil the meat until done, basting with marinade.

- Yield: 4 servings

PORK CHOPS À LA ROGUE

An appropriate main course for an elegant dinner.

8 pork chops
½ teaspoon oil
salt and pepper
6 fresh pears, peeled, halved and cored
3 tablespoons orange juice

¼ cup brown sugar, firmly packed
¼ teaspoon cinnamon
⅓ cup dry sherry
1½ tablespoons butter or margarine
1 teaspoon cornstarch
1 tablespoon water

- Preheat oven to 350 degrees.

- In a skillet, over medium heat, brown pork chops in oil.

- Place pork chops in shallow pan, sprinkle with salt and pepper. Place pears rounded side down on and around pork chops. Pour orange juice over all; sprinkle with brown sugar and cinnamon. Pour sherry over all. Divide butter and place in hollows of pears. Cover and bake 20 minutes. Continue baking uncovered for an additional 20 minutes.

- Remove from oven and place pears and pork chops in a warm serving dish.

- Dissolve cornstarch in water, add to juices in pan, and cook until mixture thickens. Pour over chops and pears.

- Yield: 6-8 servings

CHINA GULCH
SWEET AND SOUR PORK

Enjoy this authentic recipe for crispy, bite-size pieces of pork wrapped in a succulent sweet-and-sour sauce.

3 pounds pork loin, cut into 1-inch cubes
3 cups boiling water
3 tablespoons soy sauce plus ½ cup soy sauce
3 tablespoons cornstarch
oil - for deep frying

1½ cups sugar
6 tablespoons cornstarch
⅔ cup vinegar
1⅓ cups water
1 green pepper, sliced and sautéed
1 (10-ounce) can pineapple chunks, drained

- In medium saucepan, simmer pork in water until tender. Meanwhile, mix 3 tablespoons soy sauce with 3 tablespoons cornstarch. Drain meat well and coat with soy sauce mixture.

- Heat oil to 390 degrees. Fry pork until brown and crisp. Drain off excess oil.

- Meanwhile, in a large saucepan, mix sugar with remaining 6 tablespoons cornstarch. Add ½ cup soy sauce, vinegar and water; mix well.

- Cook sauce over medium-low heat, stirring constantly until transparent and thickened.

- Add pork, sautéed green pepper, and pineapple to thickened sauce; heat through. If sauce is too thick, add a little water to attain desired consistency.

- Serve with any kind of rice.

- Yield: 6 servings

RASPBERRY HERB PORK TENDERLOIN

½ cup raspberry vinegar
2 cloves garlic, minced
1 tablespoon Dijon mustard
1 tablespoon honey
¼ teaspoon marjoram

¼ teaspoon sage
¼ teaspoon thyme
½ teaspoon coarsely ground pepper
2 (1-pound) pork tenderloins,
   trimmed of fat

This lean pork main dish will add elegance to your summer barbecues. Accompany with "Orzo with Myzithra and Basil" and get ready for rave reviews.

- In a bowl, combine raspberry vinegar, garlic, mustard, honey and dry herbs to make marinade.

- Pour marinade into a quality, sealable plastic bag and add tenderloins. Refrigerate for at least 2 hours up to 24 hours, occasionally turning the bag.

- When ready to cook, remove tenderloins from marinade and set remaining marinade aside. Place tenderloins on grill of barbecue, over gas or briquets. Cook on medium heat for 20-30 minutes, being careful not to overcook. Baste often with remaining marinade. Meat will look slightly pink but will fade when removed from heat. May check with meat thermometer at 165 degrees.

- To serve, slice thinly across grain.

- Yield: 4-6 servings

MARINATED PORK LOIN

½ cup dry sherry
½ cup soy sauce
3 cloves garlic, pressed
1 tablespoon dry mustard
1 teaspoon ground ginger
1 teaspoon dried thyme, crushed

1 (4-5 pound) pork loin roast,
   boned, rolled and tied
or 1 bone-in sirloin pork roast,
   about 4 pounds
3-4 cloves garlic, cut in slivers

For best results in determining the degree of doneness in meats, use a meat thermometer. Place in the center of uncooked roast so that the bulb of the thermometer reaches the thickest part of the meat, being careful that it is not resting on bone or fat. When desired temperature is reached, push thermometer into roast further. If the temperature drops, continue cooking until correct temperature is achieved.

- This recipe needs to marinate at least 2 hours before roasting.

- To marinate: Combine sherry, soy sauce, garlic, dry mustard, ginger and thyme in a good quality sealable plastic bag. Place roast in bag and seal tightly. Rotate bag carefully to thoroughly coat roast and mix marinade.

- Marinate at least 2 hours at room temperature or overnight in refrigerator. Occasionally turn bag to distribute marinade.

- To cook: Drain roast and reserve marinade in a small bowl. Using a shallow 9x13-inch roasting pan, place roast on a rack sprayed with a non-stick coating. With a knife, randomly cut slits in roast and insert desired number of garlic cloves.

- Roast uncovered, at 325 degrees for 2½ to 3 hours or until thermometer registers 165-170 degrees. Baste with marinade during last hour.

- Note: The bone-in roast will be done in about 2½ hours.

- Yield: 6-8 servings

BRAISED PORK LOIN

Braising is a technique where food is browned in a little fat, seasonings are added with a small amount of liquid, then covered tightly and cooked slowly on a range or in an oven until tender.

2 teaspoons salt
1 teaspoon pepper
1 teaspoon sage
1 teaspoon thyme
3 pound boneless pork loin roast, rib end, (boned and tied)

2 tablespoons vegetable oil
2 cups onion, chopped
2 large cloves garlic, chopped
½ cup apple cider

- Place roast on a large sheet of wax paper. Combine salt, pepper, sage, and thyme and rub mixture into pork roast. Wrap in wax paper and chill overnight.

- Preheat oven to 325 degrees.

- In large Dutch oven, heat oil and brown roast. Transfer meat to platter, drain off all but 2 tablespoons of fat and sauté onion and garlic over medium heat for 1 minute.

- Return roast to Dutch oven; add cider and bring to boil.

- Cover Dutch oven and place in oven. Cook for 50-60 minutes.

- Let stand 10 minutes before carving.

- Drain fat from Dutch oven. Pour remaining juices and solids into a blender and puree. Strain liquid and serve with roast.

- Yield: 6 servings

PEAR PUREE

An excellent accompaniment for pork.

3 pounds Bartlett pears, cut, peeled and cored
3 pounds Bosc pears, cut, peeled and cored

¾ cup water
⅔ cup pear vinegar
⅔ cup sugar
⅔ cup pear brandy

- In a heavy saucepan, simmer pears and water until pears are tender. Stir occasionally.

- Place cooked pears and water in a blender or food processor and puree.

- Return mixture to saucepan and mix in vinegar and sugar. Simmer on low heat until mixture is reduced to the consistency of applesauce. Add pear brandy and stir until well blended.

- Serve at room temperature.

- Yield: 6 cups

VEAL PICCATA

1¼ pounds veal scallops, cut
   ¼-inch thick
¾ cup all-purpose flour
salt and pepper
8 tablespoons butter, divided

2 tablespoons fresh lemon juice
1 tablespoon capers
1 tablespoon parsley, chopped for
   garnish

Top quality veal is prized for its subtle, elegant flavor. Our choices to round out this menu include, "Garlic Roma Tomatoes and Croutons" and "Pear Dumplings with Cream Custard".

- Lightly dust veal with flour, salt and pepper.

- Melt 6 tablespoons of butter in a large skillet. Brown the veal in the butter for 2 minutes on each side at a medium high temperature.

- Remove meat from the pan and place on a warm serving dish.

- Add remaining 2 tablespoons of butter to meat juices cooking at a medium high temperature until mixture takes on a medium brown color. Add lemon juice and capers.

- Pour over the veal. Sprinkle with chopped parsley and serve immediately.

- Yield: 4 servings

BETTS HOLE BEEF PARMIGIANA

1½ to 2 pounds beef round steak
3 tablespoons flour
salt and pepper, to taste
1 egg, beaten with 1 tablespoon
   water
½ cup fine, dry bread crumbs
¼ cup Parmesan cheese, freshly
   grated

¼ teaspoon basil
4 tablespoons oil
1 cup tomato sauce
1 clove garlic, crushed
½ tablespoon oregano
6 slices mozzarella cheese

Located on the Upper Rogue River, the Betts Hole is just above the ranch that was formerly owned by screen legend Ginger Rogers. It is known as one of the best fishing holes on the river.

- Cut steak into serving size pieces. Combine flour, salt and pepper. Dredge meat in flour to coat. Pound meat with mallet to tenderize.

- Mix egg and water in a dish. Combine dry bread crumbs, Parmesan cheese and basil in another dish. Dip meat into egg mixture and then into bread crumbs, making sure to coat well. Brown meat lightly in oil and place in a buttered 9x13-inch baking pan.

- Preheat oven to 350 degrees.

- Combine tomato sauce, garlic, and oregano and pour over meat. Cover with foil and bake for 1 hour.

- Remove from oven, place a slice of mozzarella cheese on each piece of meat and return to oven until cheese is melted.

- Yield: 6 servings

FILLETS OF BEEF IN CREAMY WINE-DILL SAUCE

This gourmet dinner recipe will surely impress the guests at your next dinner party.

2 fillets of beef, (approximately 2½-pounds each) tied, at room temperature

¼ cup vegetable oil
salt and pepper, to taste

SAUCE

½ cup unsalted butter, softened
⅓ cup Dijon mustard
¾ cup shallots, minced
2½ cups dry white wine
¼ cup fresh tarragon, minced

¼ cup heavy cream
⅛ teaspoon white pepper
½ (22-ounce) jar baby kosher dill pickles, cut into julienne strips

- Preheat oven to 550 degrees.

- Rub fillets with oil and season with salt and pepper. Place on rack in a large roasting pan, leaving space between fillets. Roast in preheated oven for approximately 20-25 minutes, or until a meat thermometer registers 130 degrees, for medium-rare meat.

- Transfer the fillets to a platter and let stand, covered loosely with foil, for 15 minutes.

- To make sauce: In a bowl, cream together butter and mustard, using an electric mixer.

- In a large saucepan, combine shallots, wine and tarragon and cook over high heat until mixture reduces to 1 cup.

- Add the heavy cream, pepper and pickles. Reduce heat to low and whisk in creamed butter and mustard, a little at a time. Add any meat juices. Keep sauce warm; do not let boil.

- To serve, slice the fillets, cover with sauce.

- Yield: 8-10 servings

During the Indian Wars of 1855-56, Battle Bar was the site of the Battle of the Rogue River on April 27, 1856.

BEER CHILI BEEF

¼ pound pepper bacon
1½ pounds sirloin, cubed
2 tablespoons flour
¼ teaspoon garlic powder
½ cup chopped scallions
12 ounces dark beer

1 cup beef broth
2-4 ounces green chilies, depending on taste
2 tablespoons flour in ½ cup water
⅓ cup cashews
sour cream for garnish

A great reason for you to try some of the new beers provided by local micro-breweries.

- In a Dutch oven, cook bacon until crisp. Remove bacon from pan and drain fat; cut into bite size pieces.

- Coat meat with flour and garlic powder. Brown meat in Dutch oven over medium-high heat. Return bacon to pan with meat adding scallions, beer, broth and green chilies. Bring to boil; cover and reduce heat. Simmer 1½ to 2½ hours until meat is tender.

- Thicken chili with 2 tablespoons flour dissolved in ½ cup water.

- Add cashews ½ hour before serving. Serve over rice. Garnish with dollop of sour cream.

- Yield: 6 servings

HOT SUMMER SPARERIBS

SAUCE

¾ cup chopped onion
7 garlic cloves, minced
¼ cup olive oil
2¼ cups tomato puree
¼ cup light brown sugar
¼ cup lemon juice

¼ cup apple cider vinegar
4¼ tablespoons Tabasco sauce
1½ tablespoons dry mustard
1¼ tablespoons salt
6 pounds spareribs, cut into 3 rib pieces.

Ribs always rate high on summertime menus. When trying to determine how many pounds of ribs to purchase, a good rule to follow is allow approximately one pound per person.

- This recipe needs to be marinated 4 to 24 hours ahead of planned cooking time.

- To prepare marinade: Sauté onions and garlic in oil until soft. Stir in tomato puree, brown sugar, lemon juice, vinegar, Tabasco sauce, mustard and salt; bring to a boil.

- Coat spareribs with ⅔ of sauce and refrigerate at least 4 hours or overnight.

- Preheat oven to 325 degrees.

- To cook: In roasting pan, arrange spareribs in a single layer. Bake for 1 hour, turning to brown. Drain most of the fat from the roasting pan and return ribs to oven for another hour, basting them with the remaining sauce. Serve warm.

- Yield: 4-6 servings

ROGUE RIVER RIBS

Brands of dry mustard vary as to how hot they are. Of course, the more you use, the hotter the ribs, so use dry mustard to taste.

beef or pork ribs (any amount)
salt
pepper

dry mustard
all-purpose flour
soy sauce

- Preheat oven to 325 degrees. Place ribs in a 13x9 inch pan. Salt and pepper to taste. Sprinkle ribs liberally with dry mustard, the flour and then soy sauce. Cover with foil and bake 1½ to 1¾ hours at 325 degrees. Remove foil and bake ½ hour longer at 350 degrees. Note: The last ½ hour may be done on a grill.

BULGOGI (KOREAN STIR FRY)

The longer the marinating time for this Korean dish, the better the flavor!

1 pound top round or sirloin, thinly sliced across grain, 2 inches long
2 tablespoons sugar
¼ cup green onion, chopped
¼ cup soy sauce
3 tablespoons sesame oil (dark preferably)

2 tablespoons sesame seeds, toasted and crushed
2 cloves fresh garlic, chopped
2 teaspoons sugar
½ teaspoon ground black pepper
2 tablespoons cooking oil

- This recipe needs to marinate 4 hours or more before cooking.

- To marinate: Lightly pound sliced meat. Sprinkle each side with 1 tablespoon of sugar and marinate for 1 hour.

- Drain excess liquid from meat if necessary. In a small bowl, combine onion, soy sauce, sesame oil, sesame seeds, garlic, the remaining 2 teaspoons of sugar and pepper. Mix and pour over meat in a shallow glass baking dish or quality sealable plastic bag. Marinate for at least 4 hours.

- To cook: Heat cooking oil in a wok or fry pan to medium-high heat. Stir fry meat until done. Remove from the pan immediately. Do not overcook.

- Serve with any kind of rice.

- Yield: 4 servings

TIPSY TENDERLOINS

¼ cup soy sauce
¼ cup whiskey
1 tablespoon sugar
1 clove garlic, minced

2 pounds pork tenderloins
hot mustard for dipping
sesame seeds for dipping

Perfect for taking on river rafting and camping trips. Serve with other Rogue River Rendezvous specials such as "Spicy Cool Watermelon Salad" and "Poppy Seed Cake".

- This recipe needs to be marinated for at least 4 hours

- In bowl, combine soy sauce, whiskey, sugar and garlic to make marinade.

- Place tenderloins and marinade in shallow glass dish or quality sealable plastic bag and refrigerate 4-5 hours or more. Turn several times during marinating time.

- Preheat oven to 350 degrees.

- Bake for 50-60 minutes or barbecue on grill for 45-60 minutes or to desired doneness.

- To serve; Carve into thin slices and serve with hot mustard and seeds.

- Yield: 4 servings

FLANK STEAK IN HONEY MARINADE

1-2 pounds beef flank steak
¼ cup mild flavored honey
¼ cup soy sauce

¼ cup vegetable oil
4 cloves garlic, pressed or minced

Flank steak is best served rare to medium doneness. It may be cooked under the broiler, over coals or on a gas grill. Serve flank steak sliced thinly, across grain.

- This recipe needs to marinate 12-24 hours before grilling.

- To marinate: Pat steak dry with a paper towel and score both sides in a diamond pattern approximately ¼-inch deep. Place in a shallow glass dish or quality, sealable plastic bag.

- Mix remaining ingredients for marinade and pour over steak. Refrigerate 12-24 hours, turning several times.

- To grill: Pour the marinade off and grill 6-7 minutes on the first side and 9-15 minutes on the second side, depending on personal taste. Slice and serve immediately.

- Yield: 4 servings

ORANGE-ROSEMARY STEAKS
THE OREGON BEEF COUNCIL

Any good quality steak, such as New York, Spencer, flank or rib eye, may be used with delicious results.

1¼ pounds boneless beef chuck top blade steaks, cut ¾ to 1-inch thick (about 4 steaks)
⅓ cup orange juice
1 tablespoon balsamic vinegar or red wine vinegar

1 tablespoon onion, finely chopped
¾ teaspoon dried rosemary, crushed
¼ teaspoon salt
¼ coarsely ground black pepper

- Combine orange juice, vinegar, onion and rosemary. Place beef steaks in plastic sealable bag; add marinade, turning to coat. Seal and marinate in refrigerator 30 minutes or up to 6 hours, turning occasionally.

- Remove steaks from marinade and place on grill over medium coals or on a gas grill at medium setting. Grill 17-22 minutes for rare (140 degrees) or medium (160 degrees), turning once. Season with salt and pepper. Carve into thin slices and serve.

- Yield: 4 servings

FLANK STEAK IN PEPPER MARINADE

After a day of whitewater excitement, settle down with fresh corn-on-the-cob, a crisp green salad, "Basil Batter Rolls" and these wonderful steaks.

1½ to 2 pounds flank steak
¼ cup salad oil
½ cup olive oil
½ cup red wine
¼ cup lemon juice
1¼ teaspoons salt

¼ teaspoon Tabasco sauce
½ teaspoon basil
1 teaspoon oregano
¼ to ½ teaspoon cayenne pepper
1 clove garlic, mashed

- This recipe needs to be marinated at least 4 hours before serving time.

- Place steak in a shallow glass baking dish or quality sealable plastic bag. In a small bowl, mix all remaining ingredients and pour over steak. Refrigerate for at least 4 hours.

- Grill or broil steak 7-8 minutes on each side for medium-rare. Slice thinly across grain and serve immediately.

- Yield: 4-5 servings

VERMOUTH FLANK STEAK

3-4 pounds flank steak
½ cup soy sauce
6 tablespoons honey
4 tablespoons vermouth (sweet or dry)

3 teaspoons garlic powder
3 teaspoons ginger
1½ cups vegetable oil

Vermouth provides a slightly sweet flavor to this simple yet sensational flank steak.

- This recipe needs to marinate for 12-24 hours before grilling.

- To marinate: Pat steak dry with a paper towel and score both sides in a diamond pattern approximately ¼-inch deep. Place in a shallow non-metal dish or a quality sealable plastic bag.

- In a small bowl, mix remaining ingredients and pour over steak. Refrigerate for 12-24 hours, turning several times.

- To grill: Pour the marinade off and grill 6-7 minutes on the first side and 9-15 minutes on the second side, depending on personal taste. Slice thinly across grain and serve immediately.

- Yield: 10-12 servings

BROWN BAG SIRLOIN STEAK

3 slices egg bread with crusts
2-3 pounds top sirloin steak, approximately 2½-inches thick
4 tablespoons butter, softened
4 tablespoons vegetable oil

1 teaspoon fresh garlic, crushed
2 teaspoons salt
1½ teaspoons ground pepper
4 ounces sharp Cheddar cheese, grated

Fun, different and very easy, but best of all - very delicious!

- Tear bread into pieces and place in food processor with metal blade. Process until crumbly. Measure 1 cup breadcrumbs.

- Trim excess fat from steak.

- In a bowl, mix butter, oil, garlic, salt and pepper. Spread on all sides of steak.

- Mix breadcrumbs with cheese. Coat steak with breadcrumb and cheese mixture. Place steak in a brown paper grocery bag. (It is not recommended to use recycled paper bags.) Fold end over and secure with staples. Steak, in bag, may be refrigerated several hours, but let steak come to room temperature before cooking.

- Place bag on rimmed baking sheet. For rare steak, bake at 375 degrees for 30 minutes. For medium-rare, bake at 425 degrees for 50 minutes. Remove steak from bag. Let stand 5 minutes and carve into thin slices.

- Yield: 8-10 servings

CREAMY HORSERADISH SAUCE

The Tulelake region is one of the world's top producers of horseradish.

¼ cup prepared horseradish
1 tablespoon white vinegar
1 teaspoon sugar

½ teaspoon salt
¼ teaspoon prepared mustard
½ cup whipped cream

- Combine the first 5 ingredients; fold into whipped cream.

- Serve with roast pork or beef.

- Yield: 4-6 servings

MRS. MURPHY'S CORNED BEEF

A wonderful St. Patrick's Day tradition, served with "Red Potatoes in Lemon Butter".

4 pounds corned beef
water
3 tablespoons prepared mustard
2½ to 3 tablespoons prepared
   horseradish

3 tablespoons red wine vinegar
¼ cup molasses
¼ cup honey

SAUCE

4 tablespoons prepared
   horseradish

2 tablespoons mayonnaise

- Place corned beef in a Dutch oven on stove and cover with water. Cover the pot and cook meat on low for 4 hours until meat is tender.

- Drain the cooked corned beef and place on an ovenproof platter or broiler pan.

- Combine the mustard, horseradish, vinegar, molasses, and honey in a small bowl. Brush mixture on all sides of the meat.

- Brown the corned beef in a 400 degree oven for about 20 minutes. Brush more mixture on several times during cooking.

- Remove the corned beef from the oven and serve. Mix the remaining horseradish and mayonnaise and serve on the side.

- Yield: 6 servings

TEQUILA CHILI

2½ pounds ground chuck
2 cups white onion, minced
2 dried de arbol chilies, crushed
3 cloves garlic, minced
salt to taste
1 teaspoon ground cumin
¼ teaspoon ground cloves
1 (29-ounce) can whole, peeled
    tomatoes, undrained and
    coarsely chopped

½ cup orange juice
½ cup tequila or water
¼ cup tomato paste
1 (15-ounce) can red kidney beans
lime wedges for garnish
fresh cilantro sprigs for garnish

A basket of warm tortillas makes a good accompaniment for this hearty main dish.

- In a skillet, crumble ground chuck and cook 6-8 minutes. Add onion, and cook until tender.

- Add crushed chilies, garlic, salt, cumin, and cloves; stir to blend.

- Add tomatoes, orange juice, tequila, tomato paste and beans; mix well.

- Heat to boiling, reduce to low and simmer, covered for about 1½ hours.

- For thicker chili, uncover skillet; cook over medium heat, stirring frequently for 10-15 minutes.

- Serve garnished with lime wedges and cilantro sprigs.

- Yield: 4-6 servings

PACIFIC BURGERS

½ cup prepared teriyaki sauce
½ cup rolled oats, uncooked
1 egg, beaten
¼ cup onion, chopped
½ teaspoon salt (optional)
¼ teaspoon pepper
1 pound lean ground beef
4 hamburger buns

lettuce
mayonnaise
prepared hot/sweet mustard
1 (8-ounce) can sliced pineapple
    rings, drained
8 slices bacon, fried crisp and
    drained

Easy to prepare, economical and delicious, it is no wonder as to why hamburgers rate number one for summer barbecues. The tangy flavor of teriyaki combined with pineapple and bacon make these burgers the outstanding choice of outdoor gourmets everywhere.

- In medium bowl, combine teriyaki sauce, oats, egg, onion, salt and pepper; mix well. Add ground beef; mix lightly but thoroughly. Divide into four equal portions. Form into ¾-inch thick patties.

- Grill over medium coals for 4 minutes. Turn patties and grill for another 4 minutes for medium-rare burgers. Adjust timing to personal preference.

- Meanwhile, prepare hamburger buns to taste with lettuce leaf, mayonnaise, and hot/sweet mustard.

- Place cooked beef patty on half a bun, top with 2 slices cooked bacon, one pineapple ring and top half of bun.

- Yield: 4 servings

HORSESHOE BEND BARBECUE SAUCE

Make extra and place in small jars with a barbecue brush tied on for a great gift to take to friends.

6 tablespoons prepared mustard
1 (14-ounce) bottle ketchup
1 (5-ounce) bottle Worcestershire sauce
4 tablespoons lemon juice
8 tablespoons sugar
1 tablespoon salt

1 tablespoon pepper
1 tablespoon chili powder
2 tablespoons vinegar
½ cup butter
a few drops liquid smoke
a few drops Tabasco sauce

- Combine mustard and ketchup in a saucepan. Add remaining ingredients and simmer for 30 minutes over low heat.

- Store in the refrigerator and serve on chicken, beef or pork.

- Yield: 1 quart

OLD-FASHIONED MEATBALLS AND NOODLES

A hearty, homey recipe that is perfect to serve after a day of cross-country skiing.

1 pound lean ground beef
⅔ cup rolled oats, uncooked
½ cup milk

1 teaspoon salt
1 tablespoon onion, chopped
1 egg

SAUCE

1 cup ketchup
2 tablespoons vinegar
1 tablespoon Worcestershire sauce
¾ cup water

1 (8-ounce) can tomato sauce
1 teaspoon sugar
1 medium onion, chopped

- Mix ground beef, oats, milk, salt, onion and egg in a medium sized bowl. Shape meatballs and brown in a large skillet with lid or Dutch oven. Drain on paper towels.

- Mix the sauce ingredients in a small bowl and add to the skillet. Gently place the meatballs in the sauce. Simmer, covered for 30-45 minutes. Sauce will thicken.

- Serve over egg noodles. (One (1-pound) bag boiled makes enough for 4-5 servings.)

- Yield: 4-5 servings

VERY ITALIAN MEATBALLS

2 pounds lean ground beef
¼ pound ground pork sausage
1 tablespoon parsley
5 eggs
1 teaspoon salt

1 teaspoon pepper
1 cup bread crumbs
¼ cup Parmesan cheese, freshly
    grated
¾ cup onion, chopped

SAUCE

1 (16-ounce) can tomato puree
1 tablespoon fresh basil, chopped
salt and pepper to taste
½ tablespoon oregano
1 teaspoon garlic salt

2 cups water
pork neck bones
1 (8-ounce) can tomato paste
1 cup water

The perfect meatball sand-wich meatball!

- Mix ground beef and pork with parsley, eggs, salt, pepper, bread crumbs, cheese and onion. Shape mixture into balls and fry until brown. Reserve pan drippings.

- Make the sauce by combining all the sauce ingredients except the tomato paste in a large pot. Add 2 cups water. Add the meatballs to this pot.

- Put the tomato paste in the frying pan with the reserved pan drippings. Simmer this mixture for a couple of minutes and then add 1 cup water.

- Combine the tomato paste mixture with the sauce and meatballs. Simmer slowly for at least 4 hours until thick. You may need to add more water as the sauce simmers down for desired consistency.

- Remove pork neck bones and serve meatballs in sauce over pasta.

- Yield: 6 servings

POULTRY

RED ANT

When fall arrives on the Rogue, the ever popular Red Ant is a top producer. Its red floss and brown bucktail wings offset the tail of golden pheasant. Frequently the wings are tied upright and divided to attract the Lower Rogue half-pounders.

OREGON CHARDONNAY CHICKEN

You'll have to wait overnight to taste this one, but it is guaranteed worth the wait. The wine tenderizes the chicken and the onion is especially savory.

¾ cup butter
3 large white onions, thinly sliced
3 cloves garlic, peeled and minced
6 whole chicken breasts, halved, boned and skinned
salt and pepper

1 (14-ounce) can artichoke bottoms, drained
2 cups grated Gruyère cheese
1½ cups French bread crumbs
1 tablespoon dried tarragon
1 bottle Oregon Chardonnay wine

- The day before: In large skillet over medium heat, melt ½ cup butter. Add onions and garlic; sauté until limp and golden.

- Spread half the onions over bottom of 8x11-inch baking dish. Arrange chicken over onions, season with salt and pepper and top each with artichoke bottom. Cover chicken with remaining onions.

- Combine cheese, bread crumbs and tarragon in medium bowl.

- Melt remaining butter and add to cheese mixture, tossing to mix. Press some of cheese mixture over each chicken breast. Pour enough wine into pan to come halfway up side. Cover with foil and refrigerate overnight.

- One hour before serving, preheat oven to 350 degrees. Bake covered for 20 minutes. Uncover and bake 20 more minutes until bubbling hot and golden brown.

- Yield: 10 servings

WILD BLACKBERRY CHICKEN

1½ cups blackberry wine
1½ cups chopped fresh mushrooms
1 teaspoon olive oil
1 cup fresh blackberries
1 teaspoon garlic salt
½ teaspoon dried basil

4 slices bacon, cooked and
  crumbled
1½ pounds boneless chicken
  breasts
1 cup grated fresh Parmesan cheese

- Combine first 7 ingredients in shallow, ovenproof pan. Add chicken and turn to coat. Refrigerate and allow to marinate for at least 2 hours, turning occasionally.

- Preheat oven to 325 degrees.

- Bake for 35-40 minutes until tender. Sprinkle with Parmesan and return to oven until cheese melts.

- Yield: 4-6 servings

Frozen berries may be used without compromising the outcome.

Oregon's blackberries are so admired, they are often flown to The White House for State dinners. They are used to their full advantage in this unusual and lovely entree.

LEMON-ROSEMARY CHICKEN

4 boneless chicken breasts
lemon juice to cover
3 cloves garlic, peeled and sliced

3 sprigs fresh rosemary or 1
  teaspoon dried rosemary
2 tablespoons olive oil

- Place chicken breasts in glass or plastic container. Pour just enough lemon juice over chicken to cover. Add garlic and rosemary; toss to distribute herbs evenly. Refrigerate 1-3 hours.

- Add oil to 12-inch skillet over medium-high heat. Remove chicken from lemon juice and place in pan. Brown well on both sides. Reduce heat to medium and continue cooking about 15-20 minutes or until chicken is cooked through.

- Or: Remove chicken from marinade and place on preheated grill. Cook, turning occasionally, for 20-25 minutes until browned and cooked through. Serve immediately.

- Yield: 4 servings

No need to marinate this chicken for hours on end. The fresh taste of lemon and rosemary are imparted to the meat rather quickly — less than 1½ hours from refrigerator to table if need be.

The rosemary plant is native to the Mediterranean region, which has a climate very similar to our own. Therefore, it thrives in our area (except in the coldest of winters) as a lovely landscape plant. We can enjoy beautiful blue flowers and snip a sprig here and there to season our food.

CHICKEN PINOT NOIR

The rich, dark brown sauce and tender chicken is just the answer on a cool fall or winter evening. Garnish with fresh parsley sprigs or, if you're feeling creative, sculpted mushroom caps add an exquisite touch.

2 tablespoons oil
8 chicken breast halves
12 pearl onions
½ pound mushrooms, quartered
1 (14-ounce) can beef broth

1 cup Oregon Pinot Noir
2 tablespoons Dijon mustard
2 tablespoons parsley, chopped
1 teaspoon water
1 teaspoon cornstarch

- Heat oil in 12 to 14-inch skillet over medium-high heat. Add chicken and onions and sauté for about 20 minutes until well browned. Remove from pan and keep warm.

- To same pan add mushrooms, cooking until lightly browned and juices have evaporated. Add mushrooms to reserved chicken. Add beef broth to skillet and boil until reduced by half. Return chicken, mushrooms and onions to pan. Stir in wine and mustard; bring to boil. Reduce heat, cover and simmer over low heat for about 30 minutes. Add parsley.

- Remove chicken and vegetables to serving dish with slotted spoon. Blend 1 teaspoon water with 1 teaspoon cornstarch and stir into cooking pan juices. Stir briskly until thickened and pour sauce over chicken.

- Yield: 6-8 servings

CURRY OVEN-FRIED CHICKEN

A deliciously spiced version of fried chicken, this recipe tends itself in the oven allowing the cook more freedom in the kitchen.

1 large fryer chicken, quartered
6 tablespoons margarine
2 teaspoons Worcestershire sauce
2 teaspoons curry powder
1 teaspoon oregano, crushed
½ teaspoon dry mustard

½ teaspoon garlic powder
¼ teaspoon paprika
3 dashes Tabasco sauce
1 chicken bouillon cube or 1
    teaspoon granules

- Preheat oven to 375 degrees.

- Wash chicken, pat dry and place skin side down in a 9x13-inch baking dish.

- Melt margarine in small saucepan. Add Worcestershire sauce, curry powder, oregano, mustard, garlic powder, paprika, Tabasco sauce and bouillon. Stir well to blend.

- Brush sauce over chicken and bake uncovered for 20 minutes. Turn skin side up and baste with sauce. Continue baking, basting occasionally, until chicken is tender and brown, about 40 minutes. Remove chicken to warm platter.

- Yield: 4 servings

ROGUE RENDEZVOUS CHICKEN

½ cup raspberry vinegar
½ cup soy sauce
½ cup fresh squeezed lime juice
¼ cup Worcestershire sauce
⅔ cup corn oil
⅔ cup olive oil
2 teaspoons freshly ground pepper

1 tablespoon minced garlic
5 pounds boneless, skinless
    chicken breasts
2 pounds sweet onions, sliced
1 each red, green and yellow
    pepper, cored and sliced

Developed for us by one of our members who is a local caterer, this dish has true Northwest flair. It also happens to hold very well, keeping several days if needed. Reheat slowly and serve. It is ideal for parties since it requires little last minute attention.

- Day one: Combine first eight ingredients in large nonmetal bowl. Add chicken and marinate 12-24 hours.

- Day two: Remove chicken from marinade, reserving marinade. Allow chicken to come just to room temperature and cold smoke over cherry wood for 20-30 minutes. Consult index for directions on cold smoking. Meanwhile, put onions in half the marinade and peppers in the other half.

- Preheat oven to 350 degrees. After smoking chicken, place on baking sheet and bake for 8-12 minutes, depending on oven. Do not overcook.

- Increase oven temperature to 375 degrees. Remove onions and peppers from marinade and bake separately until crisp cooked, 20-30 minutes.

- Meanwhile, slice chicken into ½-inch by 3-inch pieces. Toss with vegetables and serve.

- Yield: 10-12 servings

BRUSHY BAR CHICKEN CASSEROLE

2 cups cooked chicken breasts,
    chopped into ½-inch pieces
2 cups chopped celery
½ cup minced onion
1 cup mayonnaise

2 tablespoons lemon juice
½ cup toasted slivered almonds
½ cup sliced stuffed green olives
½ cup grated sharp Cheddar cheese
1 cup potato chips, crushed

The fresh taste and crisp texture of this casserole make it a natural alternative to those with rich and creamy sauces and it comes together in a snap!

- Preheat oven to 375 degrees. Combine chicken, celery, onion, mayonnaise and lemon juice in large bowl. Add almonds, green olives and cheese; fold gently to mix. Spread in 9x13-inch casserole and top with potato chips. Bake for 20-30 minutes, until heated through and cheese melts.

- Yield: 6-8 servings

FUZZY NAVEL CHICKEN

Deglaze means to add some sort of liquid, usually wine, to a pan in which meat has been cooked or browned. The resulting liquid is then used in a sauce incorporating the flavor of the meat into the sauce.

The subtle flavor of peach adds a luscious touch to the moist and tender chicken. Try this with our steamed "Snow Peas with Pine Nuts" for a nice combination.

1 cup freshly squeezed orange juice
½ teaspoon salt
¼ teaspoon pepper
1 clove garlic, minced
¼ teaspoon ground cloves
1 tablespoon cornstarch

3 whole chicken breasts, halved, skinned and boned
3 tablespoons vegetable oil
½ cup Peach Schnapps
½ cup whole roasted cashews
fresh orange slices for garnish

- Combine orange juice, salt, pepper, garlic, cloves and cornstarch. Set aside.

- Pound chicken breasts to ¼-inch thickness. Heat oil in large skillet and add chicken. Brown well over medium heat and remove from skillet. Add Schnapps to skillet and deglaze pan over medium-high heat reducing liquid by half. Return chicken breasts to skillet and cook, coating on all sides with browning Schnapps. Remove chicken to platter and keep warm.

- Add cashews to skillet and stir to coat well. Remove. Add orange juice mixture to skillet and cook over medium heat, stirring until sauce is thick and smooth.

- Pour sauce over chicken and top with cashews. Garnish with orange slices.

- Yield: 4-6 servings

CHICKEN SAN CARLOS

South of the border chicken in a spicy, creamy sauce. Make it hot or mild by adjusting the amount of chili powder and cumin used.

1 tablespoon vegetable oil
½ cup onion, finely chopped
1 clove garlic, crushed
1 pound boneless chicken breast, in bite size pieces
1-2 teaspoons chili powder
¾-1 teaspoon ground cumin

¼ teaspoon salt
¼ cup diced red pepper
2 ounces diced green chilies
¾ cup chicken broth
2 teaspoons cornstarch
2 tablespoons white wine or water
½ cup sour cream

- Add oil to skillet over medium heat. Add onion and garlic and sauté until translucent.

- Toss chicken with chili powder, cumin and salt. Add to skillet and sauté with onion and garlic until chicken is lightly browned. Add red pepper, green chilies and chicken broth; simmer covered until chicken is no longer pink, 5-10 minutes.

- Mix cornstarch with wine or water and add to chicken, stirring until sauce is thickened.

- Remove from heat and add sour cream. Serve immediately.

- Yield: 3-4 servings

FRENCH CHICKEN PÂTE

**breasts, thighs and legs of 4
  chickens, skinned**
**4 medium onions, peeled and
  sliced in rings**
3-4 bay leaves

10 whole cloves
2 tablespoons salt
1 bottle hearty red wine
pie crust dough
¼ cup butter, softened

- 2-3 days in advance: Place chicken pieces in large nonmetal bowl. Add onions, bay leaves, cloves and salt. Stir to distribute seasonings evenly. Pour wine over chicken mixture and cover with plastic wrap. Refrigerate 2-3 days stirring each day.

- Preheat oven to 425 degrees.

- Make pie crust. Roll out to 12x15-inch square. Spread with ½ softened butter and fold two opposite edges over to meet in center. Refrigerate 2-3 minutes and repeat process. Divide dough in half. Roll one half to fit bottom of 10-inch pie pan.

- Line pie pan with crust. Remove chicken pieces from wine and seasonings; place in bottom of pie pan. Sprinkle with 2 tablespoons of wine broth and dot with 2 tablespoons butter.

- Roll out remaining pie dough and cover chicken, making slits in crust to allow steam to escape.

- Bake for 20 minutes; reduce heat to 350 degrees and bake 1 hour until chicken is cooked through and crust is golden brown. Spoon onto plates and serve. Meat should fall easily from bones.

- Yield: 6 servings

For a beautiful presentation, roll out pastry scraps and cut into the shape of a grape leaf. Place on top crust and brush with egg whisked together with 1 tablespoon water. Bake as directed.

The word "pâte" is actually a French word for pie or pastry and this is exactly that. A rich, savory chicken pie. This is an authentic recipe from a little French woman handed down three generations.

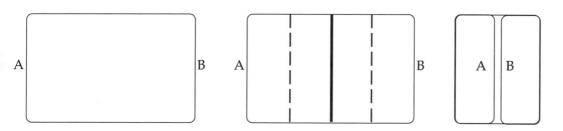

CREAMY BOW TIES WITH CHICKEN AND SPINACH

Delightful bow tie pasta adds a special twist to this delicious dish. It's fun, it's creamy and it comes with a built in vegetable.

1½ teaspoons salt
1 (12-ounce) package bow tie pasta
3 quarts boiling water
2 teaspoons olive oil
2 teaspoons butter
1 small onion, chopped
1 pound boneless chicken breasts, skinned and cut in 1-inch pieces

½ teaspoon pepper
10 ounces fresh spinach, cleaned, stemmed and coarsely chopped
½ cup half-and-half
½ cup freshly grated Parmesan cheese

- Cook pasta in boiling water with 1 teaspoon salt. Drain.

- Meanwhile, heat oil and butter in skillet over medium heat until butter is melted. Add onions and sauté stirring often. Add chicken and sprinkle with remaining salt and pepper. Sauté, stirring often, until chicken is lightly browned. Add spinach to skillet, cooking and stirring until wilted. Add cream and bring to boil. Simmer until mixture is slightly thickened.

- Combine pasta, chicken mixture and cheese in large bowl and toss gently to mix. Serve immediately.

- Yield: 4 servings

WILD MUSHROOM CHICKEN STROGANOFF

Many varieties of mushrooms are now available in most grocery stores. Use whatever combination you happen to find. Shiitake, oyster, enoki and brown crimini are all good choices. If you are really lucky and know what to look for, the morel mushrooms found in the foothills and forests throughout Southern Oregon are some of the most prized in the world. Never gather your own mushrooms unless you are experienced, as the great taste is not worth the risk of accidental poisoning.

5 chicken breasts, skinned, boned and cut into 1 inch pieces
salt
freshly ground pepper
3 tablespoons butter
1 medium onion, sliced
½ pound mixed wild mushrooms

1 tablespoon flour
½ cup chicken broth
½ cup dry white wine
½ cup sour cream
2 tablespoons Dijon mustard
fresh parsley, chopped, for garnish
cooked rice

- Season chicken with salt and pepper. Melt 2 tablespoons butter in heavy large skillet over medium-high heat. Add chicken and cook until opaque, stirring occasionally, about 5 minutes. Transfer to serving dish, cover and keep warm. Add onion and mushrooms to skillet; cook until light brown, stirring frequently, 6-8 minutes. Add to chicken in dish and keep warm.

- Melt remaining butter in small saucepan over medium-low heat. Add flour and stir 3 minutes. Whisk in broth and wine; stir constantly until sauce is thickened and smooth, about 5 minutes. Stir in sour cream and mustard. Heat sauce until warmed through, about 3 minutes: do not boil. Pour over chicken and mushrooms; garnish with parsley. Serve with rice.

- Yield: 4-6 servings

WEST COAST CHICKEN

1 cup frozen orange juice
  concentrate, thawed
⅓ cup butter, melted
4 teaspoons soy sauce
2 teaspoons ground ginger

2 teaspoons salt
¼ teaspoon black pepper
5 pounds chicken thighs, skinned
  orange slices for garnish

The flavor of citrus perks up the tender chicken. It's a cinch to prepare the night before and have it ready for a busy evening. Try with "Wild Rice with Hazelnuts" for a nice taste combination.

- Day before, combine orange juice, butter, soy sauce, ginger, salt and pepper. Oil two 11x7-inch glass pans. Arrange chicken in single layer in pans and baste well with sauce. Cover and refrigerate overnight. Save remaining sauce.

- Preheat oven to 350 degrees. One hour before serving, bake uncovered for 1 hour basting once with orange sauce. Garnish with fresh orange slices.

- Yield: 8-10 servings

GRILL ROASTED TURKEY

9-11 pound turkey
fresh lemon juice
1 teaspoon thyme or fines herbes
1 apple, quartered

1 orange, quartered
1 large onion, quartered
4 cloves garlic, peeled and halved
6 slices bacon

The indirect heat method is one in which the heat source is not directly below the food. (1) In a charcoal kettle grill the coals are burning at each side of kettle with a drip pan below the food. (2) In a covered gas grill, only one of the grill's burners is ignited while the food is positioned on the other side and rotated occasionally. See illustration.

- Clean and rinse bird with water and pat dry. Remove neck and gizzard package; rinse cavity with small amount of lemon juice. Sprinkle cavity with thyme or fines herbes. Fill cavity with apple, orange, onion and garlic, using as much as required to fill cavity and neck end. Pin flaps closed if you desire. Lay bacon strips across top of bird and place directly on grill. Roast 3½-4 hours in a covered barbecue using indirect heat method or; preheat oven to 325 degrees and place in shallow roasting pan and cook 3½ - 4 hours or until meat thermometer reads 170-175 degrees.

- Remove from grill or oven and let rest 10-15 minutes before slicing.

- Yield: 6-8 servings

If you put this turkey in the barbecue early in the afternoon and head out for a day of yard work, you'll be able to enjoy the aroma of your cooking dinner as you toil. The smoky herb flavor of the meat makes a delicious sandwich the next day.

BLACK SATIN CHICKEN

The one pot method used to prepare this moist and tender whole chicken is a favorite of gourmet and dishwasher alike. Rice and stir-fried vegetables complete the picture.

1 whole roasting chicken
1 clove garlic, peeled and crushed
fresh ground pepper
salt
1 tablespoon sweet sherry plus ¼ cup

1 whole green onion
½ cup soy sauce
¼ cup water
2 tablespoons sugar

- Rub outside of chicken with garlic, pepper, salt and 1 tablespoon sherry. Place green onion inside chicken.

- Mix soy sauce, sherry, water and sugar in saucepan large enough to contain chicken. Bring to boil and add whole chicken. Cover and simmer over low heat, turning often, for about 1 hour or until chicken is tender.

- Yield: 3-4 servings

WOK CORNISH HENS

Oriental noodles, along with oyster sauce, are found in the Oriental food section of most grocery stores.

The subtle flavor of sherry and oriental seasonings permeates the meat of these tender little birds. Showy results without a great investment of time and effort.

3 Rock Cornish game hens, rinsed and dried
1 tablespoon peanut oil
6 green onions, cut julienne style
4 cloves garlic, crushed
2 tablespoons coarsely grated fresh ginger
1½ tablespoons soy sauce
1½ tablespoons oyster sauce

¼ teaspoon pepper
¼ teaspoon Chinese Five Spice
¼ cup dry sherry
2 teaspoons sugar
1 tablespoon sesame oil
¼ cup water
6 ounces oriental noodles, cooked
¼ cup coarsely chopped cilantro for garnish

- Preheat wok over high heat. Add oil and place hens in wok, skin-side-down. Reduce heat to medium and cook covered for 6 minutes, turning hens once. Add remaining ingredients, except cilantro, and simmer covered, over medium-low heat for 30 minutes turning once.

- Remove birds to platter of cooked oriental noodles. Continue to cook sauce until reduced to a thick glaze, about 10-15 minutes. Pour sauce over hens and noodles, and garnish with fresh cilantro.

- Yield: 3 servings

BARBECUED GAME HENS

6 Rock Cornish game hens
garlic salt
white wine vinegar, in small spray
    bottle

3 tablespoons butter
2 tablespoons Kitchen Bouquet®

Kitchen Bouquet gives the hens a lovely mahogany color while the vinegar gives them a wonderful flavor. The spray bottle technique adds a little fun.

- Wash and drain game hens. Salt well inside and out with garlic salt. Set 3-4 quarts of well burning charcoal in one end of grill and place game hens in other end. Close lid. Temperature should reach 350-450 degrees. Cook 35-45 minutes.

- Melt butter in small saucepan and add Kitchen Bouquet, stirring to blend. Spray hens well with wine vinegar then baste with butter mixture. Rotate hens to ensure even cooking. Close lid and cook 35-45 minutes.

- Yield: 6 servings

PACIFIC NORTHWEST GAME HENS

4 Rock Cornish game hens
2 cups fresh or frozen blueberries
1 cup blueberry vinegar, purchased
    or see recipe below

¾ cup olive oil
salt and pepper to taste
2 good quality, resealable plastic
    bags

These birds are an amazing color of blue when they hit the grill, but when cooked are transformed to a lovely golden brown. Try fresh raspberries with raspberry vinegar or blackberries with blackberry vinegar. You get the idea! The results are superb.

- The night before serving or very early that day, rinse hens and dry with paper towels.
- Combine blueberries and vinegar in medium saucepan over medium-high heat. Bring to boil and simmer 1 minute; set aside. Stir in remaining ingredients and cool.
- Place hens in plastic bags (2 per bag) and pour in vinegar mixture.
- Refrigerate 8-10 hours or overnight, turning often.
- Grill 35-40 minutes, turning occasionally, or roast in 400 degree oven for approximately 45 minutes, basting with marinade.
- Yield: 4 servings

FRUIT VINEGAR

2 cups white wine vinegar
2 tablespoons sugar

1 cup fresh or frozen blueberries,
    raspberries or blackberries
cheesecloth

- Measure vinegar into small saucepan. Heat to boiling and add sugar. Stir and simmer 5 minutes. Meanwhile place washed berries into clean quart jar. Pour boiling vinegar over fruit. Let stand 24 hours. Strain vinegar through cheesecloth into clean, scalded quart jar. Cover and store in cool place.
- Yield: 1 quart

SMOKY GARLIC CHICKEN PIZZA

Pizza without the tomato sauce. It's a nice change and worth a try. The chicken makes for a refreshing difference.

1 recipe pizza dough or purchased crust
1 whole boneless breast of chicken
3 cloves garlic, pressed
2 tablespoons olive oil
2 tablespoons pesto with sun-dried tomato

6 ounces sliced provolone
2 tablespoons sliced green olives
½ cup sliced mushrooms
red onion, thinly sliced
¼ cup grated fresh Parmesan cheese

- Rub chicken with crushed garlic and set aside for 2-4 hours.

- Prepare pizza dough or use purchased crust, placing it on 12 to 14-inch pizza pan or cookie sheet.

- Grill or sauté chicken until cooked through and golden. Slice into thin strips.

- Preheat oven to 425 degrees. Brush crust with olive oil and spread on pesto. Cover with slices of provolone. Place chicken over cheese and sprinkle with olives, mushrooms, onion and Parmesan. Bake for 20-25 minutes until crust is golden brown and top is bubbly.

- Yield: 4 servings

PASTA SAUVIGNON BLANC

Try serving this beautiful pasta dish with a green salad, a loaf of focaccia (Italian flatbread) and the left-over wine. Close your eyes and imagine you are on the Italian Riviera. A little cappuccino after dinner completes the scene.

6 chicken breasts, skinned, boned and sliced into thin strips
salt and pepper
½ cup butter
6 cloves garlic, peeled and halved
2 green onions, chopped
2 tablespoons flour
¾ cup Sauvignon Blanc wine
2½ cups heavy cream

3 ounces cream cheese, softened and cut in pieces
⅛ teaspoon cayenne pepper
1 (8.4-ounce) jar marinated sun-dried tomatoes, drained and chopped
3 large fresh basil leaves
12 ounces spinach fettucine
freshly grated Parmesan cheese

- Sprinkle chicken with salt and pepper.

- Melt butter in large heavy skillet over medium heat. Sauté garlic, but do not allow it to brown. Remove with slotted spoon, add chicken and cook until lightly browned. Set aside.

- Add onions to same skillet and sauté until softened. Add flour and blend well to make a soft paste. Add wine and cream in thirds, stirring constantly to blend well between additions. Add cream cheese; stir until melted and well incorporated.

- Return chicken to pan; add cayenne pepper, sun-dried tomatoes and basil leaves. Simmer gently for 15-20 minutes to blend flavors.

- Cook fettucine until al dente. Drain and place on platter or in shallow bowl. Spoon chicken and sauce over pasta; sprinkle with grated cheese.

- Yield: 6-8 servings

CHICKEN STRIPS WITH JALAPEÑO SAUCE

3 whole chicken breasts, skinned
    and boned
buttermilk to cover
½ cup butter
2 cloves garlic, peeled and minced
¾ cup ground hazelnuts

¼ teaspoon salt
1 teaspoon paprika
¾ cup mayonnaise
2 tablespoons chopped jalapeño
    peppers

- Cut chicken breasts into strips and soak in buttermilk for 1 hour.

- Preheat oven to 375 degrees. Drain chicken and set aside. Melt butter over medium heat and add garlic. Mix paprika and salt with hazelnuts. Coat chicken with melted butter and roll in seasoned hazelnuts. Place on greased baking sheet. Bake until cooked through and golden brown, about 20 minutes.

- Blend mayonnaise and peppers; serve with chicken strips.

- Yield: 4-6 servings as entree or 8-10 as appetizer

Make these nutty chicken strips for a Saturday night in front of the television. Add a green salad and a Mexican brew and settle in for the evening; or try as an appetizer when you need a meaty addition to a cocktail buffet.

CHICKEN IN PHYLLO PASTRY
JACKSONVILLE INN

2 whole chicken breasts, split
1 jar artichoke hearts, drained and
    chopped
1 cup mayonnaise
1 cup Parmesan cheese

½ cup Port Salut cheese
12 sheets phyllo pastry
1 cup oil
Dijonnaise Sauce (recipe on page
    166)

- Trim chicken breasts of all fat and tendons. Pound thin.

- Mix artichokes, mayonnaise and Parmesan together. Place heaping tablespoon of artichoke mixture in the center of a chicken breast. On top of that, place one-fourth of the Port Salut. Fold breast around filling. Repeat with remaining breasts.

- Brush one sheet of phyllo pastry with oil. Repeat with two additional layers. Place one stuffed breast at the end of a 3-layer phyllo sheet. Roll phyllo around chicken. After two rolls, fold sides in, then continue rolling. Brush lightly with oil.

- Bake in a 375 degree oven 30 minutes or until a thermometer registers 165 degrees. (It is always best to use a thermometer when cooking chicken.) Phyllo should be lightly browned.

- Serve with Dijonnaise Sauce ladled over top.

- Yield: 4 servings

Located in historic Jacksonville and constructed in 1863, the Jacksonville Inn has been home to a bank and a hardware store. While dining in the fine restaurant, one can still see specks of gold dust in the mortar of the original brick walls.

CHICKEN LASAGNA

A creamy and refreshing version of lasagna just made for "Herbed Walnut Salad" and a chilled glass of white wine.

1 pound boneless, skinless chicken breasts
½ teaspoon garlic powder
¼ teaspoon Italian seasoning
freshly ground pepper
½ cup butter or margarine
½ cup flour
3 cups milk
1 cup fresh grated Parmesan cheese, divided
1 cup white wine

salt
1 cup chopped red onion
2 tablespoons chopped fresh basil
1 (10-ounce) package frozen chopped spinach, cooked and drained well
1 (15-ounce) package ricotta cheese
2 eggs
1 (16-ounce) package lasagna noodles, cooked and drained
1½ cups grated mozzarella cheese

- Place chicken in shallow microwave proof dish. Sprinkle chicken with garlic powder, Italian seasoning, and freshly ground pepper. Cover with plastic wrap and cook 9-11 minutes on high or until chicken cooked through. Cool.

- Melt butter in small saucepan over medium-low heat. Blend in flour to make thick, smooth paste and cook about 1 minute, stirring constantly. Gradually stir in milk and continue to cook until thickened. Add ½ cup Parmesan and stir until melted. Add wine and season with salt and pepper. Set aside.

- Tear chicken into 1-inch pieces and place in medium size bowl. Add red onion and basil. Stir to blend and set aside.

- Squeeze water out of spinach and place in small mixing bowl. Add ricotta, eggs and remaining Parmesan. Stir until blended. Set aside.

- Preheat oven to 350 degrees.

- To assemble coat bottom of 9x13-inch pan with ¾ cup of sauce. Arrange single layer of noodles over sauce. Top with ricotta mixture. Add second single layer of noodles. Spoon ¾ cup of sauce over noodles. Spread with chicken mixture and drizzle with ¾ cup sauce. Cover with noodles and pour remaining sauce over casserole. Top with mozzarella.

- Bake 50 minutes at 350 degrees until top is browned and bubbly. Let stand 15 minutes before serving.

- Yield: 8-10 servings

In the 1800's, miners dug for gold at Alameda Mine. Today, rafters and fishermen use the gravel shore for a resting point.

PACIFIC FLYWAY CHRISTMAS MALLARD

3 wild ducks (preferably mallards)
½ cup dry sherry
½ teaspoon marjoram
1 apple, cored and cut in sixths
½ medium onion, cut in thirds
6 dried juniper berries
2 teaspoons salt

1 teaspoon pepper
1 tablespoon marjoram
½ cup red wine
½ cup water
¼ cup seedless raspberry jam
1 tablespoon cornstarch

- Preheat oven to 350 degrees. Sprinkle the cavity of each duck with sherry and a pinch of marjoram. Stuff each bird with 2 pieces of apple, 1 wedge of onion and 2 juniper berries. Combine salt, pepper and 1 tablespoon of marjoram in a small bowl and rub mixture into the skin of the ducks.

- Place birds side by side in shallow pan, pouring wine and water around ducks and cover tightly with foil. Bake for 1 hour or until juice runs rosy pink when duck is pierced with a fork. Remove ducks to warm platter.

- Stir raspberry jam into pan juices and bring to boil stirring constantly. Add cornstarch while briskly stirring and boil until sauce thickens.

- Serve birds whole or slice meat from bone placing on platter with the tiny drumsticks and pass sauce separately. Spoon sauce over meat or wild rice.

- Yield: 3-4 servings

Be careful not to overcook your wild ducks. The meat is naturally dark red in color and should be medium-rare to be at its best.

The lovely red sweet-tart sauce takes the "wild" out of these birds and transforms them into elegant fare.

BARBECUED WILD DUCK

1 cup oil
½ cup red wine vinegar
¼ cup soy sauce
6 cloves garlic, minced
1 tablespoon celery seed

1 teaspoon salt
¼ teaspoon pepper
1 teaspoon rosemary
2-3 wild ducks, halved

- Early in the morning or the night before serving, combine first 8 ingredients in small saucepan. Simmer 10 minutes over medium-low heat. Cool to room temperature.

- Pour marinade into glass pan or bowl large enough to contain duck. Add duck halves, coating well and refrigerate for 12 hours.

- Grill over hot coals turning occasionally until done, about 12 minutes total.

- Yield: 2-4 servings

Barbecuing duck is popular with the hunting crowd. This flavorful marinade brings out the unique flavor of the birds while taming the "gamey" taste that is sometimes apparent with some wild fowl.

PEACH AND SESAME GLAZED DUCKLING WITH WILD RICE PANCAKES

MCCULLY HOUSE INN

Domestic Duckling vs. Wild Duck: It is very important to know the difference! When you think of duckling think of the fluffy white ducks in fairy tales. They are large and have a thick layer of fat, which means they require much different treatment than their wild cousins who are small, muscular and have almost no fat on their bodies. After all, while ducklings have been feasting on grain in the barnyard, the wild ducks have had to fly the length of the continent twice each year. One needs to know which you are dealing with.

½ gallon apple cider vinegar
2½ cups sugar
1 tablespoon fresh ginger, grated
3 ripe peaches, pureed

salt and pepper to taste
2 domestic ducklings
½ cup toasted sesame seeds
fresh peach slices for garnish

- Early in day or day before, prepare peach glaze by combining vinegar, sugar and ginger in a 4-quart saucepan. Bring to boil over medium-high heat, stirring until sugar dissolves. Continue to simmer until reduced by half and is syrupy. Add peaches, salt and pepper and continue to cook for 10-15 minutes. Strain. Makes 1 quart.

- 4 hours before serving, remove legs and excess fat from ducklings. Place in small roasting pan and cook at 275 degrees for 2½-3 hours or until tender. Cook breasts at 450 degrees for ½ hour or until rare.

- Brush legs and breasts with glaze and sprinkle with sesame seeds. Serve with "Wild Rice Pancakes" and garnish with additional sauce and fresh peach slices.

- Yield: 2 servings

WILD RICE PANCAKES

1 tablespoon butter
1 tablespoon olive oil
½ small onion, diced
1 tablespoon fresh thyme, chopped
1 cup cooked wild rice
2 tablespoons fresh parsley, chopped

3 eggs, separated
3 tablespoons flour
3 tablespoons milk
salt and fresh ground pepper to taste

- Add butter and olive oil to small sauté pan. Add onion and thyme; cook over medium heat until soft. Remove from heat and chill. Combine rice, chilled onion, parsley, egg yolks, flour, milk, salt and pepper and stir until just blended. Beat egg whites until stiff peaks form. Gently fold into rice mixture. Cook on greased griddle or frying pan. Turn when bubbles appear and cakes are golden brown.

- Yield: Twelve 2½-inch pancakes

PHEASANTS WITH CHANTERELLES

1 package dried Chanterelle
    mushrooms
1¾ cups hot water
¼ cup brandy
2 tablespoons olive oil
2 wild pheasants (2-2½ pounds
    each)
4 slices bacon
4 tablespoons butter, divided

1 cup coarsely chopped onion
1 cup coarsely chopped carrot
1 cup coarsely chopped celery
2 tablespoons chopped parsley
4 whole cloves
2 cloves garlic, pressed
¼ teaspoon dried sage
2 tablespoons flour
½ cup milk

If you are fortunate enough to have a fearless hunter who brings home wild pheasant, this is the perfect way to showcase the prize fowl. The meat is moist and tender and the creamy mushroom sauce is delightful. Serve "Wild Rice Roxy Ann" to complete the "wild" theme.

- Place dried mushrooms in small bowl and cover with ¾ cup hot water and ¼ cup brandy. Set aside for 2 hours to rehydrate mushrooms.

- Preheat oven to 400 degrees. Place oil in large skillet over medium- high heat. Add birds and brown on all sides. Place birds side by side in roasting pan and cover breasts with bacon; roast 30-40 minutes, basting often with pan drippings.

- Meanwhile, to same skillet add 2 tablespoons butter, onion, carrot, celery, parsley, cloves, garlic and sage. Cook over medium heat until onion is soft. Drain mushrooms and add liquid to skillet plus one cup of water. Boil uncovered 10-15 minutes until liquid is reduced to ½ cup. Strain and reserve liquid for mushroom sauce.

- To make sauce, melt 2 tablespoons butter in saucepan over medium heat. Add flour stirring to make paste. Cook for 1 minute. Stir in ½ cup reserved liquid and ½ cup milk and cook stirring until thick, smooth and hot. Chop mushrooms and add to sauce.

- Slice meat from roasted pheasants and place on platter. Serve with mushroom sauce.

- Yield: 4-6 servings

VEGETABLES, RICE & BRUNCH

TIGER'S PAW

The newest of the Rogue collection, the Tiger's Paw, was developed by Joe Howell for the Umpqua River. First tied in the early 1980's, it has been refined for the Rogue and currently sports "krystal flash" wings.

STEAMED VEGETABLES WITH DIJONNAISE SAUCE
JACKSONVILLE INN

This savory sauce is the perfect accompaniment for vegetables as well as the Inn's "Chicken in Phyllo Pastry" on page 159.

1 large bunch broccoli or 1½ pounds asparagus
2 shallots, minced
1 tablespoon olive oil
½ cup dry white wine or vermouth
½ cup whipping cream

1 cup butter, unsalted, room temperature
2 tablespoons Dijon mustard
salt and pepper
1 squeeze or 1 teaspoon lemon juice, fresh

- Steam vegetables until tender.

- Sauté shallots in olive oil. Pour in wine, scraping up any browned bits from bottom of pan. Stir in cream; cook until thickened. Reduce heat to low and gradually whisk in butter, then mustard. Do not boil. Season with salt and pepper to taste; add lemon juice. Serve over steamed vegetables.

- Yield: 4-6 servings

Jacksonville carved out a place in Oregon's history and the nearby hillsides when miners took millions of dollars of gold from the ground in the mid-1800's. But the gold vein ran out, and with it, Jacksonville's luck, as the once thriving mining town became virtually a ghost town. Today the boom times have returned, thanks in part to the town's designation as a National Historic Landmark. During the summer, enjoy performances on the grounds of the Peter Britt Estate during the Britt Music Festival.

SESAME ASPARAGUS

4 cups water
1 pound asparagus, tough ends
    removed
2 tablespoons soy sauce

2 tablespoons sesame oil
¼ teaspoon sugar
1 clove garlic, finely chopped
1 teaspoon sesame seeds

To remove tough ends, hold the asparagus stalk near the bottom and bend. It will snap at the point where it turns tough.

- Bring water to a boil. Add asparagus, boil 1 minute. Drain; rinse with cold water.

- Mix soy sauce, sesame oil, sugar, garlic and sesame seeds in small bowl. Pour over asparagus.

- Yield: 4 servings

ASPARAGUS WITH PEACH HAZELNUT TOPPING

1 pound asparagus, tough ends
    removed
1 teaspoon butter

1½ tablespoons hazelnuts, coarsely
    chopped
¼ cup peach preserves

A lovely combination using three of Oregon's finest flavors: asparagus, hazelnuts and peaches.

- Place asparagus in a steamer basket over boiling water in a covered saucepan and cook for 4 minutes or until crisp and tender. Drain and keep warm.

- Melt butter in small saucepan over low heat. Add hazelnuts and sauté until lightly toasted.

- Stir in preserves, cook until heated.

- Spoon over asparagus and serve.

- Yield: 4 servings

SAUTÉED STRING BEANS

⅓ cup vegetable oil
2 pounds whole green beans,
    washed, dried and stems
    removed
3 cloves garlic, minced

3 tablespoons soy sauce
2 tablespoons sherry, dry or sweet
1 teaspoon sugar
½ teaspoon crushed red pepper
    flakes

For those who thought green beans had no sophistication or style, try these.

- Heat oil in skillet on medium-high heat. Sauté beans with garlic until crisp tender, about 3 minutes.

- Combine soy sauce, sherry, sugar and red pepper flakes. Add to beans and continue cooking another 1-2 minutes. Serve immediately.

- Yield: 6 servings

SPINACH STUFFED ARTICHOKE CROWNS

Attractive as a vegetable course, these may also be served as an appetizer.

8 canned artichoke bottoms, drained
1 clove garlic
2½ tablespoons green onion, minced
1 tablespoon butter
2 tablespoons mayonnaise

1 package (10-ounce) frozen chopped spinach, cooked and drained
2 tablespoons sour cream
¼ teaspoon salt
4 ounces Bonbel® or SAFR Port Salut®

- Preheat oven to 325 degrees.

- Rub artichoke bottoms with garlic. Place in greased shallow dish.

- Sauté onion in butter until golden. Add mayonnaise, spinach, sour cream and salt. Spoon mixture over bottoms.

- Cut cheese into 8 thin slices and then into 4 strips each. Arrange strips lattice-like over spinach.

- Bake for 20 minutes. Remove from oven, cut cheese into spinach.

- Return to oven and bake until cheese is melted.

- Yield: 8 servings

BROCCOLI BAKE

Serve with "West Coast Chicken" for a Sunday dinner.

24 ounces broccoli spears
½ pound mushrooms, thinly sliced
2 tablespoons chopped onion
2 tablespoons butter
2 eggs
1½ cups cottage cheese

½ teaspoon salt
½ teaspoon pepper
1 teaspoon Worcestershire sauce
½ cup Cheddar cheese, shredded
½ cup butter, melted
2 cups cubed bread

- Preheat oven to 350 degrees.

- Steam broccoli and place in greased shallow casserole dish.

- Sauté mushrooms and onion in butter. Place mushrooms, onion and butter they were sautéed in over broccoli.

- In small bowl, mix eggs, cottage cheese, salt, pepper, Worcestershire and Cheddar cheese. Put mixture over broccoli.

- Mix melted butter and cubed bread to make croutons. Cover top of casserole with croutons.

- Bake for 30 minutes.

- Yield: 6-8 servings

BLOSSOM BAR BROCCOLI

1 bunch broccoli, cut into flowerets
⅓ cup fresh parsley, chopped
2 cloves garlic, crushed
1½ teaspoons salt
¼ teaspoon pepper

⅓ cup cider vinegar
1 tablespoon prepared mustard
3 tablespoons brown sugar, firmly packed
1 teaspoon onion powder

Experienced boaters know the way through the rapids of Blossom Bar: Stay right of the line of rocks dubbed "The Picket Fence."

- Blanch broccoli in boiling water for 2 minutes. Rinse with cool water.

- Combine remaining ingredients and stir until smooth paste consistency. Toss with broccoli.

- Refrigerate several hours before serving.

- Yield: 6 servings

INDIAN SUMMER CORN

2 tablespoons vegetable oil
1 pound zucchini, trimmed and sliced (about 3 cups)
½ green pepper, diced
3 ears fresh corn, cut off cob
2 medium ripe tomatoes, diced
½ teaspoon sugar

salt
pepper, freshly ground
½ teaspoon ground cumin seed, or to taste
½ cup Monterey Jack cheese, shredded

When everything is ripening all at once in your garden, this is a perfect dinner choice.

- Heat oil in heavy pan over medium heat. Add zucchini and pepper; cook, stirring constantly, for 2 minutes.

- Add corn, tomatoes, sugar, salt, pepper, and cumin. Mix well.

- Simmer, covered for 8-10 minutes or until vegetables are tender.

- Sprinkle with cheese before serving.

- Yield: 6 servings

ANISE CARROTS

Anise is the fruit of a small plant belonging to the carrot family. Anise, usually popular in bakery products or candy, makes these carrots into a treat.

1½ pounds carrots, peeled and cut diagonally into ½-inch slices
3 tablespoons butter or margarine
¾ teaspoon anise seed, crushed

6 tablespoons orange juice
1 tablespoon plus 1½ teaspoons fresh parsley, chopped
salt and pepper to taste

- Place carrots in steamer basket over boiling water in a covered 3-quart saucepan, or cook covered in a 1-quart casserole in the microwave, stirring several times until almost tender, about 12 minutes. Don't cook past tender crisp stage.

- Place butter and anise seed in a small saucepan. Heat on medium setting to melt butter and blend flavor. Add to carrots.

- Stir in orange juice, parsley, salt and pepper. Heat in saucepan or microwave 1-2 minutes.

- Turn into serving dish and sprinkle with additional parsley if desired.

- Yield: 4 servings

CARROTS IN WINE SAUCE

A very easy way to make an otherwise ordinary vegetable taste delicious.

3 tablespoons butter or margarine
8 medium carrots, sliced ¼-inch thick
6-8 green onions, sliced, tops included
¼ teaspoon salt

1 tablespoon water
4 teaspoons flour
⅔ cup half-and-half
3 tablespoons Madeira wine
parsley, finely chopped as garnish

- Melt butter in 10-inch skillet with lid. Add carrots and onions. Sauté over medium heat for 3 minutes.

- Add salt and water. Cover and cook until carrots are almost tender, about 7 minutes.

- Sprinkle with flour. Cook, stirring until bubbly. Remove from heat.

- Gradually stir in half-and-half and wine. Cook until thickened, may thin with half-and-half for desired consistency.

- Garnish with parsley.

- Yield: 6 servings

WHISKEY BAKED BEANS

6 slices bacon
1 large onion, chopped
1 (32-ounce) can pork and beans,
    drained
3 tablespoons brown sugar, firmly
    packed

1½ teaspoons Worcestershire sauce
1 teaspoon dry mustard
1 cup ketchup
1 tablespoon molasses
¼ cup whiskey

The better the brand of whiskey, the better the baked beans.

- Preheat oven to 350 degrees.

- Cut bacon into thin strips, fry, remove from pan and drain all but 2 table-spoons drippings.

- Sauté onion in drippings until limp.

- Combine, in an oiled 2-quart deep casserole dish, the onions, beans, brown sugar, Worcestershire sauce, mustard, ketchup, molasses and whiskey. Stir well.

- Crumble bacon and sprinkle on top of casserole. Bake uncovered for 40-45 minutes until bubbly and liquid is reduced.

- Yield: 8 servings

PICNIC BEANS

1 (15-ounce) can kidney beans,
    drained
2 (15-ounce) cans green beans,
    regular cut, drained
1 (15-ounce) can yellow wax beans,
    drained

1 (15-ounce) can butter beans,
    drained
8 slices bacon, fried, drained and
    diced
⅓ cup onion, chopped
¾ cup sharp Cheddar cheese,
    shredded

Perfect for those old fashioned potlucks where baked beans in a crock pot are a must.

SAUCE

¾ cup brown sugar, firmly packed
¾ cup ketchup

3 teaspoons Worcestershire sauce
½ cup corn syrup

- Preheat oven to 325 degrees. Mix beans in large baking dish.

- Mix sauce ingredients in small bowl and toss with beans. Bake, uncovered for 1 hour.

- Yield: 10-12 servings

GINGER GARLIC CAULIFLOWER

Served over hot steaming rice, this vegetable becomes an entire meal.

2 tablespoons oil (peanut or sesame)
2 cloves garlic, chopped
2-3 tablespoons fresh ginger, chopped
½ head of cauliflower, cut into small flowerets
3 green onions, chopped
½ red pepper, sliced in strips

¼ cup chicken broth
2 tablespoons oyster sauce
1 tablespoon soy sauce
½ teaspoon cornstarch
¾ cup bean sprouts or ¾ cup fresh spinach, sliced into strips
¼ cup dry roasted peanuts, coarsely chopped

- Heat oil in wok; add garlic and ginger. Stir fry for 1 minute. Add cauliflower, stir fry until browned. Add ¾ cup water, cover and steam approximately 3 minutes or until cauliflower softens.

- Remove lid (water should be cooked off). Add green onions and red pepper strips.

- Mix chicken broth, oyster sauce, soy sauce and cornstarch; stir until mixed. Add to cauliflower; heat until thickened.

- Remove from heat; add bean sprouts or spinach. Garnish with peanuts.

- Yield: 4 servings

GERMAN RED CABBAGE

The deep purple color and intriguing taste will enhance a simple main course.

3 strips bacon, chopped
1 medium onion, chopped
1 small head purple cabbage, thinly sliced
1 red apple with peel, chopped

1-2 tablespoons vinegar
1 tablespoon sugar
½ tablespoon salt
¼ teaspoon ground cloves

- In saucepan, brown bacon and onion together at medium-high temperature on stove. Drain off most of the bacon grease leaving a small amount in pan. Add thinly sliced purple cabbage, chopped apple, vinegar, sugar, salt and cloves to the onion-bacon mixture. Heat at medium temperature until thoroughly mixed. Reduce temperature and simmer for approximately 20 minutes until cabbage is softened. Serve immediately.

- Yield: 6 servings

ROASTED PEPPER TRIO

2 red peppers, sliced lengthwise,
    discard seeds
2 green peppers, sliced lengthwise,
    discard seeds
2 yellow peppers, sliced
    lengthwise, discard seeds

⅓ cup olive oil
1 teaspoon salt
1½ tablespoons chives, chopped

Purchase the freshest peppers with smooth, shiny skin, free of soft or black spots.

DRESSING

½ teaspoon garlic, minced
½ teaspoon salt
2 tablespoons red wine vinegar
6 tablespoons olive oil

⅛ teaspoon Tabasco sauce
2 teaspoons Dijon mustard
½ teaspoon sugar

- To roast peppers: Grease large baking sheet with small amount olive oil. Place peppers, skin side down, in single layer in pan. Pour remaining olive oil over peppers. Sprinkle with salt. Roast for 20 minutes then let cool at room temperature.

- To prepare dressing: Mash garlic and salt into a paste; add to remaining ingredients in a jar with a lid. Shake to mix well.

- To serve, overlap peppers on a platter and spoon dressing over. Garnish with chives.

- Yield: 6 servings

PEAS WITH TRIPLE SEC

1 (10-ounce) package frozen peas
½ teaspoon salt, or less
¼ teaspoon pepper
⅛ teaspoon nutmeg
1 tablespoon butter

1 tablespoon triple sec or orange
    liqueur
1 teaspoon freshly grated orange
    peel, or more

Nutmeg comes from the kernel of the same fruit which also gives us mace.

- Cook peas according to package. Drain. Season with salt, pepper and nutmeg. Add butter and triple sec. Stir to blend.

- Pour into serving dish and sprinkle liberally with orange peel.

- Yield: 4 servings

SNOW PEAS WITH PINE NUTS

A delicate vegetable that would be excellent served with "Fuzzy Navel Chicken."

1 pound fresh snow peas, trimmed
   and rinsed
2 tablespoons butter

2 tablespoons water
¼ cup pine nuts, toasted
salt and pepper to taste

- Toast pine nuts by spreading nuts on a cookie sheet. Bake at 350 degrees for 4 minutes, stirring occasionally. Set aside.
- In a 10-inch frying pan over high heat or an electric skillet set on highest heat, melt butter. Add snow peas then add water; stir and cover. Cook for 3 minutes, stirring occasionally. Add pine nuts to snow peas. Season with salt and pepper; cook 30 seconds more. Pour into serving bowl and serve immediately.
- Yield: 4 servings

GARLIC SPINACH

Well-known for its therapeutic properties, garlic was held in high esteem by the Greeks and Romans.

This spinach dish would enhance any meal, but would be especially good with fish.

1 bunch spinach, washed, stems
   removed and coarsely chopped
⅓ cup olive oil

2 cloves garlic, minced
¼ cup seasoned bread crumbs

- Preheat oven to 375 degrees.
- Oil a shallow baking dish with 2 tablespoons olive oil. Mix minced garlic with remaining oil. Place spinach in dish. Sprinkle bread crumbs evenly over spinach then drizzle garlic oil mixture over bread crumbs.
- Bake 35 minutes; serve immediately.
- Yield: 4 servings

WINDY CREEK POTATOES

Pimiento is a variety of Spanish sweet pepper. Combined with green pepper, this dish becomes a colorful version of scalloped potatoes.

6 medium potatoes
2 cups Cheddar cheese, shredded
¼ cup butter or margarine
1½ cups sour cream
½ cup onion, chopped

½ cup green pepper, chopped
½ cup red pimientos, chopped
1 teaspoon salt
¼ teaspoon pepper
¼ to ½ teaspoon paprika

- Preheat oven to 350 degrees.
- Wash potatoes and bake for 1 hour at 350 degrees or boil until cooked but still firm. Cool, peel and slice or shred coarsely.
- Melt cheese and butter in saucepan over low heat.
- Remove from heat and stir in sour cream, onion, green pepper, pimientos, salt and pepper.
- Mix with potatoes and place in a 13x9-inch dish. Sprinkle with paprika.
- Bake uncovered for 30 minutes.
- Yield: 6-8 servings

RIVER TRAIL VEGETABLES

4 carrots, peeled
2 small zucchini
3 cups cauliflower flowerets
2 cups broccoli flowerets
1 (6-ounce) can black pitted olives, drained

1 (6-ounce) jar marinated artichoke hearts, drained
¾ pound mushrooms, halved
2 cups cherry tomatoes, washed and stems removed

DRESSING

½ cup chili sauce
2 tablespoons vegetable oil
¼ cup lemon juice
¼ cup red wine vinegar
4 cloves garlic, minced

½ teaspoon dry mustard
1 teaspoon oregano leaves
1 teaspoon basil leaves
1 teaspoon thyme

Meeting friends for that annual fishing trip? Place these marinated vegetables in a sealable plastic bag and serve with the catch of the day.

Fly fishermen challenge the steelhead waters of the Rogue, taking on the rapids of Dunn Riffle and, farther downstream, Ennis Riffle.

- Chop and slice carrots and zucchini.

- Steam carrots for 3 minutes. Add remaining vegetables and steam for an additional 2 minutes.

- In saucepan, combine chili sauce, oil, lemon juice, vinegar, garlic, dry mustard and spices. Bring to a boil and pour over steamed vegetables. Toss gently.

- Add olives, artichoke hearts, mushrooms and tomatoes. Mix to marinate evenly. Chill before serving.

- Yield: 12 servings

BARLEY CHEESE BAKE

6 tablespoons butter, divided
1¾ cups pearl barley
2 onions, chopped

2 (4-ounce) cans mushrooms, drained
4 cups chicken broth
Monterey Jack cheese, sliced

Pearl barley is barley that has been husked and polished. It is presteamed before packaging, making it the quick cooking type of barley. Medium barley needs to be cooked longer than pearl barley.

- Preheat oven to 350 degrees.

- Melt 2 tablespoons butter in skillet. Add barley and brown. Put in large greased casserole dish.

- Sauté onion in 2 tablespoons butter. Add to barley.

- Sauté mushrooms in 2 tablespoons butter. Add to barley.

- Pour 4 cups broth over barley and bake for 1 hour.

- Check for moistness adding additional liquid if necessary and baking for an additional 15 minutes.

- Place cheese slices over top and return to oven to melt cheese.

- Yield: 6-8 servings

BAKED APPLES AND NEW POTATOES

Allspice is commonly thought of as a mixture of cloves, nutmeg and cinnamon but is actually the berry of a kind of myrtle tree grown only in the Caribbean.

The aroma of allspice mixed with baking apples fills your kitchen with the smell of autumn.

2 pounds thin skinned potatoes, 1½ to 2-inch wide, washed
2 medium onions, cut into 1-inch wedges
2 tablespoons olive oil
1 pound red apples, Jonathan or Winesap, cored and cut into ¾-inch wedges

1¼ cups beef broth
¾ cup apple juice
2 tablespoons cornstarch
¾ teaspoon ground allspice

- Preheat oven to 400 degrees.

- Place prepared potatoes in 9x13-inch baking dish. Break apart onion wedges and sprinkle over potatoes. Add oil and mix well.

- Bake, uncovered, for 25 minutes, stirring occasionally.

- Mix apples, broth, apple juice, cornstarch and allspice. Stir apple mixture into potatoes.

- Return to oven and bake another 25 minutes, or until very tender when pierced. Serve hot.

- Yield: 6 servings

RED POTATOES IN LEMON BUTTER

Potatoes should be stored in a cool, dry place but not the refrigerator. When chilled, the starch in potatoes changes to sugar resulting in an unpleasant taste and color.

16-20 small red potatoes (2 pounds), washed
¼ cup butter or margarine
2 tablespoons fresh chives, chopped (or more to taste)

1 tablespoon plus 1 teaspoon fresh lemon juice
salt and pepper to taste

- Cook potatoes in a large covered pan of boiling water until tender, 15-25 minutes. Drain potatoes.

- In saucepan, melt butter over medium heat and add chives, lemon juice, salt and pepper. Toss gently with potatoes to coat.

- Yield: 4-6 servings

TOMATOES MARINADE

ripe tomatoes
olive oil
red wine garlic vinegar
garlic salt
seasoning salt

seasoning pepper
dried parsley
oregano
chopped onions

Tomatoes are a treat fresh from the garden, during the Rogue Valley's warm Indian summers.

- Slice tomatoes and place on a platter. Cover with oil and vinegar, then sprinkle with seasonings following the order listed.

- Add chopped onions, cover and marinate at room temperature for 3 hours before serving.

- Yield: varies with amount of tomatoes used

SWEET POTATOES WITH APRICOTS

2 (30-ounce) cans sweet potatoes
1 cup brown sugar, firmly packed
1½ tablespoons cornstarch
¼ teaspoon salt
⅛ teaspoon cinnamon

1 teaspoon grated orange peel
1 (16-ounce) can apricot halves
2 tablespoons butter or margarine
½ cup walnuts, chopped

This recipe is colorful and a nice change for traditional holiday dinners.

- Preheat oven to 375 degrees.

- Place sweet potatoes in a greased 10x6x1½-inch baking dish.

- Combine brown sugar, cornstarch, salt, cinnamon and orange peel in a small saucepan. Drain apricots and reserve the syrup. Stir 1 cup of the syrup into the cornstarch mixture. If necessary, add water to the syrup to make one cup. Cook and stir this mixture over medium heat until boiling. Boil for 2 minutes.

- Add the apricots, butter and nuts to mixture. Pour over potatoes. Bake uncovered for 25 minutes.

- Yield: 6 servings

GREEK POTATO WEDGES

4 large potatoes, washed, cut
    lengthwise into wedges
1 tablespoon olive oil

paprika to taste and color
salt to taste

Today's version of healthier French fries.

- Preheat oven to 450 degrees.

- In a large bowl, toss potatoes with olive oil until well coated. Sprinkle with paprika and further toss to add color. Spread on a cookie sheet.

- Bake for 25 to 30 minutes until fork tender. Turn once or twice, with a metal spatula during cooking. Salt lightly and serve.

- Yield: 6 servings

PEPPER CHEESE ZUCCHINI

This dish may be refrigerated before cooking. Just add 10 minutes to the cooking time.

4 eggs
2 cups Monterey Jack cheese, shredded
2 cups Cheddar cheese, shredded
2-3 teaspoons jalapeño peppers, pickled, finely minced

½ cup crushed croutons, divided
2 cloves garlic, minced
¼ cup onion, finely minced
4 cups zucchini, coarsely shredded
½ cup Parmesan cheese, grated

- Preheat oven to 350 degrees.

- Beat eggs in a large mixing bowl. Stir in Jack and Cheddar cheeses, jalapeño peppers, all but 2 tablespoons of croutons, garlic and onion. Fold in the zucchini.

- Turn into a well greased 2-quart baking dish. Top with Parmesan cheese and remaining crushed croutons.

- Bake uncovered in a 350 degree oven for 45-50 minutes until browned and set in the center. Allow to cool 5-10 minutes before serving.

- Yield: 8 servings

HERBED ZUCCHINI PANCAKES

These pancakes make a beautiful side dish with roast meat or sauerbraten. May be served with butter and lemon wedges, or even a brown gravy.

2 cups zucchini, coarsely grated
2 eggs, beaten
¼ cup onion, minced
½ cup all-purpose flour
½ teaspoon baking powder

½ teaspoon salt
¼ teaspoon oregano
¼ teaspoon sweet basil
vegetable oil

- Place grated zucchini in a strainer. Use soup spoon to press out as much moisture as possible. In a small bowl, mix zucchini, eggs and onion. Add flour, baking powder, salt, oregano and basil; stir.

- Place griddle or large skillet over medium heat, preheat oil. Drop batter into pan, making pancakes approximately 2 inches in diameter. Brown on both sides, making sure pancakes are not doughy inside. Serve immediately.

- Yield: 4 servings

SAFFRON RAISIN RICE

½ cup golden or regular raisins
2 cups rice, uncooked
2 tablespoons butter
⅛ teaspoon saffron

½ cup milk, warmed
3⅓ cups water
¼ teaspoon cinnamon
¼ teaspoon salt

- Sauté raisins and rice in butter for several minutes.

- Soak saffron in warm milk. Pour into rice and add 3⅓ cups water, cinnamon and salt.

- Cover and cook until rice is done, about 20 minutes.

- Yield: 8 servings

Saffron, a greatly savored spice, may be at its best as a seasoning for rice. Saffron's high price is an indication of its high quality and unique results. Using more saffron does not increase its flavor but instead only its bitterness and color. Saffron needs to be stored away from light in an airtight container and, under these conditions, lasts up to a year.

WILD RICE WITH HAZELNUTS

4 cups chicken broth
1 cup wild rice, rinsed
1 cup white rice
salt to taste
pepper, freshly ground, to taste

2 tablespoons butter
4 shallots, minced
1 cup hazelnuts, toasted and
	husked

- In saucepan, bring chicken broth to boil. Stir in wild rice. Reduce heat, cover and simmer 20 minutes.

- Add white rice, cover and simmer until liquid has been absorbed, 20-25 minutes. Season with salt and pepper.

- Melt butter in small, heavy skillet over medium-low heat. Add shallots and cook until softened, stirring occasionally, about 5 minutes.

- Combine rice, shallots and hazelnuts in bowl. Mix together and serve immediately.

- Yield: 8 servings

This special recipe, a wild rice lovers dream, features our Oregon grown hazelnuts.

WILD RICE ROXY ANN

Wild rice is not rice, but actually a seed native to America. Great with turkey, chicken and pheasant.

2 cups wild rice
1 teaspoon salt
½ cup butter or margarine
1 onion, finely chopped
2 cups celery, finely diced

¼ pound mushrooms, thinly sliced (more if desired)
¼ teaspoon pepper
pinch of ginger
¼ cup white wine (optional)
½-1 cup half-and-half

- In medium saucepan, add wild rice and salt to boiling water. Reduce heat and simmer until rice is about half done, slightly firm but not crunchy (cooking time varies with different rice and pans). Drain, rinse rice with cool water and set aside.

- Preheat oven to 350 degrees.

- Melt butter; add onion and celery. Cook slowly until onion is clear. Add mushrooms, pepper and ginger. Mix thoroughly and put in casserole dish. If desired, add the white wine and mix.

- Cover and cook in oven for 1 hour and 15 minutes. While baking, add the half-and-half; keep adding and mixing in to keep rice very moist throughout the cooking time.

- Yield: 8 servings

INDIAN PILAF

Turmeric has its own distinct yellow color and flavor, but is also an indispensible ingredient in both mustard and curry powder.

¼ cup butter
1 medium onion, chopped
1½ cups uncooked rice, long grain
½ teaspoon salt
½ teaspoon allspice

½ teaspoon turmeric
½ teaspoon curry powder
⅛ teaspoon pepper
3½ cups chicken broth
¼ cup blanched slivered almonds

- Preheat oven to 350 degrees.

- Melt the butter in a heavy skillet. Add onion and rice; cook until rice is yellow and onion is tender. Stir in salt, allspice, turmeric, curry powder and pepper. Pour into ungreased 2-quart casserole dish.

- Heat chicken broth to boiling, then stir broth into rice mixture. Cover tightly. Bake for 30-40 minutes or until liquid is absorbed and rice is tender. Stir in almonds and serve.

- Yield: 8-10 servings

ORZO WITH MYZITHRA AND BASIL

3 tablespoons butter
1½ cups orzo (rice-shaped pasta)
2 cloves garlic, minced
3 cups chicken broth
⅔ cup Myzithra cheese, grated
    (may substitute Parmesan)

6 tablespoons fresh basil, chopped
    or 1½ teaspoons dried basil
salt to taste
coarse ground pepper to taste
fresh basil sprigs for garnish

Orzo means "barley" but is actually a pasta made of wheat flour as most pastas are. The name refers to its shape, much like that of grains of barley or long grains of rice.

- Melt butter in 10-inch skillet over medium heat. Add orzo and garlic; sauté 2 minutes.

- Add stock and bring to boil. Reduce heat, cover and simmer on low until orzo is tender and liquid is absorbed, about 20-minutes.

- Mix in Myzithra cheese, basil, salt and pepper. Garnish with fresh basil sprigs.

- Yield: 6 servings

ROGUE POLENTA

2-3 cups chicken broth
1 cup corn grits (polenta)

6 ounces Oregon blue cheese
parsley sprigs for garnish

The combination of corn grits with Oregon blue cheese gives a down-to-earth cornmeal an up-town taste.

- In medium saucepan, bring 2 cups broth to boil. Stir in grits. Cook over low heat about 25 minutes, stirring occasionally to avoid sticking. Add broth as needed to keep grits the consistency of oatmeal.

- As grits cook, slice blue cheese in ¼ to ½-inch slices and place in serving dish, reserving one slice.

- Add reserved slice of cheese to grits close to the end of cooking time. Stir in completely.

- Spoon grits over blue cheese in serving dish, garnish with parsley and serve immediately.

- Yield: 6 servings

CHANTICLEER PARSNIP APPLE PANCAKES WITH (HOT) SMOKED SALMON AND SHERRIED CRÈME FRAÎCHE

CHANTICLEER INN

Chanticleer Inn's architecture is reminiscent of a post-Victorian 1920's Craftsman style house. Located in a quiet residential neighborhood in Ashland, this cozy Bed and Breakfast reflects a European country charm.

1 pound parsnips, peeled and grated
1 medium green apple (Granny Smith), peeled, cored and grated
½ medium sweet (mild) white onion, peeled and grated
½ cup flour
1 teaspoon salt

¼ teaspoon pepper
3 eggs
1 tablespoon mixed fresh herbs such as thyme, sage, parsley, dill and/or chervil, chopped
clarified butter or equal parts of vegetable oil and whole butter for frying

- Combine grated parsnip, apple and onion in bowl. Sprinkle with flour, salt and pepper. Beat eggs, mix in and add herbs. (If mixture seems loose, add a little more flour.)

- Heat ⅛-inch or less butter or oil in skillet over moderately high heat. Drop by generous tablespoonsful and cook until golden; turn and repeat. (May hold warm while you finish frying the remainder.)

TO ASSEMBLE:

½ cup crème fraîche
2 tablespoons dry sherry
1 tablespoon minced chives and plucked chive blossoms

salt to taste
Tabasco sauce to taste
Worcestershire to taste
½ pound hot smoked salmon

- Lightly whip the crème fraîche to soft peaks; add sherry, whip a little longer and fold in the herbs. Season with the salt, Tabasco sauce and Worcestershire. Refrigerate until needed. Flake the salmon or slice if it's very firm.

- Arrange pancakes on plates, top lightly with dollops of the crème fraîche and then with the salmon.

- Yield: 6-8 servings

ROMEO INN'S WELSH RAREBIT
ROMEO INN

6 English muffins, lightly toasted
6 hard-cooked eggs, halved

SAUCE:

2 tablespoons butter
2 tablespoons flour
1 cup half-and-half, room
    temperature
½ cup dark beer, room temperature
1 cup Oregon Cheddar cheese,
    grated

Rarebit sauce

½ cup Oregon Jack cheese, grated
1 tablespoon Dijon mustard
½ teaspoon white Worcestershire
    sauce
dash of Tabasco sauce

Romeo Inn, a classic Cape Cod house built in the early 1930's, sits amid towering Ponderosa pines but is also close to downtown Ashland to accommodate visitors.

- Make a roux of the butter and flour; cook 3-4 minutes. Gradually add the half-and-half and dark beer; bring to a simmer and cook, stirring constantly, till mixture thickens.

- Remove from heat and add cheeses, mustard, Worcestershire and Tabasco sauce. Stir until cheese melts.

- To serve, place two muffin halves on a plate; cover with sauce, place an egg half on each sauce-covered muffin; top with additional sauce.

- Yield: 6 servings

ADAMS COTTAGE EGGS
ADAMS COTTAGE

10 eggs
½ cup all-purpose flour
1 teaspoon baking powder
16-ounces cottage cheese
12 ounces Swiss cheese, shredded

½ large yellow onion
½ bell pepper
10 large mushrooms
8 ounces ground turkey sausage

Old records show that the cottage was built in 1900 as a boarding house for the gold miners of Jackson County. Through the years, the quaint charm of Adams Cottage has pleased many travelers who have visited Ashland.

- Preheat oven to 375 degrees.

- Beat eggs. Add flour and baking powder; mix well. Stir in cottage cheese and swiss cheese.

- In a blender or food processor finely chop onion, bell pepper and mushrooms. Add to egg mixture.

- Form turkey sausage into patties. Cook thoroughly in skillet. Finely chop cooked sausage with food processor or blender. Add to egg mixture.

- Grease inside of 10 large custard cups. Fill each cup ⅔ full. Bake 20 minutes or until custard sets. Serve immediately.

- Yield: 10 servings

ROGUE RIVER BLUE CHEESE CUSTARDS

HERSEY HOUSE

Hersey House was built in Ashland in the year 1904 and five generations of the Hersey family have lived there. The Victorian charm of the Bed and Breakfast has been preserved and a lovely English country garden graces the premises.

½ cup milk
2 green onions, sliced including some green tops
2 ounces Oregon blue cheese
2 ounces herb-flavored cheese
2 ounces cream cheese

⅓ cup cream or half-and-half
2 eggs
nutmeg, freshly grated
salt and pepper, to taste
fresh parsley and/or basil and chives for garnish

- Boil ½ cup milk with onions. Set aside.

- In food processor or blender, combine cheeses and cream; add eggs and process. Stir in hot milk and onions. Add sprinkle of freshly grated nutmeg, salt and pepper.

- Fill 4 small ramekins. Place ramekins in glass baking casserole and add boiling water to cover ¾ of the ramekins exterior.

- Preheat over to 350 degrees. Bake for 20-40 minutes until custard is set by clean knife test. Garnish with fresh herbs.

- Yield: 4 servings

The Coffee Pot of Mule Creek Canyon boils a brew of river water that can catch unawares the rafter who's not prepared.

SAVORY TOMATO AND ASPARAGUS PIE
THE WOODS HOUSE

- **Prepare pastry for a 10-inch pie plate and line the pan.**

1 cup Swiss cheese
¼ cup sharp Cheddar cheese
2 tablespoons all-purpose flour
1 (8-ounce) package frozen asparagus or several fresh stalks
4 tablespoons butter

2 large white onions, sliced
8-10 fresh basil leaves, chopped
2 large, firm tomatoes, sliced
salt and pepper to taste
2 large eggs
¾ cup cream

The Woods House, located in Ashland's historic district, was built in 1908 and visitors may enjoy a stay in the original carriage house located across the courtyard from the main house.

- Preheat oven to 350 degrees.

- Grate cheese and toss in bowl with flour. Spread about ⅓ of this mixture over the bottom of pie shell.

- If frozen, microwave to defrost asparagus stalks. Split lengthwise in half.

- Melt butter in large skillet, sauté onion slices (separate into rings); spread over cheese in pie shell.

- In remaining butter in skillet, sauté basil and tomato slices for a minute or two, season with salt and pepper. Arrange the slices over the onions. Place asparagus halves over tomatoes, then cover with remaining cheese.

- Beat eggs with cream and pour over cheese. Bake for about 35 minutes, or until the top browns nicely. Slice into 6 wedges and serve hot.

- Yield: 6 servings

DESSERTS

SILVER HILTON

The unique, simple pattern of the Silver Hilton lends itself well to day fishing as its elegance sparkles in the crisp clear waters of the Rogue. The Silver Hilton is an old traditional steelhead fly.

FROZEN MOCHA-MINT CHEESECAKE

25 species of mint are grown in temperate regions around the world and this aromatic herb lends a special touch to this cheesecake.

2 cups plus 2 tablespoons chocolate wafer cookie crumbs
½ cup sugar
½ cup butter, melted
1 (8-ounce) package cream cheese
1 (14-ounce) can sweetened condensed milk

⅔ cup chocolate syrup
1 tablespoon instant espresso powder
1 teaspoon hot water
1 teaspoon peppermint extract
1 cup heavy cream, whipped

- Combine 2 cups crumbs, sugar and butter. Pat into buttered 9-inch springform pan. Chill.

- In large bowl, beat cheese until fluffy. Add condensed milk and chocolate syrup. In small bowl, dissolve coffee in hot water and add peppermint extract. Add to milk mixture; mix well. Fold in whipped cream. Pour into crust. Cover with aluminum foil and freeze at least 6 hours before serving. Garnish with additional cookie crumbs.

- Yield: 10-12 servings

3-MINUTE CHOCOLATE MOUSSE

8 ounces semi-sweet chocolate
  chips
½ pound unsalted butter

¾ cup sugar
6 eggs

As rich and smooth a mousse as found in any French restaurant. Indulge and serve this at your next dinner party. Bon Appetit!

- Melt chocolate chips in microwave 30-60 seconds on half power.

- In a food processor, process butter and sugar until smooth. Add melted chocolate and eggs; process until well blended and very smooth.

- Spoon into individual dishes, serving bowl or chocolate crumb crust.

- Refrigerate at least 2 hours or overnight.

- Yield: 6-8 servings

WHITE CHOCOLATE MACADAMIA NUT CHEESECAKE

2 cups chocolate wafer cookie
  crumbs
½ cup sugar
½ cup butter or margarine, melted
1 pound white chocolate, chopped
4 (8-ounce) packages cream cheese,
  softened
3 tablespoons milk

1 tablespoon vanilla
⅛ teaspoon nutmeg
4 eggs
4 ounces milk chocolate, chopped
4 ounces macadamia nuts, chopped
  (reserve some whole, for
  garnish)

If you don't have a 10-inch springform pan, make this cheesecake in one 9-inch springform or three 6-inch purchased chocolate crumb crusts. Bake the 9-inch cheesecake 55-60 minutes; the 6-inch ones 15-20 minutes. Check for doneness 5-10 minutes before the end of baking time.

The Macadamia nut, also known as the Queensland nut, is the delectable fruit of an Australian tree and adds a distinctive flavor to this dessert.

- Preheat oven to 350 degrees. Butter sides of a 10-inch springform pan. Combine cookie crumbs, sugar and melted butter. Press into bottom and partially up sides of springform pan. Place on cookie sheet.

- Melt white chocolate in microwave at 50% power, stirring often, or in double boiler over barely simmering water.

- In large mixing bowl, beat melted white chocolate, cream cheese, milk, vanilla and nutmeg until well blended. Add eggs and beat on low speed until just mixed. Stir in milk chocolate and macadamia nuts. Pour into crust.

- Bake for 50-60 minutes or until edges puff. If cheesecake begins to brown on top, cover loosely with foil until baking time reaches 50 minutes; remove from oven. Cool on wire rack. Chill 6 hours or overnight. To serve, remove sides of pan; garnish with whole macadamia nuts.

- Yield: 12-16 servings

CHOCOLATE ESPRESSO CHEESECAKE

A rich chocolate dessert that is the perfect finale to a light meal.

1 cup graham cracker crumbs
¼ cup butter or margarine, melted
2 tablespoons sugar
½ teaspoon cinnamon
3 (8-ounce) packages cream cheese, softened
¾ cup sugar
3 large eggs
1 (8-ounce) package semi-sweet chocolate squares

2 tablespoons heavy cream
1 cup sour cream
1 teaspoon espresso powder dissolved in ¼ cup hot water, cooled
¼ cup coffee liqueur
2 teaspoons vanilla
Whipped cream and chocolate covered espresso beans for garnish

- Preheat oven to 350 degrees. Butter sides of 8-inch springform pan. Combine graham cracker crumbs, butter, 2 tablespoons sugar and cinnamon, thoroughly. Press evenly into bottom of pan.

- Beat cream cheese with mixer, on medium speed, until smooth. Gradually add ¾ cup sugar mixing until well blended. Add eggs, one at a time, and beat at low speed until smooth.

- Melt chocolate in top of double boiler, or in microwave, stirring frequently until smooth. Add to cream cheese mixture, blending well. Mix in heavy cream and sour cream, then coffee, and liqueur. Add vanilla and beat until smooth.

- Pour into springform pan and bake for 45 minutes at 350 degrees or until sides are slightly puffed. (Center will firm up when chilled.) Cool on rack. Refrigerate at least 12 hours. To serve, remove sides of pan and garnish with dollops of whipped cream topped with chocolate covered espresso beans.

- Yield: 12-15 servings

BROWN SUGAR HAZELNUT CHEESECAKE

1 cup graham cracker crumbs
¼ cup hazelnuts, toasted and
    chopped
¼ cup butter, melted
3 (8-ounce) packages cream cheese,
    softened
1 cup brown sugar, firmly packed

4 eggs
2 teaspoons vanilla
1 cup heavy cream
½ cup brown sugar, firmly packed
¼ cup butter
whipped cream and whole
    hazelnuts for garnish

- Preheat oven to 450 degrees. Combine graham cracker crumbs, hazelnuts and melted butter in small bowl; mix well. Press into the bottom and 1½ inches up the sides of a 9-inch springform pan.

- Beat cream cheese, 1 cup brown sugar, eggs and vanilla in a bowl until fluffy. Blend in heavy cream. Pour into graham cracker crust and bake at 450 degrees for 10 minutes. Reduce oven temperature to 250 degrees and bake for 65-75 minutes or until edges are firm. Cool completely.

- For topping, combine ½ cup brown sugar and remaining butter in a small saucepan and cook over medium heat, stirring constantly, until thick. Spread topping over cooled cheesecake. Refrigerate at least 2 hours before serving.

- Carefully remove sides of springform pan and garnish with whipped cream and whole hazelnuts.

- Yield: 8-10 servings

Oregon grows 99% of the U.S. commercial hazelnut crop and exports mainly to Canada and West Germany. Oregon hazelnuts, also known as filberts, are prized for their unique flavor and texture.

CINNAMON CHEESECAKE

1⅓ cups graham cracker crumbs
½ cup butter, melted
¼ cup sugar
1 pound cream cheese, room
    temperature
1½ cups sugar, divided

3 eggs
1½ cups dairy sour cream
1 teaspoon vanilla
ground cinnamon for garnish
slivered almonds for garnish

- Preheat oven to 350 degrees. Place graham cracker crumbs in mixing bowl. Work in the melted butter and ¼ cup sugar until well distributed. With the back of a spoon, press mixture onto the bottom only of a 9-inch springform pan with sides in place. Bake for 5 minutes. Cool on rack.

- Using an electric mixer, beat cream cheese until fluffy. Beat in ½ cup of sugar, then the eggs, one at a time. Beat only until smooth. Pour into prepared crust. Bake for 15-20 minutes or until firm in center. Cool 10 minutes on a rack away from drafts.

- Combine sour cream with remaining 1 cup sugar and vanilla. Spoon over slightly cooled cheesecake. Dust with cinnamon and sprinkle almonds over entire top. Return to oven and bake 15 minutes. Cool on a rack to room temperature. Chill in refrigerator at least 4 hours before serving.

- Yield: 10-12 servings

Cinnamon, a spice that comes from the bark of tropical cinnamon trees, adds a sweet, spicy flavor to this cheesecake. The most popular varieties of cinnamon are from Sri Lanka and China. Ancient cultures often used it to flavor wine.

PEAR POSSIBILITIES

Medford, Oregon is the winter pear capitol of the world with over 2 million boxes of Anjou, Bosc, Comice, Seckel and other winter pears produced annually. This figure represents nearly ⅓ of the winter pears produced in the United States. In addition to winter pears, over one million boxes of Bartlett pears are grown annually—half of which are packed and half canned.

This 40 million dollar industry started with the first commercial plantings in 1884. Today more than 8,000 acres in Jackson County grow pears.

Pears are nutritious as well as versatile. The average size pear is full of vitamins and contains only 75 calories. Pears may be eaten fresh, baked, poached, dried, or canned.

Buy pears when firm and ripen at room temperature several days. Inspect them daily until the flesh near the stem yields slightly to thumb pressure. Ripe pears may be held for several days in the refrigerator. Their mellow flavor will be enhanced by chilling before serving. Sprinkle cut pears with lemon juice to prevent discoloration.

Pear	Distinguishing Shape	Color	Availability	Uses
Anjou (rhymes with *"banjo"*)	round, heart-shape	green-yellow	October - May	eating fresh, salads, with wine and cheese, desserts
Bosc (*"bosk"*)	long, slender necks, curving stem	golden brown	September - May	best pear for cooking and canning
Bartlett	classic bell	green to yellow when ripe	August - December	eating fresh, baking, canning, drying, poaching
Comice (*"Cumees"*)	round chubby	green-yellow, often with red blush	October - May	best for eating fresh
Seckel	smallest, often "bite-sized"	green with dark red blush to dark red	August - January	eating fresh

OREGON HAZELNUT PEARS

4 well shaped pears with stems
1 cup finely ground hazelnuts
1 tablespoon sugar
2 tablespoons butter

½ teaspoon Frangelico liqueur or
   vanilla
6 ounces dark European semi-
   sweet chocolate

This beautiful no-bake dessert combines pears, hazelnuts and chocolate. Slice pears just before serving.

- Using an apple corer, begin from the blossom end and carefully remove the cores from the pears (be careful not to core out the stems.) Drain thoroughly on paper towels. In a small bowl, mix hazelnuts, sugar, butter and flavoring. Stuff hazelnut mixture into the cavity firmly.

- Melt the chocolate over hot water. Using the back of a teaspoon, frost the pears with chocolate from the stem down to the blossom end. Dry on waxed paper.

- To serve, slice rounds of pear and arrange on a dessert plate—two to three slices per serving. This is best made the same day you plan to serve it.

- Yield: 4-6 servings

ROGUE PEARS

1 tablespoon butter
4 large, but firm pears (Bosc
   preferred) cored, peeled, and
   thinly sliced
¼ cup packed light brown sugar
¼ cup orange liqueur or light rum

1 teaspoon grated orange peel
3 tablespoons orange juice
1 quart vanilla ice cream, good
   quality
Sugared Orange Peels for garnish

The best of the Rogue Valley doesn't get any better than this!

- In a large skillet, melt butter. Add pears and cook over low heat until slices are golden, about 20 minutes.

- Mix sugar, liqueur, peel and juice in a small bowl. Add to pears and bring to a boil. Boil on high heat until sauce thickens and clings to fruit (about 2-3 minutes). Keep warm

- Scoop ice cream into 6 individual dessert bowls. Spoon pears and sauce equally over ice cream. Garnish with one sugared orange peel. Serve immediately.

- Yield: 6 servings

SUGARED ORANGE PEELS

- Using a vegetable peeler or sharp knife, make 6 narrow 1½-inch long orange peels, using only the outer layer of orange. Place peels in small bowl and cover with sugar until serving. Twist attractively to garnish.

POACHED AMARETTO PEARS
OAK HILL COUNTRY INN

This charming home, built in 1910, was the original farmhouse of a large fruit orchard in the south end of Ashland. Uniquely decorated in country style, each room in the Oak Hill Country Inn offers a warm welcome to those who enter its door.

4 nearly ripe pears
1 teaspoon nutmeg
2 tablespoons butter

2 tablespoons brown sugar
2 tablespoons amaretto liqueur

- Preheat oven to 325 degrees. Slice pears into halves; core leaving small hole in each pear half. Place hole up in shallow, well-buttered baking dish. Sprinkle with nutmeg.

- Melt butter in small saucepan. Add brown sugar and amaretto. Heat just until sugar dissolves. Pour over pears. Bake 20-25 minutes.

- Yield: 8 pear halves

RASPBERRY CREAM PEARS

This grand prize winning recipe marries vanilla-flavored poached pears with liqueured raspberries. For a make ahead dessert sensation, poach pears and make raspberry sauce a day in advance. Assemble several hours before serving.

1 quart water
2 cups sugar
1 vanilla bean, split
6 pears, peeled, halved and cored
1 (10-ounce) package frozen
    raspberries in syrup

1 tablespoon raspberry liqueur
1 (8-ounce) package cream cheese,
    room temperature
⅓ cup powdered sugar
½ teaspoon almond extract
3 tablespoons chopped roasted
    almonds

- Combine water, sugar and vanilla bean in a large saucepan and bring to a boil. Add pears, reduce heat to low and cook gently until tender, about 15-20 minutes. Refrigerate pears in syrup for 24 hours.

- Puree raspberries and juice in blender until smooth. Over a small bowl, push mixture through a fine sieve to remove seeds. Add liqueur to pulp and stir. Refrigerate in a small pitcher. (This raspberry sauce will keep in a covered container in the refrigerator for 2 weeks.)

- In a small bowl, blend cream cheese thoroughly with powdered sugar and almond extract. Stir in chopped roasted almonds.

- Remove pears from syrup and pat dry. Gently spread all of the cream cheese mixture over 6 of the pear halves, carefully covering entire cut surface. Top each with another pear half, pressing slightly. Spoon enough raspberry sauce onto each dessert plate to cover the bottom. Place each pear upright in the sauce. Pour a few drops of raspberry sauce on top of the pears and garnish with a fresh mint sprig. Pass additional sauce when serving.

- Yield: 6 servings

PEAR DUMPLINGS WITH CREAM CUSTARD

1½ cups flour
½ cup butter, softened
4 ounces cream cheese, softened
½ teaspoon ground cinnamon
1½ teaspoons sugar
3 ripe medium-size Bartlett pears,
    peeled, halved and cored

1 egg, separated
2 cups heavy cream
4 teaspoons cornstarch
¼ teaspoon salt
4 tablespoons sugar
½ teaspoon vanilla
6 mint leaves

These pears prepare ahead beautifully, making them a great choice for a dinner party. Serve with grilled turkey and spend your pre-meal time visiting with guests.

- Preheat oven to 375 degrees. In a medium mixing bowl, combine flour, butter and cream cheese. Knead by hand until blended. On a lightly floured surface, roll half of pastry to ⅛-inch thickness using floured rolling pin. Cut three 7-inch circles (a salad plate may be used as a pattern) from the rolled out pastry. Repeat with remaining pastry.

- Mix cinnamon and sugar in a small bowl; sprinkle evenly over pastry circles. Place a pear half, with cut side up, in the middle of each pastry circle. Fold pastry around pears, brush pastry with egg white and place seam side down on ungreased cookie sheet. Bake dumplings 30 minutes or until golden. Remove from oven and cool slightly on a wire rack.

- To prepare custard, combine cream, cornstarch, salt, egg yolk and 4 tablespoons sugar. Cook over medium heat, stirring constantly, until custard coats back of spoon. Remove from heat, add vanilla and allow to cool.

- When ready to serve, place some custard in a dessert dish and put pear dumpling on top. Garnish dumpling with mint to resemble a pear leaf. Dumplings and custard may be made ahead of time and refrigerated, separately, to be served chilled later.

- Yield: 6 servings

BURNT CREAM

1 pint whipping cream
4 egg yolks
½ cup granulated sugar

1 tablespoon vanilla
4 tablespoons sugar
1 teaspoon brown sugar

To create a peaches and cream dessert, spoon sliced peaches on top of each custard. This would be a good finale to a Cajun dinner.

- Preheat oven to 350 degrees. To prepare Burnt Cream, heat cream over low heat until bubbles form around the edge of the pan.

- In a bowl, beat egg yolks and ½ cup sugar together until thick, about 3 minutes. Gradually beat cream into egg yolks. Stir in vanilla and pour into 6 (6-ounce) custard cups. Place custard cups in baking pan that has about ½ inch hot water in bottom. Bake until set, about 45 minutes. Remove custard cups from water and refrigerate until chilled.

- To prepare topping, combine 4 tablespoons granulated sugar and brown sugar. Mix well. Divide topping evenly among custard cups. Place on top rack under broiler and cook until topping is medium brown. Chill before serving.

- Yield: 6 servings

FRESH FRUIT TRIFLE

This dessert is simple to prepare and would be quite spectacular on a buffet table or for a summer dinner party.

2 cups milk
4 egg yolks
⅓ cup sugar
3 tablespoons cornstarch
¼ teaspoon salt
2 tablespoons butter
1 teaspoon vanilla
Pound cake cut into ½ inch slices

¼ cup rum
1 pound strawberries, sliced
2 bananas, peeled and sliced
2 cups blueberries
2 kiwi fruit, peeled and sliced
1 cup whipping cream
2 tablespoons powdered sugar

- In food processor or blender, combine milk, yolks, sugar, cornstarch and salt until thoroughly blended. Pour into medium size glass bowl. Cook in microwave oven on high for 6-7 minutes, stirring halfway through cooking time. Whisk in butter and vanilla. Cover custard and refrigerate until cool and softly set.

- Brush cake slices with rum. Arrange half of slices in single layer in trifle bowl or other deep bowl. Layer with half of each of the types of fruit. Spoon half of custard over top. Repeat layering with remaining cake, custard and fruit.

- Whip cream until soft peaks form. Add powdered sugar and continue beating until stiff peaks form. Pipe whipped cream on top of trifle and garnish with fresh fruit. Chill.

- Yield: 10-12 servings

STRAWBERRIES IN LEMON MOUSSE

This light dessert is both flavorful and refreshing. Choose strawberries that are red, shiny, firm and fragrant.

4 egg yolks
½ cup sugar
5 tablespoons lemon juice
2 teaspoons grated lemon peel
2 egg whites, beaten to stiff peaks

½ cup heavy cream, whipped to stiff peaks
1¼ cups fresh strawberries, sliced, reserve ¼ cup for garnish

- In bowl beat 4 egg yolks until thick and pale. Beat in sugar, lemon juice and lemon peel. Cook this mixture in a double boiler, over hot water, stirring constantly, until mixture is thick. Remove from heat; cool.

- Into lemon mixture, fold egg whites, whipped cream and 1 cup strawberries. Pour into 4 stemmed glasses; garnish with remaining berries. Chill thoroughly and serve. Fresh blueberries may be substituted for strawberries.

- Yield: 4 servings

MACADAMIA-BANANA PIE ON CHOCOLATE SAUCE

9-inch pie shell, baked and cooled
⅔ cup sugar
¼ cup cornstarch
½ teaspoon salt
3 cups milk
4 egg yolks
2 tablespoons butter or margarine

1 tablespoon vanilla
½-⅔ cup macadamia nuts, roasted
    and chopped
1 large banana, sliced
macadamia nuts and chocolate
    curls for garnish

To roast macadamia nuts, spread on cookie sheet and bake at 250 degrees for 12-15 minutes, stirring often.

- In a 3-quart saucepan, mix sugar, cornstarch and salt. In a medium bowl, blend milk and egg yolks using a wire whip. Gradually stir egg mixture into cornstarch mixture. Stirring constantly, cook over medium heat until mixture thickens and boils. Boil and stir vigorously 1 minute. Remove from heat; add butter and vanilla.

- Press plastic wrap onto surface of filling in saucepan or transfer filling to cool mixing bowl and press with plastic wrap. Cool to room temperature.

- Sprinkle macadamia nuts in bottom of pie shell. Top with banana. Pour cooled filling carefully over layers. Chill at least 2 hours. To serve, pour a pool of Chocolate Sauce on dessert plate and place a slice of chilled pie in the sauce. Decorate with whole macacamia nut and a chocolate curl or a dab of sauce, if desired.

- Yield: 8 servings

CHOCOLATE SAUCE

⅔ cup sugar, divided
½ cup cold water
4 ounces unsweetened chocolate,
    chopped into large pieces

½ cup heavy cream
1 teaspoon vanilla

- In a small, heavy saucepan stir together ⅓ cup sugar and water. Bring to a boil over high heat. Reduce heat to low; simmer 1 minute. Remove from heat.

- In a food processor or heavy duty blender, process ⅓ cup sugar and chocolate in bursts until mixture is ground finely. While processor or blender is running, pour hot syrup through feed opening in a slow stream. Without stopping machine, add cream and vanilla. Process 30 seconds.

- Yield: 2 cups

CHOCOLATE ALMOND TART
MCCULLY HOUSE INN

McCully House Inn, an elegant and stately mansion located in Jacksonville, was constructed in 1861 and is on the National Registry of Historic Places. The interior is furnished with exquisite European and American antiques.

PASTRY DOUGH

1 cup all-purpose flour
¼ teaspoon salt
1 teaspoon sugar
1 teaspoon lemon zest

¼ pound butter
4 teaspoons water
¼ teaspoon vanilla

- Combine flour, salt and sugar. Add lemon zest. Cut butter into cubes and cut into flour. Combine water and vanilla and add to flour mixture just until dough holds together. Form into ball, wrap and chill.

- Preheat oven to 425 degrees. Roll out pastry and place in a 10-inch fluted tart pan. Weight down with foil and dry beans. Bake crust 15-20 minutes at 425 degrees until golden brown. Reduce oven temperature to 350 degrees.

FILLING

1 cup almonds, slivered and toasted
2 cups heavy cream, divided
3 ounces dark chocolate
2 tablespoons brown sugar
2 egg yolks

1 teaspoon vanilla
½ teaspoon almond extract
½ cup powdered sugar
1 teaspoon vanilla
shaved chocolate for garnish

- Place almonds in bottom of tart shell. In a saucepan, scald 1 cup cream. Lower heat; add chocolate and brown sugar. Stir to melt (about 5 minutes). In a medium bowl, whisk egg yolks; slowly add chocolate, stirring until well combined. Add 1 teaspoon vanilla and almond extract and pour into pie shell. Bake at 350 degrees for 10 minutes. Cool.

- Whip remaining cream with powdered sugar and 1 teaspoon vanilla. Fit pastry bag with star tip and cover tart shell with whipped cream. Garnish with shaved chocolate.

- Yield: 12-14 servings

FRESH STRAWBERRY PIE

1 (9-inch) pie shell, cooked and
    cooled
¾ cup strawberries, pureed
¾ cup cold water
3 tablespoons cornstarch
2 tablespoons lemon juice
1 cup plus 2 tablespoons sugar
½ teaspoon red food coloring
    (optional)

2 (3-ounce) packages cream cheese,
    softened
1 teaspoon vanilla
¼ cup sugar
6 cups whole strawberries, cleaned
    and stemmed
Whipped cream, ice cream or
    yogurt for topping (optional)

*Juicy, sweet, fresh straw-
berries are as beautiful as
they are tasty in this summertime special.*

- In a saucepan, combine pureed berries, cold water, cornstarch, lemon juice and sugar. Cook over high heat, stirring constantly, until mixture thickens and becomes translucent. Add food coloring, if desired. Cool to room temperature while preparing remainder of recipe.

- Mix cream cheese with vanilla and ¼ cup sugar; spread in bottom of pie shell and up the sides. Fill pie shell with berries placed upright with small end pointing up. Fill gaps with smaller berries or sliced berries. Pour cooled sauce over berries filling gaps; chill. Serve with one of the optional toppings.

- Yield: 8-10 servings

KIWI PAVLOVA

4 egg whites
pinch of salt
1 cup sugar
½ teaspoon vinegar
1½ teaspoons cornstarch

½ teaspoon vanilla
1 pint whipping cream
2 tablespoons powdered sugar
1 teaspoon vanilla
2-3 kiwi fruits, peeled and sliced

*This family favorite recipe
was given to us by a New
Zealand exchange student
whose family farm supplies
a large portion of the kiwi
fruit available from
Medford's Harry and
David's.*

- Preheat oven to 225 degrees. Beat egg whites with salt until stiff peaks form. Continue to beat, gradually adding 1 cup sugar. Add vinegar, cornstarch and ½ teaspoon vanilla.

- To prepare meringue bowl, place a piece of foil on a cookie sheet. Draw a circle onto foil the size of the serving plate to be used. Spoon ⅔ of the meringue onto the center of the circle on the foil. Spread meringue with a spatula making a disk slightly smaller than the drawn circle. Drop the remaining ⅓ meringue by spoonfuls on top of the disk along the edge. Smooth spoonfuls with spatula making a rim around the outer edge to form the meringue dish. Bake the meringue dish for 1½-2 hours or until just beginning to brown; cool completely. Meringue dish may be stored covered, at room temperature for days.

- Whip cream to soft peaks; gradually add powdered sugar and vanilla. Continue beating to stiff peaks. Spoon whipped cream into meringue bowl; top with kiwi fruit.

- Yield: 8-10 servings

FROZEN PUMPKIN DESSERT

When the last Trick-or-Treaters have gone home to bed, enjoy this colorful autumn dessert with coffee and neighbors!

1 cup golden raisins, soaked overnight in rum to cover
1½ cups ginger snap crumbs
¼ cup butter or margarine, melted
2 tablespoons ground almonds (optional)
½ gallon good quality vanilla ice cream
1 cup pumpkin (canned)

¾ cup sugar
1 teaspoon vanilla
½ teaspoon nutmeg
¼ teaspoon ginger
1 cup slivered almonds, toasted
15 ginger snap cookies, crushed
whipped cream and almonds for garnish (optional)

- Preheat oven to 350 degrees. Drain raisins; set aside. Mix 1½ cups ginger snap crumbs with butter and ground almonds. Press along bottom and 1 inch up sides of a lightly oiled 9-inch springform pan. Bake 10 minutes. Cool.

- Cut ice cream into chunks to soften. Stir in pumpkin, sugar and spices; mix well. Add slivered almonds, crushed ginger snaps and drained raisins; mix well. Pour into prepared crust and freeze 3-4 hours or overnight.

- To serve, run a knife blade around edge of pan and loosen sides of pan. Place on serving plate.

- Yield: 10-12 servings

CHOCOLATE RASPBERRY TART

This chocolate lover's special is pictured on page 13.

1 (9-inch) tart shell, baked and cooled
1 cup semi-sweet chocolate, chopped
2 tablespoons butter, melted
2 tablespoons cherry liqueur

¼ cup powdered sugar
1 tablespoon water
1½ - 2 cups raspberries (fresh, beautiful ones)
fresh mint leaves or flowers for garnish

- Melt chocolate slowly in a double boiler, taking care that water does not touch bottom of inserted pan. (Alternate method: Melt at reduced power in microwave.) Heat until chocolate may be stirred smooth with a spoon. Overheating may cause it to seize (become dry and crumbly.) Remove chocolate from heat, add butter, liqueur, powdered sugar and water. Stir until smooth.

- Spread warm filling in tart shell. While chocolate is still warm, but not hot, arrange berries symmetrically directly on top. Cover entire surface. Garnish with fresh mint leaves or small flowers such as violets, flax, etc.

- Yield: 10-12 servings

FRESH FRENCH RHUBARB GREENWOOD
UNDER THE GREENWOOD TREE

4 cups rhubarb, trimmed and
　　cleaned
1 cup sugar
1 cup water
1-3 tablespoons cornstarch

1 tablespoon vanilla
1-2 cups fresh strawberries, diced
1 drop red food coloring (optional)
1 pint heavy cream

Under the Greenwood Tree, homesteaded in 1861 by the Walz family, provides a parklike ambiance which includes magnificent gardens, sweeping croquet lawns and 300 year old oak trees. This romantic Bed and Breakfast is located in Medford.

- Cut rhubarb into 1-inch pieces and place into a large pot with sugar and water. Boil until rhubarb is soft and comes apart when pushed with a spoon. Stir often. Mix cornstarch with just enough water to dissolve it (1- 3 tablespoons water). Gradually add cornstarch mixture until desired thickness is reached. Add vanilla.

- Pour rhubarb into large measuring cup. Divide into two equal batches. Leave one batch as is; to the other batch add one cup strawberries for each cup of rhubarb and a drop of red food coloring if desired.

- To serve, cover bottom of serving plate with plain rhubarb mixture. Place ½ cup of strawberry/rhubarb mixture in center of plain rhubarb. Pour unwhipped whipping cream around edges, or flute sweetened whipped cream around edges. Garnish with white pansies or fresh mint with a sliced strawberry, fanned. Recipe may be doubled or tripled and served warm or cold.

- Yield: 4 servings

BLUE RIBBON APPLE PIE

pie crust for a two-crust pie
2 tablespoons butter, melted
¼ teaspoon salt
¼ teaspoon mace
½ cup sugar
½ cup brown sugar, firmly packed
¼ teaspoon nutmeg

¼ teaspoon cinnamon
3 tablespoons all-purpose flour
7 cups pie apples, peeled and sliced
　　or cubed
2 tablespoons butter, room
　　temperature

Both mace and nutmeg are spices derived from the fruit of the nutmeg tree. Nutmeg is the seed; mace the netting which surrounds the nutmeg. Both are dried. Mace is sold in chips called blades while nutmeg is sold ground or whole. (1 grated nutmeg = 2-3 teaspoons ground nutmeg). Though similar in flavor, each spice adds a unique taste to this deliciously different apple pie.

- Preheat oven to 450 degrees. Place bottom crust in 9-inch pie pan; brush with melted butter.

- Mix salt, mace, sugars, nutmeg, cinnamon and flour in a small bowl. Sprinkle ¼ sugar mixture over bottom crust. Mound apple slices in pie crust and sprinkle remaining sugar mixture over top of apples. Randomly place pieces of remaining butter on top of apples. Cut air vents in top crust and place on pie. Cover pie edges with strips of foil.

- Bake at 450 degrees for 30 minutes. Reduce oven temperature to 325 degrees and bake 30 minutes. Remove foil strips for last 10-15 minutes of cooking time. Apples should be soft when pie is completely done.

- Yield: 6-8 servings

BLACKBERRY PEACH COBBLER WITH GRAND MARNIER CREAM

If peaches or black-berries are especially tart, add more sugar before turning into baking dish. Ripe blackberries should be very black, plump and firm. See about selecting peaches on page 203.

¼ cup sugar
¼ cup brown sugar, firmly packed
1 tablespoon cornstarch
½ cup water
1 tablespoon lemon juice
2 tablespoons Grand Marnier
2 cups peaches, peeled and sliced
1 cup blackberries, fresh or frozen

1 cup all-purpose flour, sifted
½ cup sugar
1½ teaspoons baking powder
½ teaspoon salt
½ cup milk
¼ cup butter, softened
2 tablespoons sugar
¼ teaspoon nutmeg

- Preheat oven to 375 degrees. In a saucepan, combine ¼ cup sugar, ¼ cup brown sugar and cornstarch. Add water, blend well. Cook over medium heat, stirring constantly, until thick. Add lemon juice, Grand Marnier, peaches and blackberries. Turn into a 2-quart baking dish.

- In a mixing bowl, sift together flour, ½ cup sugar, baking powder and salt. Add milk and softened butter; beat until smooth. Spoon over fruit. Combine 2 tablespoons sugar with nutmeg and sprinkle over cobbler. Bake for 40-45 minutes or until lightly browned; cool. Serve topped with Grand Marnier Cream.

- Yield: 8-10 servings

GRAND MARNIER CREAM

1 cup whipping cream
1 tablespoon powdered sugar

1 tablespoon Grand Marnier

- Whip cream until foamy. Add sugar and Grand Marnier; whip until thick but not stiff.

BLUEBERRY PEACH GLACÉ TART

1 (10-inch) tart shell, baked and
    cooled
1 cup sugar
3 tablespoons cornstarch
1 cup peaches, peeled and crushed
¼ cup water

1 tablespoon lemon juice
3 cups fresh peaches, peeled and
    sliced
1 cup blueberries
whipped cream for garnish
    (optional)

- Combine sugar and cornstarch in medium saucepan. Add crushed peaches and water. Cook over medium heat, stirring constantly, until thick and clear. Add lemon juice and cover. Set aside until cooled.

- Arrange sliced peaches in tart crust in circular design and sprinkle with blueberries. Pour cooled sauce over fruit. Chill at least 2 hours before serving. Garnish with whipped cream if desired.

- Yield: 10 servings

Fresh fruit tarts rely on the ripeness of the fruit for proper texture, sweetness and flavor. As peaches do not ripen well once picked, be sure to select well-ripened fruit. Peaches should have non-broken, colorful skins and feel soft and juicy when slightly squeezed, but not mushy. Perfectly ripened blueberries may be identified by their firm, plump exteriors and dusky gray coloring.

Nectarines may be substituted for peaches and do not require peeling.

FROZEN BLUEBERRY PIE

1 pound frozen blueberries
2 egg whites
1 cup sugar
1 tablespoon lemon juice

½ pint heavy cream
1 (9-inch) pie shell, cooked and
    cooled
fresh blueberries for garnish

- In a large chilled bowl, combine berries, egg whites, sugar and lemon juice. Beat on high speed for 10 minutes until firm and frothy.

- Whip cream until stiff peaks form. Fold into berry mixture. Spoon into pie shell and freeze at least 8 hours. Garnish with fresh berries when serving.

- Yield: 6-8 servings

Blueberries freeze well, retaining their juice and shape. If fresh blueberries are in season, select firm, ripe ones and freeze them in a single layer on a cookie sheet. When frozen, place in a recloseable plastic bag for use with this recipe or for delicious midwinter muffins. Freeze twice as many as you think you will use as the temptation to sample semi-frozen berries is impossible to resist.

CHRISTMAS DATE CAKE

Make this quickly prepared dessert during the hectic Holiday Season and start a family tradition.

3 eggs, separated
1 cup sugar
1 tablespoon all-purpose flour
2 teaspoons baking powder

¼ teaspoon salt
1 cup dates, pitted and chopped
1 cup walnuts, broken
whipped cream for garnish

- Preheat oven to 350 degrees. Butter and flour an 8x8-inch pan. Beat egg yolks, gradually adding sugar. Mix in flour, baking powder and salt. Stir in dates and nuts. Beat egg whites just until stiff. Fold whites into batter mixture.

- Bake 30 minutes. Cool. Top with a dollop of whipped cream.

- Yield: 8 servings

SOUR CREAM FUDGE CAKE

Look no further for the best chocolate cake you've ever tasted!

3 ounces unsweetened chocolate
2¼ cups all-purpose flour
2 tablespoons baking soda
½ teaspoon salt
½ cup butter, room temperature
2¼ cups brown sugar, packed

3 eggs
1½ teaspoons vanilla
1 cup sour cream
1 cup boiling water
Chocolate Fudge Frosting

- Preheat oven to 350 degrees. Melt chocolate slowly, over low heat, in a double boiler, or at reduced power in a microwave. Set aside to cool.

- Grease and flour two 9-inch round cake pans. Wax paper may be cut to fit bottoms for easy removal. If using wax paper, grease pans, insert wax paper, grease wax paper, then flour pans.

- Sift flour, soda and salt into a medium bowl and set aside. In mixing bowl, beat butter until soft and fluffy. Add sugar and eggs. Beat 3-5 minutes until light and increased in volume. At low speed, beat in vanilla and chocolate. Add sifted ingredients alternately with sour cream, beating with a spoon or low speed of mixer after each addition. Stir in boiling water until smooth.

- Pour into prepared pans and bake for 35 minutes. Let cool on rack 10 minutes; remove from pans and place on rack until completely cooled. Frost with Chocolate Fudge Frosting.

- Yield: 10-12 servings

CHOCOLATE FUDGE FROSTING

½ cup butter or margarine, room temperature
4 ounces unsweetened chocolate, melted

1 (1-pound) box powdered sugar, sifted
½ cup milk
2 teaspoons vanilla

- Beat butter in mixing bowl until light. Add melted chocolate. Add powdered sugar alternately with milk. Mix in vanilla.

FILBERT-HAZELNUT TORTE
UNDER THE GREENWOOD TREE

6 eggs separated
1 whole egg
1 cup ground hazelnuts, also
    known as filberts
¾ cup sugar, divided
2 teaspoons flour

⅓ cup dry bread crumbs
⅓ cup ground hazelnuts for garnish
1 pint of whipped cream,
    sweetened and whipped
6 whole hazelnuts for garnish
Very Berry Raspberry Sauce

This cake can be doubled for a greater effect. If raspberries are unavailable, use strawberries for a delicious substitute.

- Preheat oven to 275 degrees. Butter and flour a 10-inch springform pan. Beat egg yolks and whole egg in electric mixer for 10 minutes; add nuts, ½ cup sugar, flour and bread crumbs.

- Whip egg whites with rest of sugar until very, very stiff. Fold gently into yolk mixture. Pour into prepared pan; bake 45 minutes. Cool; freeze.

- To serve, cut frozen cake into two layers. Fill between layers and cover top of cake with sweetened whipped cream. Decorate with whole hazelnuts. Cut into 6 pieces and top with 1-2 tablespoons Very Berry Raspberry Sauce.

- Yield: 6 servings

VERY BERRY RASPBERRY SAUCE

1 teaspoon cornstarch
¼ cup sugar
¼ cup water
1 pint fresh raspberries or 10
    ounces frozen unsweetened
    raspberries

¼ cup raspberry liqueur (very
    important)

- Combine all sauce ingredients in a large saucepan. Cook over medium heat until translucent and slightly thickened. Strain seeds at this point if you wish. Add liqueur. Refrigerate.

- Yield: approximately 1 cup

RENATE'S PLUM CAKE
UNDER THE GREENWOOD TREE

This is one of the most popular, simple yet delicious summer treats, served at breakfast or tea time.

1 cup butter, softened
1½ cups sugar, divided
1½ cups flour
About 40 Italian plums

1 pint whipping cream
2 tablespoons powdered sugar
1-2 tablespoons plum schnapps or brandy

- Preheat oven to 375 degrees. Combine butter, 2 tablespoons sugar and flour; press into bottom of a 9x13-inch dish. Bring a sharp knife to fruit and cut quickly across and once across the other way. Remove the stone. Now you have a little flower-like fruit. Place plums "petals up", close together on top of flour mixture. Sprinkle with ½ cup sugar.

- Bake 45 minutes. Sprinkle immediately with remaining sugar; cool. For topping, whip cream until frothy. Gradually add powdered sugar and continue beating until stiff peaks form. Stir in schnapps. Serve cooled cake topped with a dollop of flavored whipped cream.

- Yield: 10-12 servings

POPPY SEED CAKE

For gift giving, bake in a Bundt pan, 2 regular loaf pans or 5 mini loaf pans. Grease and flour pans; bake regular loaves 45-50 minutes, mini loaves 40-45 minutes.

For a lovely continental breakfast, serve slices with fruit and jasmine tea.

3 cups all-purpose flour
1½ teaspoons salt
1½ teaspoons baking powder
2¼ cups sugar
1⅛ cups vegetable oil
1½ cups milk

3 eggs
1½ teaspoons butter flavoring
1½ teaspoons almond extract
1½ teaspoons vanilla
1½ tablespoons poppy seeds

- Preheat oven to 350 degrees. Grease and flour a Bundt pan. Combine flour, salt, baking powder and sugar. Mix in vegetable oil, milk, eggs, butter flavoring, almond, vanilla and poppy seeds. Pour batter into pan. Bake at 350 degrees for 45-50 minutes until cake tester comes out clean. Glaze warm cake; let cake cool before removing from pan.

GLAZE

½ teaspoon butter flavoring
½ teaspoon almond extract
½ teaspoon vanilla

¼ cup orange juice
¾ cup sugar

- To prepare glaze, combine all glaze ingredients in a small saucepan. Heat just until sugar is dissolved. Pour over warm cake.

- Variation: for Amaretto Poppy Seed Cake, decrease the milk to 1 cup and add ½ cup amaretto liqueur to cake ingredients.

- Yield: 1 Bundt cake

GRAND MARNIER BROWNIES

6 ounces unsweetened chocolate
1 cup butter
2 cups sugar
4 eggs
2 tablespoons Grand Marnier

1½ cups all-purpose flour
½ teaspoon baking powder
½ teaspoon salt
2 tablespoons chopped candied
   orange peel

A brownie elegant enough for the grandest dinner yet easy enough to take along on a river trip.

- Preheat oven to 350 degrees. In saucepan melt chocolate and butter. Beat in sugar, eggs and Grand Marnier. Combine flour, baking powder and salt; add to chocolate mixture. Add orange peel and mix well.

- Spoon into 8-inch square pan and bake for 20 minutes. Cool. Prick top of brownies with toothpick and sprinkle additional Grand Marnier over top. Frost with Orange Buttercream. Brownies may be frozen at this time.

- Yield: 16 brownies

ORANGE BUTTERCREAM

1½ cups unsalted butter
2 tablespoons orange juice or 1
   tablespoon Grand Marnier

2 cups powdered sugar
1 tablespoon orange zest

- Combine all frosting ingredients in mixing bowl. Beat until creamy.

CRANBERRY PEAR CRISP
MT. ASHLAND INN

1½ cups fresh cranberries
½ cup sugar
1 teaspoon orange peel
3 cups thinly sliced pears
½ cup brown sugar, firmly packed
1 cup oats (Or multigrain cereal
   mix)

1 cup whole wheat pastry flour
¼-½ cup butter or margarine,
   melted
¼ teaspoon baking soda
¼ teaspoon baking powder
¼ teaspoon salt

Mt. Ashland Inn, located three miles from the summit, is a cozy cedar log home which offers spectacular views of Mt. Shasta and Mt. McLaughlin. The beauty and serenity of the forested hills may be enjoyed year round and the Inn is a short drive from the city of Ashland.

- Preheat oven to 350 degrees.
- Cook cranberries in ⅓ cup water until skins start to pop. Add ½ cup sugar and stir until sugar dissolves; remove from heat. Add orange peel and pears. Place cranberry mixture in a lightly greased 7x11-inch pan.
- For topping: Mix remaining ingredients together and spread over cranberry mixture in baking dish. Bake for 30 minutes until fruit is bubbly and topping is lightly browned.
- Yield: 6 servings

GINGER PEACH ROLL

When sliced, the peachy cream cheese filling is a nice contrast against the gingerbread cake roll. You'll win rave reviews for this one!

½ cup all-purpose flour
1 teaspoon ground ginger
½ teaspoon baking soda
½ teaspoon baking powder
¼ teaspoon nutmeg
¼ teaspoon ground cloves
4 eggs
½ cup sugar

¼ cup molasses
½ cup powdered sugar, divided
1 (16-ounce) can cling peach halves
1 (8-ounce) package cream cheese
1 teaspoon grated lemon peel
1 tablespoon lemon juice
1 teaspoon vanilla
½ cup heavy cream

- Preheat oven to 350 degrees. Line a 10x15x1-inch jelly roll pan with foil. Lightly grease and flour foil. Sift together first six ingredients.

- In a mixing bowl, combine eggs, sugar and molasses. Beat with mixer until thick and light, about 5 minutes. Gently fold in flour mixture. Spoon batter into prepared pan, smoothing top. Bake at 350 degrees for 15 minutes. Remove from oven, sift 2 tablespoons powdered sugar over cake and cover with a cloth towel. Invert cake pan; carefully remove foil. Roll cake, starting from short side. Cool.

- Meanwhile, drain peaches, reserve one peach half for garnish. Chop remaining peaches. In a mixing bowl, beat cream cheese with remaining 6 tablespoons powdered sugar, lemon peel, juice and vanilla. Set aside.

- In another bowl, beat heavy cream until stiff peaks form. Fold peaches and cream into cream cheese mixture. Unroll cake. Spread with peach mixture and reroll. Place on serving plate. Slice reserved peach to form a fan garnish.

- Yield: 8-10 servings

Every backporch step in town should have its own pot of mint each summer. Mint is easy to grow, requiring watering only. The more you pinch it off to use, the bushier the plant gets. Wonderful varieties are available including pineapple, lemon, orange and chocolate. Use them in salads and desserts or to garnish that summer drink.

CREAM CHEESE POUND CAKE

1 cup butter
½ cup margarine
1 (8-ounce) package cream cheese
3 cups sugar

6 eggs
2½ cups sifted cake flour
2 teaspoons vanilla

- Preheat oven to 325 degrees. Generously grease a 10-inch tube pan. Combine butter, margarine and cream cheese; beat well. Gradually add sugar and beat until fluffy. Add eggs one at a time. Stir in flour; then vanilla. Pour batter into pan and cook at 325 degrees for 1 hour and 25 minutes. Cool in pan for 10 minutes; remove from pan and cool completely.   Optional: Top slices with Raspberry Sauce.

- Yield: 12-16 servings

Cake flour is an unenriched superfine flour milled from soft wheat and produces a cake with a fine, feathery grain.

Rich and buttery, you don't need to add a topping to this outstanding brunch or dessert choice. Wrapped in a basket, this cake travels well and will be moist and delicious when you reach your destination. Try baking in tiny loaf pans, add a ribbon and give as a perfect gift.

RASPBERRY SAUCE

1 (12-ounce) package whole frozen
   raspberries, thawed
8 cloves

½ teaspoon cinnamon
½ cup sugar

- In a saucepan, combine raspberries with cloves, cinnamon and sugar. Cover; heat until simmering. Simmer 3-5 minutes. Remove from heat; cool. Strain mixture to remove seeds and cloves. Chill sauce.

- Yield: approximately 2 cups

APPLE CAKE WITH RUM SAUCE

Many varieties of apples may be used in baking but the following types seem to provide especially fine flavor and texture: Jonathan, McIntosh, Newton, Pippin and Winesap.

½ - ¾ cup sugar (depending on sweetness of apples)
¼ cup shortening (or ⅛ cup butter and ⅛ cup shortening)
1 egg

1 cup all-purpose flour
⅛ teaspoon mace
¾ teaspoon cinnamon
¼ teaspoon salt
2 cups apples, peeled and chopped

- Preheat oven to 350 degrees. Grease and flour a 9-inch square pan. In a mixing bowl, cream sugar and shortening until fluffy. Add egg and beat well.

- In a separate bowl, combine flour, mace, cinnamon and salt. Blend into sugar mixture. Gently stir in apples. Pour into prepared pan and bake for 35 minutes or until cake tester comes out clean. Cool on rack.

- Yield: 8-10 servings

RUM SAUCE

½ cup butter
1 cup sugar

½ cup heavy cream
1½ teaspoons rum flavoring

- In the top of a double boiler, combine butter, sugar, cream and rum flavoring. Stir constantly over simmering water until sugar dissolves. Spoon warm sauce over warm cake and serve.

- Yield: about 1½ cups

PECAN TURTLE BARS

As these bars are very rich, a 1½-inch square is the ideal serving size. Enjoy!

2 cups all-purpose flour
1 cup brown sugar, firmly packed
½ cup butter
1¼ - 1½ cups pecans, chopped
1 cup butter

¾ cup brown sugar, packed
½ cup milk chocolate chips (or a combination of semi-sweet and milk chocolate)

- Preheat oven to 350 degrees. Combine flour, 1 cup brown sugar and ½ cup butter in large bowl; blend with pastry cutter until fine. Pat firmly into ungreased 9x13-inch pan. Sprinkle pecans evenly over unbaked crust.

- In a heavy 1-quart saucepan, combine 1 cup butter and ¾ cup brown sugar; cook over medium heat, stirring until mixture comes to a boil. Boil 1 minute, stirring constantly. Pour evenly over pecans and unbaked crust.

- Bake 18-20 minutes until caramel mixture is bubbly and crust is golden brown. Remove from oven and sprinkle chocolate chips on top. Allow to melt 2-3 minutes and swirl slightly—do not spread evenly. Cool and cut into small squares.

- Yield: 4 dozen

CHOCOLATE BOURBON PECAN PIE BARS

3 cups all-purpose flour
2 cups sugar, divided
1 cup butter, softened
½ teaspoon salt
1¼ cups light corn syrup

6 ounces semi-sweet chocolate
¼ cup bourbon
4 eggs, beaten
1½ teaspoons vanilla
3 cups pecans, chopped

A variation of this sumptuous cookie might include substituting walnuts or Oregon hazelnuts for the pecans. Recipe may be successfully halved or doubled.

- Preheat oven to 350 degrees. Grease bottom and sides of a 9x13-inch baking pan. In a large mixing bowl, beat flour, ½ cup sugar, butter and salt at medium speed until mixture resembles coarse crumbs. Press firmly and evenly into pan. Bake for 20 minutes.

- Meanwhile in a 3-quart saucepan, stir corn syrup and chocolate over low heat until chocolate melts. Remove from heat. Stir in bourbon, remaining sugar, eggs and vanilla until blended. Stir in pecans. Pour over crust and spread evenly. Bake for 30 minutes or until filling is firm around edges. Cool before cutting.

- Yield: 24 bars

PECAN PIE COOKIES

1 cup butter or margarine
½ cup sugar
½ cup dark corn syrup
2 eggs, separated
2½ cups all-purpose flour, unsifted

½ cup powdered sugar
¼ cup butter or margarine
3 tablespoons dark corn syrup
½ cup pecans, chopped

These cookies are especially good warm from the oven and would be a special treat as an after-school snack. Recipe may be halved, doubled and freezes well.

- In a large bowl, blend 1 cup butter and ½ cup sugar together using an electric mixer set on low speed. Add ½ cup corn syrup and egg yolks; beat until thoroughly blended. Stir in flour. Chill several hours.

- To prepare pecan filling, combine powdered sugar, ¼ cup butter and 3 tablespoons corn syrup in a saucepan; stir to blend. Cook over medium heat, stirring occasionally, until mixture reaches a full boil. Remove from heat, stir in pecans. Chill.

- Preheat oven to 375 degrees. Beat egg whites slightly; set aside. Using 1 tablespoon of dough for each cookie, roll into balls, brushing each very lightly with egg white. Place on greased cookie sheet, leaving a 2-inch space between cookies. Bake at 375 degrees for 5 minutes.

- Remove from oven. Roll ½ teaspoon of the chilled pecan filling into a ball and firmly press into the center of each cookie. Bake 5 minutes longer or until lightly browned. Cool 5 minutes on cookie sheet. Remove; cool completely on rack.

- Yield: 4 dozen

LEMON TEA COOKIES

COOKIES

1⅔ cups all-purpose flour
1 cup butter, softened

⅓ cup powdered sugar
1 teaspoon vanilla

FILLING

1 egg, beaten
2-3 teaspoons lemon peel, grated
salt
⅔ cup sugar

1 teaspoon cornstarch
3 tablespoons butter
powdered sugar

An excellent choice for afternoon tea, perhaps served with lemon grass or Rosehip tea. This recipe may be doubled and freezes well.

- Preheat oven to 350 degrees. In medium bowl, combine all four cookie ingredients. Blend well. Chill dough at least one hour. Shape dough into 1-inch balls. Place 2 inches apart on ungreased cookie sheets. With thumb or finger make imprint in center of each cookie. Bake 8-10 minutes until lightly browned. Cool.

- In medium saucepan, combine filling ingredients except powdered sugar. Cook over low heat, stirring constantly, until smooth and thickened. Cool. Top each cookie with ¼ teaspoon filling; sprinkle with powdered sugar.

- Yield: 3-4 dozen

LEMON GEMS

2⅓ cups all-purpose flour, divided
2 cups sugar, divided
1 teaspoon lemon peel, grated
1 cup butter, softened

4 eggs
½ cup fresh lemon juice
½ teaspoon baking powder

An open house or Easter brunch would be two places to share these "gems" with friends. These could be cut into shapes by using cookie cutters.

- Preheat oven to 350 degrees. In a 9x13-inch baking pan, combine 2 cups flour, ½ cup sugar, and lemon peel. With pastry blender, cut butter into flour mixture until coarse and crumbly. Pat crumbs evenly along bottom of pan. Bake for 20-25 minutes until lightly browned.

- Meanwhile combine in blender or food processor remaining ingredients: ⅓ cup flour, 1½ cups sugar, eggs, lemon juice and baking powder. Cover and blend or process 5 seconds. Scrape sides and process another 10-15 seconds. Pour over baked crust. Return to oven and bake another 20-25 minutes until lightly browned. Cool in pan and cut into squares or diamond shapes.

- Yield: 8 dozen 1-inch squares

CREAM CHEESE COOKIES

4 ounces cream cheese, room
    temperature
½ cup butter

1 cup all-purpose flour
½ cup sugar
¼ cup walnuts, finely chopped

This delicate cookie would be good served alongside a bowl of spumoni ice cream; a perfect dessert after an Italian meal.

- Preheat oven to 350 degrees. Cream together cheese and butter. Add flour, sugar and walnuts; mix together well. Drop by teaspoonfuls onto an ungreased cookie sheet. Pour 1 cup water into a small bowl. Dip fingers into water and flatten cookie dough on cookie sheet with a circular motion. Bake 10 minutes.

- Yield: 2 dozen cookies

CHOCOLATE COVERED SHORTBREAD

1 cup brown sugar, firmly packed
½ cup butter, room temperature or
    softened
½ cup shortening
1 egg yolk

1 teaspoon vanilla
2 cups all-purpose flour
8 ounces semi-sweet chocolate
½ cup finely chopped nuts

Originating from Scotland, shortbread is traditionally eaten at Christmas and New Year but this chocolate covered version can be enjoyed anytime, anywhere.

- Preheat oven to 350 degrees. Combine brown sugar with butter and shortening. Add egg yolk and vanilla; beat until creamy. Mix in flour. Spread mixture on ungreased cookie sheet. Bake 20 minutes.

- Melt chocolate and spread on baked mixture while still warm. Sprinkle nuts onto warm chocolate. While warm, score with sharp knife and cut into 24 squares.

- Yield: 24 cookies

CHOCOLATE WALNUT EUPHORIA COOKIES

12 ounces semi-sweet chocolate
    chips, divided
3 tablespoons butter
¾ cup sugar
1 egg
1½ teaspoons vanilla

½ cup all-purpose flour
¼ teaspoon baking powder
½ teaspoon salt
1 tablespoon milk
1¼ cups walnuts, chopped

These cookies are a chocolate lover's dream come true. They would surely be a hit at a cookie exchange. This recipe can easily be doubled.

- Preheat oven to 350 degrees. Melt half the chocolate chips in double boiler or in microwave until smooth. In separate bowl, beat butter, sugar, egg and vanilla until smooth. Sift together dry ingredients. Stir melted chocolate and milk into butter mixture. Mix in dry ingredients, then remaining chocolate chips and walnuts. Drop by teaspoonfuls onto ungreased cookie sheet and bake 8 minutes.

- Yield: 3 dozen

The Junior Service League of Jackson County would like to thank its members, families and friends who contributed their recipes, time and creative ideas.

*Kathryn Abbott
Tami Abeloe
*Kris Ackerman
*Adams Cottage
*Jan Alexander
Barbara Andazola
*Dorathy Anderson-Thickett
Christy Apodaca
*Galen Astle
*Cyd Bagley
Susan Baker
*Hilde Bandy
*Crissy Barnett
De Barnett
*Barbara L. Barnum
*Catherine Marie Barr
*Judith A. Barr
*Carolyn Barrett
LeAnn Bartley
Susan Becker
*Nancy Bendickson
*Richard Berks
Karen Berlandi
*LaVonne Bernard
Gloria Bloomberg
Stacey Boals
*Nancy J. Boeck
Regina Boeck
Jerilyn Bourdon
Alex Boutacoff
Karin Boutacoff
*Linda Boutacoff
*Jean Bolton Boyer
*Lorrie Brawner
*Ann Brewer
*Anne Brooke
Brown, Chudleigh, Schuler and
  Associates
Gere Brown
*Joan Brown
*Helen Bulkin
Connie Burns
*Sharman Busch
*Linda Butler
Jan Carey
*Margie Hornecker Carey
Eric Carter
*Gene Chamberlain
Debbie Chambers

*Chanticleer Inn
Ann Cichon
*Wendy Boyd Close
*Kelly Collins
*Nancy Miller Collins
Chris Cook
*Jan Coplen
*Hope Corbett
*Clare Cotta
Heather Couch
Bob Cowling
Tim Cowling
*Doris Cretton
*Margaret Cutler
*Pat Cutler
Karin Dailey
Denise Dake
Pam Danford
*Jay D'Angelo
Karen Darby
*Kathy Eggers Dawson
Nancy Day
*Elaine DeCarlow
Ann DelRosso
*Lawnedia Devlin
*Debra Trujillo Dixon
*Donna L. Dixon
Don Donegan
Pam Donegan
*Sandy Dowling
*June Duhaime
*Susan Duquette
Janice Earl
*Patti Ellis
*Linda Evans
*Carolyn Yerkovich Ferguson
*Reni Ferguson
Sandra Fletcher
Karen Foster
Mary Foster
Stuart E. Foster
Foster, Purdy, Allen, Peterson &
  Dahlin
Richard Fox
Foxtail Farms
Marilyn Gardner
*Cathy Gerking
*Barbara B. P. Gibson
Janine Gonyea

*Deanna Gossner
*Robert D. Grathwol
*Sally Ann Gravon
Jennifer Greer
*Ann Gressett
*Rhonda Gressett
Jobie Grether
*Judi Griffith
Carolyn Groves
Debbie Gruber
Mary Gustafson
Marcia Haggard
*Bonnie R. Hall
*Heidi Hall
Marta Hall
*Myra Hall
Thelma F. Halverson
*Carol Lindbloom Hamlin
*Barbara Hammack
*Katie Hornecker Hansen
Pam Hansen
Rosemary Harrington
*William Harris
*Dody Thomason Boehnke Hart
Jennifer Haugen
*Hazelnut Marketing Board
*Ben Hefley
Mark Hefley
Marvel Hefley
*Michelle Tague Hefley
Mary Heimann
*Peg Hemple
*Hersey House
*Dawn Heysell
Linda Higgins
*Ruth Hockersmith
Judy Hodge
Betsy Hoell
Diane Holcom
*Cheri Horsley
*Carole Holzkamp
Ann Horton
*Freddi Harr Hudlett
*Lynne Hunter
Robert Hunter
HVR Company
Rita Hyatt
Debra Ingram
*Carol D. Jackson

Denotes recipe contributors

Jackson County/OSU Extension
  Service
*Jacksonville Inn
*Bernadette Jacobs
*Janet Jamieson
*Mary Kay Jones
*Michele Jones
*Pauline M. Jones
*Sharon M. Jones
Linda Katzen
*Martha Kieffer
John Kilejian
Mary Ann Kilejian
*Carol Klouda
*Elaine L. Kuszmaul
Lawrence's Jewelers
Claudia Lawton
Bill Leever
*Nancy Leever
*Jane Leonardo
*Hazel Lindsey
Judy Lininger
*Jeannie Littrell
*Laura Jane Littrell
*Mike Littrell
Lisa Luce
Tina Lucich
*Kathryn E. Mahar
Jan Mahon
*Nancy Malone
*Peggy Malos
Dee Marchi
*Louretha Martin
*Jeannie Matthews
*Pat J. Mayerle
*McCully House Inn
*Debra K. McFadden
McIlhenny Co.
*Virginia McIlroy
*Donn McIntosh
*Medford Mail Tribune
Elliott Meyerding
Eugene Meyerding
*Karen Meyerding
*Leslie Holl Meyerding
Connie Miller
*Ellen Miller
William M. Miller
*Lovella Moore
*Caprice R. Moran
*Judy Morris
*Mt. Ashland Inn
*Anne Murphy

*Nancy Murphy
Nabisco Brands, Inc.
*Ellen B. Naumes
*Susan G. Naumes
Lance Nimmo
*Alma Hepner O'Connor
*Cheryl O'Reilly
*Oak Hill Country Inn
Nancy Ockunzzi
*Old Stage Inn
*Oregon Beef Council
Jeanie Payne
*Susan Penwell
Paul Peterson
Kate Phillips
*Barbara J. Pinkham
Jeffrey Pons
R. Kenneth Pons
Scott Pons
*Betty Lou Pratt
*Steve Pratt
Nancy Preston
*Bertha Ralls Prewitt
*Cindy Prewitt
Craig Prewitt
Ancel Proctor
Donna Puett
*Susan L. Rachor
*Sue Rasmussen
*Erika Rosenberg Reinke
*Shawn Retzlaff
*Janet Buck Roach
Jim Robinson
*Romeo Inn
Valerie Root
*Bev Thunem Ruck
Kathie Rulon
*Marty Hefley Rummel
*Constance Sams
*Fran Scannell
Doug Schmor
*Sandi Schmor
*Jill Schroeder
*Carole Abbott Schuler
*Greg Schuler
*Ruth Ann Schwada
*Sandy Scott
*Beverly A. Shoup
Phil Shugart
*Maggie Silverman
*Kris Singler
*Jan Sinner
Carol Skinner

*Mignon Skinner
*Vicki Skinner
Cindy Smith
Greg Smith
*Joan Boehnke Smith
Theresa Smith
*Diane Somers
*Bob Spani
*Kathy Spano
Judy Steadman
*Mary M. Stebbins
Barbara Stout
*Arlene Stover
*Barbara Stuart
*Carol Stuart
*Dan Stumpf
Bob Swanson
Danny Swanson
*Marjorie L. Swanson
*Sharon Swartsley
*Kennett G. Sublette
*Mickey Sublette
Chris Tarrant
*Mary Ann Taylor
*Gini Teemer
*Cathy Garrity Theen
*Peggy Tomlins
*Under the Greenwood Tree
Val Vakoc
*Connie Van Slack
*Gildee A. Vaughn
*Lynette Vesty
Ken Vines
*Barbara M. Walter
*R. B. Webber
Ralph Wehinger
Murray Weiss
Twyla Weiss
*Elaine Wells
*Ann Wenger
West Main Rentals and Sales
*Marsha Wilkins-Shugart
*Pam Wilkinson
Bill Williams
*Brenda Williams
*Winchester Country Inn
*Sharon Lindsay Withers
*The Woods House
Pam Wooton
Denise Workman
*Susie Wright
*Cindi Yorde
Beth Zerkel

Tabasco® is a registered trademark of
McIlhenny Co., Avery Island, LA 70513

*Denotes recipe contributors

Index

Adams Cottage Eggs, 183
Aegean Eggplant Shell, 34
Almond Puff Pastry, 93
Almond Sesame Salad, 78
Almonds
Almond Puff Pastry, 93
Apricot-Almond Butter, 99
Chocolate Almond Brioche, 104
Anaheim Chile Chicken Soup, 62
Anise Carrots, 170
Appetizers
Aegean Eggplant Shell, 34
Ashland Artichoke Triangles, 35
Baked Stuffed Shrimp, 29
Cheese Filled Pastry Puffs, 39
Cheesy Artichoke Rounds, 35
Chicken Strips with Jalapeño
Sauce, 159
China Bar Chicken, 31
China Riffle Mushrooms, 33
Chinook Salmon in Phyllo, 27
Chutney Cheese Ball, 40
Curried Cashew Pâtè, 33
Focaccia Roma, 43
Garlic Brie, 42
Gin Lin Char Shu Pork, 30
Gougère (French Pastry Puff), 34
Mediterranean Not To Worry, 43
Molded Triple Layer Hors
D'Oeuvres, 42
Newport Shrimp, 28
Oregon Blue Prosciutto Tarts, 40
Oregon Shrimp Pâtè, 28
Pear Chutney, 41
Pears, Parmesan, and Pepper, 41
Pecan-Crab Ball, 30
Pesto and Cream Cheese on Sun-
Dried Tomatoes, 37
Salmon Baguette, 27
Shrimp-Dill Puffs, 29
Smoked Salmon Cheesecake, 26
Spinach Torte, 32
Tarragon Chicken Pâté, 32
Tomatoes and Cheeses on
Phyllo, 36
Apples
Apple Cake with Rum Sauce, 210
Apple Cinnamon Muffins, 86
Baked Apples and New
Potatoes, 176
Blue Ribbon Apple Pie, 201
Carrot-Apple Potage, 50
Chanticleer Parsnip Apple
Pancakes with (Hot) Smoked
Salmon and Sherried Crème
Fraîche, 182
Spinach Apple Salad, 76
Apricot-Almond Butter, 99
Artichokes
Artichoke and Hazelnut Soup, 51

Ashland Artichoke Triangles, 35
Cheesy Artichoke Rounds, 35
Illahe Artichoke Soup, 46
Oregon Chardonnay
Chicken, 148
Spinach Stuffed Artichoke
Crowns, 168
Asparagus
Asparagus Mushroom Salad, 76
Asparagus Soup, 46
Asparagus with Peach Hazelnut
Topping, 167
Savory Tomato and Asparagus
Pie, 185
Sesame Asparagus, 167
Steamed Vegetables with
Dijonnaise Sauce, 166
Bacon Wrapped Salmon Steaks, 112
Baked Apples and New
Potatoes, 176
Baked Stuffed Shrimp, 29
Bar Cookies
Chocolate Bourbon Pecan Pie
Bars, 211
Lemon Gems, 212
Pecan Turtle Bars, 210
Barbecued Game Hens, 157
Barbecued Wild Duck, 161
Barley
Barley Cheese Bake, 175
Basil Batter Rolls, 94
Beans
Black Bean and Jalapeño
Soup, 63
Cilantro Black Bean Chicken, 80
Garbanzo-Feta Salad, 74
Italian Sausage and Bean
Soup, 60
Picnic Beans, 171
Sautéed String Beans, 167
Tomatoes Stuffed With Green
Beans, 75
Whiskey Baked Beans, 171
Beef
Beer Chili Beef, 137
Betts Hole Beef Parmigiana, 135
Brown Bag Sirloin Steak, 141
Bulgogi (Korean Stir Fry), 138
Fillets of Beef in Creamy Wine-Dill
Sauce, 136
Flank Steak in Honey
Marinade, 139
Flank Steak in Pepper
Marinade, 140
Hot Summer Spareribs, 137
Mrs. Murphy's Corned Beef, 142
Old-Fashioned Meatballs and
Noodles, 144
Orange-Rosemary Steaks, 140
Pacific Burgers, 143

Rogue River Ribs, 138
Steak and Fresh Spinach
Soup, 58
Takelma Taco Soup, 53
Tequila Chili, 143
Vermouth Flank Steak, 141
Very Italian Meatballs, 145
Beer Chili Beef, 137
Bell Peppers
Confetti Shrimp, 124
Eggplant and Sweet Red Pepper
Soup, 55
Roasted Pepper Trio, 173
Three Pepper Cajun Shrimp, 123
Betts Hole Beef Parmigiana, 135
Beverages
Rogues' Fizz, 31
Black Bean and Jalapeño Soup, 63
Black Satin Chicken, 156
Black-eyed Peas
Wildcat Black-Eyed Pea Soup, 60
Blackberries
Blackberry Peach Cobbler with
Grand Marnier Cream, 202
Fruit Vinegar, 157
Oregon Berry Salad, 67
Red, White, and Blue Fruit
Salad, 66
Wild Blackberry Chicken, 149
Blossom Bar Broccoli, 169
Blue Cheese
Blue, Shrimp, and Spinach, 74
Oregon Blue Cheese Butter, 39
Oregon Blue Prosciutto Tarts, 40
Rogue Polenta, 181
Rogue River Blue Cheese
Custards, 184
Blue Ribbon Apple Pie, 201
Blue, Shrimp, and Spinach, 74
Blueberries
Blueberry Peach Glacé Tart, 203
Chilled Blueberry and Strawberry
Soup, 50
Fresh Fruit Trifle, 196
Frozen Blueberry Pie, 203
Fruit Vinegar, 157
Northwest Blueberry Muffins, 88
Oregon Berry Salad, 67
Red, White, and Blue Fruit
Salad, 66
Braised Pork Loin, 134
Brandied Fruit Braid, 102
Breads
Croutons, 73, 81
Quick
Apple Cinnamon Muffins, 86
Cherry Nut Bread, 88
Chocolate Chip Pumpkin
Muffins, 87

Fresh Oregon Pear Bread, 89
Golden Pumpkin Biscuits, 93
Hazelnut Scone Hearts, 91
Northwest Blueberry
    Muffins, 88
Orange Pecan Muffins, 85
Orange Scones with Sun-Dried
    Cherries or Cranberries, 90
Oregon Raspberry-Hazelnut
    Muffins, 85
Pear Tea Cake, 89
River Lodge Refrigerator
    Muffins, 87
Spicy Pear Muffins, 84
Tiny Vanilla Gems, 86
Sourdough French Bread
    Starter, 100

Yeast
Basil Batter Rolls, 94
Brandied Fruit Braid, 102
Chocolate Almond
    Brioche, 104
Cream Cheese Braid, 103
Curry Baguettes, 97
Gold Nugget Bread, 101
Heavenly Yeast Biscuits, 95
Orange Sunflower Bread, 96
Overnight Light Rolls, 94
Overnight Yeast Waffles, 91
Peasant Black Bread, 99
Pesto and Sun-Dried Tomato
    Twist, 98
Pineapple Buttermilk
    Bread, 95
Sourdough French Bread, 100
Brie Soup, 59

Broccoli
Blossom Bar Broccoli, 169
Broccoli and Cheddar Soup, 57
Broccoli Bake, 168
Fresh Broccoli Salad with Custard
    Dressing, 70
Steamed Vegetables with
    Dijonnaise Sauce, 166
Brookings Clam and Red Potato
    Frittata, 120
Brown Bag Sirloin Steak, 141
Brown Sugar Hazelnut
    Cheesecake, 191

Brownies
Grand Marnier Brownies, 207

Brunch
Adams Cottage Eggs, 183
Brookings Clam and Red Potato
    Frittata, 120
Chanticleer Parsnip Apple
    Pancakes with (Hot) Smoked
    Salmon and Sherried Crème
    Fraîche, 182
Cranberry Pear Crisp, 207
Hazelnut Honey Butter, 92
Hazelnut Scone Hearts, 91
Melon Puree, 68
Orange Scones with Sun-Dried
    Cherries or Cranberries, 90

Overnight Yeast Waffles, 91
Rogue River Blue Cheese
    Custards, 184
Rogues' Fizz, 31
Romeo Inn's Welsh Rarebit, 183
Savory Tomato and Asparagus
    Pie, 185
Shrimp and Crabmeat Pancakes
    Greenwood, 114
Whole Wheat Hazelnut
    Pancakes, 92
Brushy Bar Chicken Casserole, 151
Bulgogi (Korean Stir Fry), 138
Burnt Cream, 195
Buttered Orzo, 122

Butters
Apricot-Almond Butter, 99
Hazelnut Honey Butter, 92
Lime-Dill Butter, 109
Oregon Blue Cheese Butter, 39

Cabbage
Almond Sesame Salad, 78
German Red Cabbage, 172
Cajun Shrimp with Pasta, 123

Cakes
Apple Cake with Rum Sauce, 210
Christmas Date Cake, 204
Cream Cheese Pound Cake, 209
Poppy Seed Cake, 206
Renate's Plum Cake, 206
Sour Cream Fudge Cake, 204
Calamari Marinara, 115

Cantaloupe
Chilled Cantaloupe Soup, 49
Chilled Melon Soup, 50
Melon Puree, 68

Carrots
Anise Carrots, 170
Carrot-Apple Potage, 50
Carrot-Dill Soup, 51
Carrots in Wine Sauce, 170
Parsnip and Curried Carrot
    Soup, 52

Cashews
Curried Cashew Pâté, 33
Mushroom Soup with
    Cashews, 52

Cauliflower
Ginger Garlic Cauliflower, 172
Winter Vegetable Salad, 69
Cayenne Trout with Buttered
    Orzo, 122
Champagne-Marionberry Jelly, 105
Chanticleer Parsnip Apple Pancakes
    with (Hot) Smoked Salmon and
    Sherried Crème Fraîche, 182
Cheddar Chowder, 57

Cheese
Ashland Artichoke Triangles, 35
Brie Soup, 59
Broccoli and Cheddar Soup, 57
Cheddar Chowder, 57
Cheese Filled Pastry Puffs, 39
Cheesy Artichoke Rounds, 35
Chutney Cheese Ball, 40

Cream Cheese Braid, 103
Garbanzo-Feta Salad, 74
Garlic Brie, 42
Gold Nugget Bread, 101
Gougère (French Pastry Puff), 34
Mediterranean Not To Worry, 43
Molded Triple Layer Hors
    D'Oeuvres, 42
Oregon Shrimp Pâté, 28
Pears, Parmesan, and Pepper, 41
Pecan-Crab Ball, 30
Pesto and Cream Cheese on Sun-
    Dried Tomatoes, 37
Romeo Inn's Welsh Rarebit, 183
Salmon Baguette, 27
Shrimp-Dill Puffs, 29
Smoked Salmon Cheesecake, 26
Spinach Torte, 32
Stilton Cheese and Onion
    Soup, 58
Tomatoes and Cheeses on
    Phyllo, 36
Cheese Filled Pastry Puffs, 39

Cheesecakes
Brown Sugar Hazelnut
    Cheesecake, 191
Chocolate Espresso
    Cheesecake, 190
Cinnamon Cheesecake, 191
Frozen Mocha-Mint
    Cheesecake, 188
White Chocolate Macadamia Nut
    Cheesecake, 189
Cheesy Artichoke Rounds, 35

Cherries
Cherry Nut Bread, 88
Cream Cheese Braid, 103
Orange Scones with Sun-Dried
    Cherries or Cranberries, 90
Cherry Nut Bread, 88

Chicken
Anaheim Chile Chicken Soup, 62
Black Satin Chicken, 156
Brushy Bar Chicken
    Casserole, 151
Chicken in Phyllo Pastry, 159
Chicken Lasagna, 160
Chicken Pinot Noir, 150
Chicken San Carlos, 152
Chicken Strips with Jalapeño
    Sauce, 159
Chicken Vegetable Soup Thai
    Style, 63
China Bar Chicken, 31
Cilantro Black Bean Chicken, 80
Creamy Bow Ties with Chicken
    and Spinach, 154
Curry Oven-Fried Chicken, 150
French Chicken Pâté, 153
Fuzzy Navel Chicken, 152
Lemon-Rosemary Chicken, 149
Oregon Chardonnay
    Chicken, 148
Pasta Sauvignon Blanc, 158
Posole, 54
Rogue Rendezvous Chicken, 151

Smoky Garlic Chicken
Pizza, 158
Tarragon Chicken Pâté, 32
Union Creek Chicken Salad, 77
West Coast Chicken, 155
Wild Blackberry Chicken, 149
Wild Mushroom Chicken
Stroganoff, 154
Chilled Blueberry and Strawberry
Soup, 50
Chilled Cantaloupe Soup, 49
Chilled Cucumber Soup, 48
Chilled Melon Soup, 50
Chilled Potato-Cilantro Soup, 47
Chilled Summer Corn, 72
Chilled Watermelon Strawberry
Soup, 49
China Bar Chicken, 31
China Gulch Sweet and Sour
Pork, 132
China Riffle Mushrooms, 33
Chinook Salmon in Phyllo, 27

Chocolate
Chocolate Almond Brioche, 104
Chocolate Almond Tart, 198
Chocolate Bourbon Pecan Pie
Bars, 211
Chocolate Chip Pumpkin
Muffins, 87
Chocolate Covered
Shortbread, 213
Chocolate Espresso
Cheesecake, 190
Chocolate Fudge Frosting, 204
Chocolate Raspberry Tart, 200
Chocolate Sauce, 197
Chocolate Walnut Euphoria
Cookies, 213
Grand Marnier Brownies, 207
Pecan Turtle Bars, 210
Sour Cream Fudge Cake, 204
3-Minute Chocolate Mousse, 189
Christmas Date Cake, 204
Chutney Cheese Ball, 40
Cilantro Black Bean Chicken, 80
Cinnamon Cheesecake, 191

Clams
Brookings Clam and Red Potato
Frittata, 120
Signature Clam Chowder, 62
Confetti Shrimp, 124

Cookies
Chocolate Covered
Shortbread, 213
Chocolate Walnut Euphoria
Cookies, 213
Cream Cheese Cookies, 213
Lemon Gems, 212
Lemon Tea Cookies, 212
Pecan Pie Cookies, 211

Corn
Chilled Summer Corn, 72
Gold Beach Shrimp and Corn
Chowder, 61
Indian Summer Corn, 169
Couscous Salad, 72

Crab
Crab and Zucchini Sauté, 115
Pecan-Crab Ball, 30
Shrimp and Crabmeat Pancakes
Greenwood, 114

Cranberries
Cranberry Pear Crisp, 207
Orange Scones with Sun-Dried
Cherries or Cranberries, 90
Cranberry Pear Crisp, 207
Cream Cheese Braid, 103
Cream Cheese Cookies, 213
Cream Cheese Pound Cake, 209
Cream Custard, 195
Creamy Bow Ties with Chicken and
Spinach, 154
Creamy Horseradish Sauce, 142
Creamy Olive Sauce, 118
Creamy Wine-Dill Sauce, 136
Croutons, 73, 81

Cucumbers
Chilled Cucumber Soup, 48
Cucumber Dill Sorbet, 80
Curried Cashew Pâtè, 33
Curry Baguettes, 97
Curry Oven-Fried Chicken, 150
Custard Dressing, 70

Desserts
Apple Cake with Rum Sauce, 210
Blackberry Peach Cobbler with
Grand Marnier Cream, 202
Brown Sugar Hazelnut
Cheesecake, 191
Burnt Cream, 195
Chocolate Almond Tart, 198
Chocolate Bourbon Pecan Pie
Bars, 211
Chocolate Covered
Shortbread, 213
Chocolate Espresso
Cheesecake, 190
Chocolate Walnut Euphoria
Cookies, 213
Christmas Date Cake, 204
Cinnamon Cheesecake, 191
Cranberry Pear Crisp, 207
Cream Cheese Cookies, 213
Cream Cheese Pound Cake, 209
Cream Custard, 195
Filbert-Hazelnut Torte, 205
Fresh French Rhubarb
Greenwood, 201
Fresh Fruit Trifle, 196
Fresh Strawberry Pie, 199
Frozen Blueberry Pie, 203
Frozen Mocha-Mint
Cheesecake, 188
Frozen Pumpkin Dessert, 200
Ginger Peach Roll, 208
Grand Marnier Brownies, 207
Grand Marnier Cream, 202
Kiwi Pavlova, 199
Lemon Gems, 212
Lemon Tea Cookies, 212
Macadamia-Banana Pie on
Chocolate Sauce, 197
Oregon Hazelnut Pears, 193

Pear Dumplings with Cream
Custard, 195
Pecan Pie Cookies, 211
Poached Amaretto Pears, 194
Poppy Seed Cake, 206
Raspberry Cream Pears, 194
Renate's Plum Cake, 206
Rogue Pears, 193
Sour Cream Fudge Cake, 204
Strawberries in Lemon
Mousse, 196
Sugared Orange Peels, 193
Cucumber Dill Sorbet, 80
White Chocolate Macadamia Nut
Cheesecake, 189
Dijonnaise Sauce, 166

Duck
Barbecued Wild Duck, 161
Pacific Flyway Christmas Mallard,
161
Peach and Sesame Glazed
Duckling with Wild Rice, 162

Eggplant
Aegean Eggplant Shell, 34
Eggplant and Sweet Red Pepper
Soup, 55

Eggs
Adams Cottage Eggs, 183
Brookings Clam and Red Potato
Frittata, 120
Romeo Inn's Welsh Rarebit, 183

Elk
Venison Pot Roast with Juniper
Berries, 128
Filbert-Hazelnut Torte, 205
Fillets of Beef in Creamy Wine-Dill
Sauce, 136

Fish (*See also specific fish listings*)
Lemon Grilled Orange
Roughy, 121
Oregon Ling Cod with Pistachio
Crust, 121
Petrale Sole Macadamia, 119
Red Snapper Oriental, 120
Flank Steak in Honey Marinade, 139
Flank Steak in Pepper
Marinade, 140
Focaccia Roma, 43
French Chicken Pâté, 153
Fresh Broccoli Salad with Custard
Dressing, 70
Fresh French Rhubarb
Greenwood, 201
Fresh Fruit Tray With Orange Cream
Dressing, 68
Fresh Fruit Trifle, 196
Fresh Oregon Pear Bread, 89
Fresh Raspberry Soup, 49
Fresh Strawberry Pie, 199
Fresh Tomato-Dill Soup, 48

Frostings
Chocolate Fudge Frosting, 204
Frozen Blueberry Pie, 203
Frozen Mocha-Mint
Cheesecake, 188

Frozen Pumpkin Dessert, 200
Fruit (*See also specific fruit listings*)
Brandied Fruit Braid, 102
Fresh Fruit Tray With Orange
Cream Dressing, 68
Melon Puree, 68
Oregon Berry Salad, 67
Fruit Vinegar, 157
Fuzzy Navel Chicken, 152
Game Hens
Barbecued Game Hens, 157
Pacific Northwest Game
Hens, 157
Wok Cornish Hens, 156
Garbanzo-Feta Salad, 74
Garlic Brie, 42
Garlic Roma Tomatoes and
Croutons, 73
Garlic Spinach, 174
German Red Cabbage, 172
Gin Lin Char Shu Pork, 30
Ginger Garlic Cauliflower, 172
Ginger Peach Roll, 208
Gold Beach Shrimp and Corn
Chowder, 61
Gold Nugget Bread, 101
Golden Pumpkin Biscuits, 93
Gougère (French Pastry Puff), 34
Grand Marnier Brownies, 207
Grand Marnier Cream, 202
Greek Potato Wedges, 177
Grill Roasted Turkey, 155
Grilled Lemon Salmon, 112
Grilled Lime-Sesame Salmon, 112
Half Moon Oven Barbecued
Salmon, 109
Ham
Molded Triple Layer Hors
D'Oeuvres, 42
Posole, 54
Hazelnuts
Artichoke and Hazelnut Soup, 51
Asparagus with Peach Hazelnut
Topping, 167
Brown Sugar Hazelnut
Cheesecake, 191
Confetti Shrimp, 124
Filbert-Hazelnut Torte, 205
Hazelnut Honey Butter, 92
Hazelnut Scone Hearts, 91
Oregon Hazelnut Pears, 193
Oregon Raspberry-Hazelnut
Muffins, 85
Roasted Hazelnut Salad, 71
Salmon and Hazelnuts in
Phyllo, 113
Whole Wheat Hazelnut
Pancakes, 92
Wild Rice with Hazelnuts, 179
Hearty Lentil Sausage Soup, 56
Hearty Minestrone Soup, 61
Heavenly Yeast Biscuits, 95
Herbed Walnut Salad, 70
Herbed Zucchini Pancakes, 178
Homemade Italian Dressing, 74
Honey Apple Pork Chops, 131

Honey Marinade, 139
Horseshoe Bend Barbecue
Sauce, 144
Hot Summer Spareribs, 137
Huckleberries
Chilled Blueberry and Strawberry
Soup, 50
Huckleberry Relish, 129
Illahe Artichoke Soup, 46
Indian Pilaf, 180
Indian Summer Corn, 169
Italian Sausage and Bean Soup, 60
Jalapeño Sauce, 159
Jams and Jellies
Champagne-Marionberry
Jelly, 105
Rhubarb-Raspberry Conserve, 90
Strawberry-Peach-Kiwi Freezer
Jam, 101
Tayberry Jam, 96
Kiwi Pavlova, 199
Lamb
Lamb Chops with Garlic and
Rosemary, 130
Leg of Lamb in Wine Sauce, 130
Savory Spring Leg of Lamb, 131
Lemon Gems, 212
Lemon Grilled Orange Roughy, 121
Lemon Tea Cookies, 212
Lemon-Rosemary Chicken, 149
Lentils
Hearty Lentil Sausage Soup, 56
Potage Esau, 56
Lime-Dill Butter, 109
Macadamia-Banana Pie on Chocolate
Sauce, 197
Mandarin Dressing, 77
Mandarin Salad, 77
Marinades
Honey Marinade, 139
Pepper Marinade, 140
Marinated Pork Loin, 133
Mediterranean Not To Worry, 43
Melon Puree, 68
Menus, 19
Molded Triple Layer Hors
D'Oeuvres, 42
Mrs. Murphy's Corned Beef, 142
Muffins
Apple Cinnamon Muffins, 86
Chocolate Chip Pumpkin
Muffins, 87
Northwest Blueberry Muffins, 88
Orange Pecan Muffins, 85
Oregon Raspberry-Hazelnut
Muffins, 85
River Lodge Refrigerator
Muffins, 87
Spicy Pear Muffins, 84
Tiny Vanilla Gems, 86
Mushrooms
Asparagus Mushroom
Salad, 76
China Riffle Mushrooms, 33
Curried Cashew Pâté, 33

Mushroom Soup with
Cashews, 52
Pheasants with Chanterelles, 163
Wild Mushroom Chicken
Stroganoff, 154
Newport Shrimp, 28
Northwest Blueberry Muffins, 88
Northwest Drifters' Salmon, 108
Nuts (*See also specific nut listings*)
Oregon Ling Cod with Pistachio
Crust, 121
Petrale Sole Macadamia, 119
Steelhead and Black
Walnuts, 118
Steelhead with Pine Nuts, 119
Old-Fashioned Meatballs and
Noodles, 144
Onions
Stilton Cheese and Onion
Soup, 58
Orange-Rosemary Steaks, 140
Oranges
Mandarin Salad, 77
Orange Cream Dressing, 68
Orange Pecan Muffins, 85
Orange Scones with Sun-Dried
Cherries or Cranberries, 90
Orange Sunflower Bread, 96
Sugared Orange Peels, 193
Oregon Berry Salad, 67
Oregon Blue Cheese Prosciutto
Tarts, 40
Oregon Blue Cheese Butter, 39
Oregon Chardonnay Chicken, 148
Oregon Hazelnut Pears, 193
Oregon Ling Cod with Pistachio
Crust, 121
Oregon Raspberry-Hazelnut
Muffins, 85
Oregon Shrimp Pâté, 28
Orzo with Myzithra and Basil, 181
Our Favorite Gazpacho, 47
Overnight Light Rolls, 94
Overnight Yeast Waffles, 91
Pacific Burgers, 143
Pacific Flyway Christmas
Mallard, 161
Pacific Northwest Game Hens, 157
Pancakes
Chanticleer Parsnip Apple
Pancakes with (Hot) Smoked
Salmon and Sherried Crème
Fraîche, 182
Herbed Zucchini Pancakes, 178
Shrimp and Crabmeat Pancakes
Greenwood, 114
Whole Wheat Hazelnut
Pancakes, 92
Wild Rice Pancakes, 162
Parsnips
Parsnip and Curried Carrot
Soup, 52
Pasta
Buttered Orzo, 122
Cajun Shrimp with Pasta, 123
Calamari Marinara, 115

Chicken Lasagna, 160
Confetti Shrimp, 124
Creamy Bow Ties with Chicken
and Spinach, 154
Hearty Minestrone Soup, 61
Old-Fashioned Meatballs and
Noodles, 144
Orzo with Myzithra and
Basil, 181
Pasta Sauvignon Blanc, 158
Pasta with Salmon in Basil
Cream, 125
Ravioli Salad, 75
Scallop Linguine, 125
Shrimp Rotini, 124
Very Italian Meatballs, 145
Pasta Sauvignon Blanc, 158
Pasta with Salmon in Basil
Cream, 125

Pastry
Almond Puff Pastry, 93
Cheese Filled Pastry Puffs, 39
Chicken in Phyllo Pastry, 159
French Chicken Pâte, 153
Gougère (French Pastry Puff), 34

Peaches
Asparagus with Peach Hazelnut
Topping, 167
Blackberry Peach Cobbler with
Grand Marnier Cream, 202
Blueberry Peach Glacé Tart, 203
Ginger Peach Roll, 208
Peach and Sesame Glazed
Duckling with Wild Rice, 162
Strawberry-Peach-Kiwi Freezer
Jam, 101

Pear Information
Pear Possibilities, 192

Pears
Chutney Cheese Ball, 40
Cranberry Pear Crisp, 207
Fresh Oregon Pear Bread, 89
Oregon Hazelnut Pears, 193
Pear Chutney, 41
Pear Dumplings with Cream
Custard, 195
Pear Possibilities (pear
information), 192
Pear Puree, 134
Pear Tea Cake, 89
Pears, Parmesan, and Pepper, 41
Poached Amaretto Pears, 194
Pork Chops À la Rogue, 132
Raspberry Cream Pears, 194
Rogue Pears, 193
Spicy Pear Muffins, 84

Peas
Peas with Triple Sec, 173
Snow Peas with Pine Nuts, 174
Peasant Black Bread, 99
Pecan Pie Cookies, 211
Pecan Turtle Bars, 210
Pecan-Crab Ball, 30
Pepper Cheese Zucchini, 178
Pepper Marinade, 140
Perfect Salmon Steaks, 111

Pesto
Basil Batter Rolls, 94
Pesto, 37
Pesto and Cream Cheese on Sun-
Dried Tomatoes, 37
Pesto and Sun-Dried Tomato
Twist, 98
Petrale Sole Macadamia, 119
Pheasants with Chanterelles, 163
Picnic Beans, 171

Pies
Blue Ribbon Apple Pie, 201
Fresh Strawberry Pie, 199
Frozen Blueberry Pie, 203
Macadamia-Banana Pie on
Chocolate Sauce, 197

Pineapple
Pineapple Buttermilk Bread, 95
Poached Amaretto Pears, 194
Poached Whole Salmon with Sesame
and Cilantro, 110
Poppy Seed Cake, 206

Pork
Braised Pork Loin, 134
China Gulch Sweet and Sour
Pork, 132
China Riffle Mushrooms, 33
Gin Lin Char Shu Pork, 30
Honey Apple Pork Chops, 131
Hot Summer Spareribs, 137
Marinated Pork Loin, 133
Pork Chops À la Rogue, 132
Raspberry Herb Pork
Tenderloin, 133
Rogue River Ribs, 138
Tipsy Tenderloins, 139
Very Italian Meatballs, 145
Posole, 54
Potage Esau, 56

Potatoes
Baked Apples and New
Potatoes, 176
Brookings Clam and Red Potato
Frittata, 120
Chilled Potato-Cilantro Soup, 47
Greek Potato Wedges, 177
Red Potato Salad with Sun-Dried
Tomatoes, 78
Red Potatoes in Lemon
Butter, 176
Sweet Potatoes with
Apricots, 177
Windy Creek Potatoes, 174

Pumpkin
Chocolate Chip Pumpkin
Muffins, 87
Frozen Pumpkin Dessert, 200
Golden Pumpkin Biscuits, 93
Pumpkin Soup, 53
Quinoa Salad, 71

Raspberries
Chocolate Raspberry
Tart, 200
Fresh Raspberry Soup, 49
Fruit Vinegar, 157
Oregon Berry Salad, 67

Oregon Raspberry-Hazelnut
Muffins, 85
Raspberry Cream Pears, 194
Raspberry Herb Pork
Tenderloin, 133
Raspberry Poppy Seed
Dressing, 66
Raspberry Sauce, 209
Red, White, and Blue Fruit
Salad, 66
Rhubarb-Raspberry Conserve, 90
Very Berry Raspberry Sauce, 205
Ravioli Salad, 75
Red Potato Salad with Sun-Dried
Tomatoes, 78
Red Potatoes in Lemon Butter, 176
Red Snapper Oriental, 120
Red, White, and Blue Fruit
Salad, 66

Relishes
Huckleberry Relish, 129
Renate's Plum Cake, 206
Rendezvous Smoked Salmon I, 116
Rendezvous Smoked Salmon II, 117
Rendezvous Smoked Salmon
III, 117
Rendezvous Smoked Salmon
IV, 117
Rhubarb-Raspberry Conserve, 90

Rice
Indian Pilaf, 180
Saffron Raisin Rice, 179
Wild Rice Pancakes, 162
Wild Rice Roxy Ann, 180
Wild Rice with Hazelnuts, 179
River Lodge Refrigerator
Muffins, 87
River Trail Vegetables, 175
Roasted Hazelnut Salad, 71
Roasted Pepper Trio, 173
Rogue Caesar Salad, 81
Rogue Pears, 193
Rogue Polenta, 181
Rogue Rendezvous Chicken, 151
Rogue River Blue Cheese
Custards, 184
Rogue River Ribs, 138
Rogue River Salmon Soup, 59
Rogues' Fizz, 31
Romeo Inn's Welsh Rarebit, 183
Rum Sauce, 210
Saffron Raisin Rice, 179

Salad Dressings
Custard Dressing, 70
Homemade Italian Dressing, 74
Mandarin Dressing, 77
Orange Cream Dressing, 68
Raspberry Poppy Seed
Dressing, 66
Sesame Dressing, 76
Spicy Dressing, 67
Strawberry Dressing, 67
Tarragon Vinaigrette, 79

Salads
Almond Sesame Salad, 78
Asparagus Mushroom Salad, 76

Blue, Shrimp, and Spinach, 74
Chilled Summer Corn, 72
Cilantro Black Bean Chicken, 80
Couscous Salad, 72
Fresh Broccoli Salad with Custard
  Dressing, 70
Fresh Fruit Tray With Orange
  Cream Dressing, 68
Garbanzo-Feta Salad, 74
Garlic Roma Tomatoes and
  Croutons, 73
Herbed Walnut Salad, 70
Mandarin Salad, 77
Melon Puree, 68
Oregon Berry Salad, 67
Quinoa Salad, 71
Ravioli Salad, 75
Red Potato Salad with Sun-Dried
  Tomatoes, 78
Red, White, and Blue Fruit
  Salad, 66
Roasted Hazelnut Salad, 71
Rogue Caesar Salad, 81
Smoked Salmon Salad, 79
Spicy Cool Watermelon Salad, 67
Spinach Apple Salad, 76
Strawberry Spinach Salad, 69
Tomatoes Stuffed With Green
  Beans, 75
Union Creek Chicken Salad, 77
Winter Vegetable Salad, 69

Salmon
Bacon Wrapped Salmon
  Steaks, 112
Chanticleer Parsnip Apple
  Pancakes with (Hot) Smoked
  Salmon and Sherried Crème
  Fraîche, 182
Chinook Salmon in Phyllo, 27
Grilled Lemon Salmon, 112
Grilled Lime-Sesame
  Salmon, 112
Half Moon Oven Barbecued
  Salmon, 109
Northwest Drifters' Salmon, 108
Pasta with Salmon in Basil
  Cream, 125
Perfect Salmon Steaks, 111
Poached Whole Salmon with
  Sesame and Cilantro, 110
Rendezvous Smoked Salmon
  I, 116
Rendezvous Smoked Salmon
  II, 117
Rendezvous Smoked Salmon
  III, 117
Rendezvous Smoked Salmon
  IV, 117
Rogue River Salmon Soup, 59
Salmon and Hazelnuts in
  Phyllo, 113
Salmon Baguette, 27
Salmon in Parchment with Lime-
  Dill Butter, 109
Salmon in White Wine
  Marinade, 111
Salmon Steaks Genoese, 114

Salmon with Sun-Dried
  Tomato Salsa, 110
Smoked Salmon Cheesecake, 26
Smoked Salmon Salad, 79
Salmon and Hazelnuts in
  Phyllo, 113
Salmon Baguette, 27
Salmon in Parchment with Lime-Dill
  Butter, 109
Salmon in White Wine
  Marinade, 111
Salmon Steaks Genoese, 114
Salmon with Sun-Dried Tomato
  Salsa, 110

Salsa
Salsa Sorbet, 79
Sun-Dried Tomato Salsa, 110

Sauces
Chocolate Sauce, 197
Creamy Horseradish
  Sauce, 142
Creamy Olive Sauce, 118
Creamy Wine-Dill Sauce, 136
Dijonnaise Sauce, 166
Horseshoe Bend Barbecue
  Sauce, 144
Jalapeño Sauce, 159
Raspberry Sauce, 209
Rum Sauce, 210
Very Berry Raspberry Sauce, 205
Wine Sauce, 130

Sausage
Hearty Lentil Sausage Soup, 56
Italian Sausage and Bean Soup, 60
Takelma Taco Soup, 53
Very Italian Meatballs, 145
Sautéed String Beans, 167
Savory Spring Leg of Lamb, 131
Savory Tomato and Asparagus
  Pie, 185

Scallops
Scallop Linguine, 125
Sesame Asparagus, 167
Sesame Dressing, 76

Shrimp
Baked Stuffed Shrimp, 29
Blue, Shrimp, and Spinach, 74
Cajun Shrimp with Pasta, 123
Gold Beach Shrimp and Corn
  Chowder, 61
Newport Shrimp, 28
Oregon Shrimp Pâtè, 28
Shrimp and Crabmeat Pancakes
  Greenwood, 114
Shrimp Rotini, 124
Shrimp-Dill Puffs, 29
Three Pepper Cajun Shrimp, 123
Signature Clam Chowder, 62

Smoked
Chanticleer Parsnip Apple
  Pancakes with (Hot) Smoked
  Salmon and Sherried Crème
  Fraîche, 182
Cold smoking, 116
Rendezvous Smoked Salmon
  I, 116

Rendezvous Smoked Salmon
  II, 117
Rendezvous Smoked Salmon
  III, 117
Rendezvous Smoked Salmon
  IV, 117
Rogue Rendezvous Chicken, 151
Smoked Salmon Salad, 79
Smoked Salmon Cheesecake, 26
Smoky Garlic Chicken Pizza, 158
Snow Peas with Pine Nuts, 174

Sorbets
Cucumber Dill Sorbet, 80
Salsa Sorbet, 79

Soups
  Cold
    Chilled Blueberry and
      Strawberry Soup, 50
    Chilled Cantaloupe Soup, 49
    Chilled Cucumber Soup, 48
    Chilled Melon Soup, 50
    Chilled Potato-Cilantro
      Soup, 47
    Chilled Watermelon Strawberry
      Soup, 49
    Fresh Raspberry Soup, 49
    Fresh Tomato-Dill Soup, 48
    Illahe Artichoke Soup, 46
    Our Favorite Gazpacho, 47
  Hot
    Anaheim Chile Chicken
      Soup, 62
    Artichoke and Hazelnut
      Soup, 51
    Asparagus Soup, 46
    Black Bean and Jalapeño
      Soup, 63
    Brie Soup, 59
    Broccoli and Cheddar
      Soup, 57
    Carrot-Apple Potage, 50
    Carrot-Dill Soup, 51
    Cheddar Chowder, 57
    Chicken Vegetable Soup Thai
      Style, 63
    Eggplant and Sweet Red Pepper
      Soup, 55
    Gold Beach Shrimp and Corn
      Chowder, 61
    Hearty Lentil Sausage Soup, 56
    Hearty Minestrone Soup, 61
    Italian Sausage and Bean
      Soup, 60
    Mushroom Soup with
      Cashews, 52
    Parsnip and Curried Carrot
      Soup, 52
    Posole, 54
    Potage Esau, 56
    Pumpkin Soup, 53
    Rogue River Salmon Soup, 59
    Signature Clam Chowder, 62
    Steak and Fresh Spinach
      Soup, 58
    Stilton Cheese and Onion
      Soup, 58

Takelma Taco Soup, 53
Wildcat Black-Eyed Pea
    Soup, 60
Zucchini Soup, 54
Sour Cream Fudge Cake, 204
Sourdough French Bread, 100
Sourdough French Bread
    Starter, 100
Spicy Cool Watermelon Salad, 67
Spicy Dressing, 67
Spicy Pear Muffins, 84

Spinach
Blue, Shrimp, and Spinach, 74
Creamy Bow Ties with Chicken
    and Spinach, 154
Garlic Spinach, 174
Spinach Apple Salad, 76
Spinach Stuffed Artichoke
    Crowns, 168
Spinach Torte, 32
Steak and Fresh Spinach
    Soup, 58
Strawberry Spinach Salad, 69

Squid
Calamari Marinara, 115
Steak and Fresh Spinach Soup, 58
Steamed Vegetables with Dijonnaise
    Sauce, 166

Steelhead
Steelhead and Black
    Walnuts, 118
Steelhead with Creamy Olive
    Sauce, 118
Steelhead with Pine Nuts, 119
Stilton Cheese and Onion Soup, 58

Strawberries
Chilled Blueberry and Strawberry
    Soup, 50
Chilled Watermelon Strawberry
    Soup, 49
Fresh Fruit Trifle, 196
Fresh Strawberry Pie, 199
Oregon Berry Salad, 67
Strawberries in Lemon
    Mousse, 196
Strawberry Dressing, 67
Strawberry Spinach Salad, 69
Strawberry-Peach-Kiwi Freezer
    Jam, 101
Sugared Orange Peels, 193

Sun-Dried Tomatoes
Pesto and Cream Cheese on Sun-
    Dried Tomatoes, 37
Pesto and Sun-Dried Tomato
    Twist, 98
Red Potato Salad with Sun-Dried
    Tomatoes, 78
Salmon with Sun-Dried Tomato
    Salsa, 110
Sun-Dried Tomato Salsa, 110
Sweet Potatoes with Apricots, 177
Takelma Taco Soup, 53
Tarragon Chicken Pâté, 32
Tarragon Vinaigrette, 79

Tarts
Blueberry Peach Glacé Tart, 203
Chocolate Almond Tart, 198
Chocolate Raspberry Tart, 200
Tayberry Jam, 96
Tequila Chili, 143
Three Pepper Cajun Shrimp, 123
3-Minute Chocolate Mousse, 189
Tiny Vanilla Gems, 86
Tipsy Tenderloins, 139

Tomatoes
Fresh Tomato-Dill Soup, 48
Garlic Roma Tomatoes and
    Croutons, 73
Pesto and Cream Cheese on Sun-
    Dried Tomatoes, 37
Pesto and Sun-Dried Tomato
    Twist, 98
Red Potato Salad with Sun-Dried
    Tomatoes, 78
Salsa Sorbet, 79
Savory Tomato and Asparagus
    Pie, 185
Sun-Dried Tomato Salsa, 110
Tomatoes and Cheeses on
    Phyllo, 36
Tomatoes Marinade, 177
Tomatoes Stuffed With Green
    Beans, 75

Trout
Cayenne Trout with Buttered
    Orzo, 122

Turkey
Grill Roasted Turkey, 155
Union Creek Chicken Salad, 77

Veal
Veal Piccata, 135

Vegetables (*See also individual
    vegetable listings*)
Anise Carrots, 170
Asparagus with Peach Hazelnut
    Topping, 167
Baked Apples and New
    Potatoes, 176
Blossom Bar Broccoli, 169
Broccoli Bake, 168
Carrots in Wine Sauce, 170
Garlic Spinach, 174
German Red Cabbage, 172
Ginger Garlic Cauliflower, 172
Greek Potato Wedges, 177
Herbed Zucchini Pancakes, 178
Indian Summer Corn, 169
Peas with Triple Sec, 173
Pepper Cheese Zucchini, 178
Picnic Beans, 171
Red Potatoes in Lemon
    Butter, 176
River Trail Vegetables, 175
Roasted Pepper Trio, 173
Rogue Polenta, 181
Sautéed String Beans, 167
Sesame Asparagus, 167
Snow Peas with Pine Nuts, 174

Spinach Stuffed Artichoke
    Crowns, 168
Steamed Vegetables with
    Dijonnaise Sauce, 166
Sweet Potatoes with
    Apricots, 177
Tomatoes Marinade, 177
Whiskey Baked Beans, 171
Windy Creek Potatoes, 174
Winter Vegetable Salad, 69

Venison
Venison McIntosh, 129
Venison Pot Roast with Juniper
    Berries, 128
Vermouth Flank Steak, 141
Very Berry Raspberry Sauce, 205
Very Italian Meatballs, 145

Vinegar
Fruit Vinegar, 157

Waffles
Overnight Yeast Waffles, 91

Walnuts
Cherry Nut Bread, 88
Chocolate Walnut Euphoria
    Cookies, 213
Christmas Date Cake, 204
Herbed Walnut Salad, 70

Watermelon
Chilled Watermelon Strawberry
    Soup, 49
Spicy Cool Watermelon Salad, 67
West Coast Chicken, 155
Whiskey Baked Beans, 171
White Chocolate Macadamia Nut
    Cheesecake, 189
Whole Wheat Hazelnut
    Pancakes, 92
Wild Blackberry Chicken, 149

Wild Game
Barbecued Wild Duck, 161
Pacific Flyway Christmas
    Mallard, 161
Pheasants with Chanterelles, 163
Venison McIntosh, 129
Venison Pot Roast with Juniper
    Berries, 128
Wild Mushroom Chicken
    Stroganoff, 154
Wild Rice Pancakes, 162
Wild Rice Roxy Ann, 180
Wild Rice with Hazelnuts, 179
Wildcat Black-Eyed Pea Soup, 60
Windy Creek Potatoes, 174
Wine Sauce, 130
Winter Vegetable Salad, 69
Wok Cornish Hens, 156

Zucchini
Crab and Zucchini Sauté, 115
Herbed Zucchini Pancakes, 178
Indian Summer Corn, 169
Pepper Cheese Zucchini, 178
Zucchini Soup, 54

ROGUE RIVER RENDEZVOUS
THE JUNIOR SERVICE LEAGUE OF JACKSON COUNTY
526 East Main Street   Medford, Oregon 97504
(503) 779-5020

Send _____ copies of your cookbook at $19.95 per copy plus $3.00*
per copy for postage and handling. (Payable in U.S. funds only.) Make checks payable
to **ROGUE RIVER RENDEZVOUS**.   * Outside USA, add $4.50.
Enclosed is my check or money order in the amount of $ _____
☐ Visa   Interbank No. ☐☐☐☐
☐ Mastercard   Card No. ☐☐☐☐☐☐☐☐☐☐☐☐☐☐☐☐

Signature: _____ Expiration: _____
Name _____
Address _____
City _____ State _____ Zip _____
Daytime phone (   ) _____

FROM: Rogue River Rendezvous
Junior Service League of Jackson County
526 East Main Street
Medford, Oregon 97504

TO:
Name _____
Address _____
City _____
State _____ Zip _____

MAILING LABEL — PLEASE PRINT

ROGUE RIVER RENDEZVOUS
THE JUNIOR SERVICE LEAGUE OF JACKSON COUNTY
526 East Main Street   Medford, Oregon 97504
(503) 779-5020

Send _____ copies of your cookbook at $19.95 per copy plus $3.00*
per copy for postage and handling. (Payable in U.S. funds only.) Make checks payable
to **ROGUE RIVER RENDEZVOUS**.   * Outside USA, add $4.50.
Enclosed is my check or money order in the amount of $ _____
☐ Visa   Interbank No. ☐☐☐☐
☐ Mastercard   Card No. ☐☐☐☐☐☐☐☐☐☐☐☐☐☐☐☐

Signature: _____ Expiration: _____
Name _____
Address _____
City _____ State _____ Zip _____
Daytime phone (   ) _____

FROM: Rogue River Rendezvous
Junior Service League of Jackson County
526 East Main Street
Medford, Oregon 97504

TO:
Name _____
Address _____
City _____
State _____ Zip _____

MAILING LABEL — PLEASE PRINT

ROGUE RIVER RENDEZVOUS
THE JUNIOR SERVICE LEAGUE OF JACKSON COUNTY
526 East Main Street   Medford, Oregon 97504
(503) 779-5020

Send _____ copies of your cookbook at $19.95 per copy plus $3.00*
per copy for postage and handling. (Payable in U.S. funds only.) Make checks payable
to **ROGUE RIVER RENDEZVOUS**.   * Outside USA, add $4.50.
Enclosed is my check or money order in the amount of $ _____
☐ Visa   Interbank No. ☐☐☐☐
☐ Mastercard   Card No. ☐☐☐☐☐☐☐☐☐☐☐☐☐☐☐☐

Signature: _____ Expiration: _____
Name _____
Address _____
City _____ State _____ Zip _____
Daytime phone (   ) _____

FROM: Rogue River Rendezvous
Junior Service League of Jackson County
526 East Main Street
Medford, Oregon 97504

TO:
Name _____
Address _____
City _____
State _____ Zip _____

MAILING LABEL — PLEASE PRINT